MCA
Microsoft Certified Associate
Azure Security Engineer
Study Guide

Exam AZ-500

T0179766

MCA
Microsoft Certified Associate
Azure Security Engineer

Study Guide

Exam AZ-500

Shimon Brathwaite

SYBEX®
A Wiley Brand

Acknowledgments

I have had the pleasure of working with professionals from Wiley to create this study guide.

I would like to thank Kenyon Brown, senior acquisitions editor, for recruiting me and working with me to get my proposal approved for production. He was very helpful in helping me to understand the requirements and getting started with writing the book.

I would like to thank Christine O'Connor and Janette Neal, who oversaw the edits for my book. They are extremely helpful in making sure that my book was up to Wiley's production standards and helped to coordinate my interactions with everyone else on the team.

I am very grateful for Magesh Elangovan, who worked as the content refinement specialist. He helped me to ensure that the quality of the images and overall content of the book was appropriate for all readers and that the ideas of the book will be conveyed clearly to all readers.

Lastly, I would like to thank Mahalingam, the technical editor who helped me refine the book's content. He was extremely knowledgeable on Microsoft Azure and provided excellent feedback on technical concepts that helped me to improve the overall quality of the book.

About the Author

Shimon Brathwaite is author and editor-in-chief of securitymadesimple.org, a website dedicated to teaching business owners how to secure their businesses and helping cybersecurity professionals start and advance their careers.

Before starting his career in cybersecurity, Shimon was a co-op student at Toronto Metropolitan University in Toronto, Canada, where he received a degree in their Business Technology Management program before deciding to specialize in cybersecurity. Through his work at Toronto Metropolitan University and post-graduation, he accumulated over five years of work experience in cybersecurity across financial institutions, startups, and consulting companies. His work was primarily focused on incident response, where he helped companies resolve security incidents and perform digital investigations.

About the Technical Editor

Mahalingam is an Azure Consultant and works with enterprises to design and implement their solutions in Azure. He also assesses large-scale applications hosted on Azure and provides recommendations to optimize them. He started his Azure journey five years ago and is a certified Azure Solutions Architect Expert, Azure Security Engineer Associate, and Azure Administrator Associate. In addition, he is a Microsoft Certified Trainer and delivers workshops on Azure IaaS and PaaS.

Contents at a Glance

Contents

Introduction

The Microsoft Azure Platform is one of the most popular and diverse cloud-computing platforms in existence. It includes a wide range of security features designed to help clients protect their cloud environments. The Microsoft Azure Security Technologies exam, AZ-500, focuses on testing a candidate's ability to be a subject matter expert on implementing Azure security controls. The exam focuses on four main areas:

- Managing identity and access
- Implementing platform protections
- Managing security operations
- Securing data and applications

What Does This Book Cover?

This book covers the topics outlined in the Microsoft Certified Associate Azure Security Engineer exam guide available at

```
https://query.prod.cms.rt.microsoft.com/cms/api/am/binary/RE3VC70
```

 Exam policies can change from time to time. We highly recommend that you check the Microsoft site for the most up-to-date information when you begin your preparing, when you register, and again a few days before your scheduled exam date.

The book's outline is as follows:

Chapter 1: Introduction to Microsoft Azure Chapter 1 outlines cloud computing best practices. The exam focuses on how to implement security controls that achieve specific goals in the Azure environment. In this chapter, you learn what these goals are for your cloud environment. Each of following chapters will correspond to one or more of these best practices. Before beginning this chapter you can may want to complete the assessment test to help you obtain a baseline of your current understanding of security and the Azure platform.

Chapter 2: Managing Identity and Access on Microsoft Azure Chapter 2 focuses on how to implement good identity and access management practices on Azure. Topics include managing Azure Active Directory (AD) identities, securing access to resources and applications, and implementing role-based access control (RBAC).

Chapter 3: Implementing Platform Protections Chapter 3 discusses how to implement good network security on the Azure platform. Topics include firewall configuration, endpoint protection, network monitoring, and how to use the Azure-specific security tools to accomplish these tasks. It begins with network security, exploring topics such as security groups; Windows Application Firewall (WAF); endpoint protection; DDoS protection; operational security, such as vulnerability management; disk encryption; and Secure Socket Layer/Transport Layer Security (SSL/TLS) certifications.

Chapter 4: Managing Security Operations   Chapter 4 focuses on how to use Azure tools like Azure Sentinel and Security Center to manage security operations. It includes discussions on creating custom alerts, policy management, vulnerability scans, and security configurations for the platforms. We then delve into how to configure good network monitoring using Azure Monitor, Azure Security Center, Azure Policy, Azure Blueprint, and Azure Sentinel.

Chapter 5: Securing Data and Applications   This chapter will focus on how to secure data and applications on the Azure platform. Topics include using secure data storage, creating data backups seamlessly, implementing database security, and leveraging Azure tools like Azure Defender and Key Vault. We also cover how to protect application backend databases by implementing database encryption, database authentication, and database auditing.

Appendix A: Azure Security Tools Overview   This appendix focuses on Microsoft Azure security tools that are used to create a secure platform. In this chapter, I review the tools' functions and how they can be used and integrated together to create security operations, compliance, networking monitoring, automated alerts, and proper logging. It also includes tools like Microsoft Azure Sentinel, Azure Key Vault, Azure Defender, Azure Firewall, Azure Policy, and Azure Monitor.

Who Should Read This Book

As the title implies, this book is intended for people who have an interest in understanding and implementing security features in Azure. These people probably fall into two basic groups:

Security Professionals in an Azure Environment   They can be IT administrators or security professionals who are responsible for securing their organization's Azure cloud environment.

Candidates for the AZ-500 Exam   This book is meant to be a study guide for anyone interested in taking the AZ-500 exam. It gives readers a clear understanding of the topics needed to pass the exam. It also comes with hundreds of practice questions/tests to help readers prepare for the type of questions they can expect on the exam.

This book is designed for people who have some experience in cybersecurity. While we give a breakdown of all key foundational concepts relevant to the course, it's impossible to give readers all the information they would need in this book. For those of you with a cybersecurity/IT background, this will be no issue, but for the rest of you this might be a steep learning curve. So we encourage you to do your research if you ever need more context for the cybersecurity concepts found in this book.

You can use this book in two ways. The most straightforward (and time consuming) is to start at the beginning and follow all the steps to gain a good overall understanding of security controls in Azure. Alternatively, you can skip around from chapter to chapter and only look at the areas of interest to you. For example, if you are having trouble understanding how to implement access management in your environment, then you may want to skip to Chapter 2 and just focus on that. Each chapter includes step-by-step instructions on how to implement the controls that we talk about in that chapter.

Study Guide Features

This study guide uses several common elements to help you prepare. These include the following:

Summaries   The summary section of each chapter briefly explains the chapter, allowing you to easily understand what it covers.

Exam Essentials   The exam essentials focus on major exam topics and critical knowledge that you should take into the test. The exam essentials focus on the exam objectives provided by Microsoft.

Chapter Review Questions   A set of questions at the end of each chapter will help you assess your knowledge and if you are ready to take the exam based on your knowledge of that chapter's topics.

The review questions, assessment test, and other testing elements included in this book are *not* derived from the actual exam questions, so don't memorize the answers to these questions and assume that doing so will enable you to pass the exam. You should learn the underlying topic, as described in the text of the book. This will let you answer the questions provided with this book *and* pass the exam. Learning the underlying topic is also the approach that will serve you best in the workplace—the ultimate goal of a certification.

Interactive Online Learning Environment and Test Bank

Studying the material in the *Microsoft Certified Associate Azure Security Engineer Study Guide* is an important part of preparing for the Azure Security Engineer Associate certification exam, but we also provide additional tools to help you prepare. The online tools will help you understand the types of questions that will appear on the certification exam:

- The practice tests include all the questions in each chapter as well as the questions from the assessment test. *In addition,* there are two practice exams with 50 questions each. You can use these tests to evaluate your understanding and identify areas that may require additional study.

- The flashcards will push the limits of what you should know for the certification exam. There are 100 questions, which are provided in digital format. Each flashcard has one question and one correct answer.

- The online glossary is a searchable list of key terms introduced in this exam guide that you should know for the exam.

To start using these tools to study for the exam, go to www.wiley.com/go/sybextestprep and register your book to receive your unique PIN. Once you have the PIN, return to www.wiley.com/go/sybextestprep, find your book, and click Register to register a new account or add this book to an existing account.

Like all exams, the Microsoft Certified Associate Azure Security Engineer certification is updated periodically and may eventually be retired or replaced. At some point after Microsoft is no longer offering this exam, the old editions of our books and online tools will be retired. If you have purchased this book after the exam was retired, or you are attempting to register in the Sybex online learning environment after the exam was retired, please know that we make no guarantees that this exam's online Sybex tools will be available once the exam is no longer available.

Additional Resources

People learn in different ways. For some, a book is an ideal way to study whereas others may find practice test sites a more efficient way to study. Some of these websites come with exam pass guarantees and consistently update their content with some of the exact exam questions you will see on the official exam. These websites include www.udemy.com, www.exam-labs.com, https://acloudguru.com, and www.whizlabs.com.

MCA Azure Security Engineer Study Guide Exam Objectives

This table provides the extent, by percentage, each section is represented on the actual examination.

Section	% of Examination
Section 1: Manage Identity and Access	30–35%
Section 2: Implement Platform Protection	15–20%
Section 3: Manage Security Operations	25–30%
Section 4: Secure Data and Applications	25–30%

Exam objectives are subject to change at any time without prior notice and at Microsoft's sole discretion. Please visit the Exam AZ-500: Microsoft Azure Security Technologies website (https://docs.microsoft .com/en-us/certifications/exams/az-500) for the most current listing of exam objectives.

Objective Map

The following objective map will allow you to find the chapter in this book that covers each objective for the exam.

Objective	Chapter
Section 1: Manage Identity and Access	2
1.1 Manage Azure Directory (Azure AD) Identities	2
1.2 Manage secure access by using Azure AD	2
1.3 Manage Application Access	2

How to Contact Wiley or the Author

If you believe you have found a mistake in this book, please bring it to our attention. At John Wiley & Sons, we understand how important it is to provide our customers with accurate content, but even with our best efforts an error may occur.

In order to submit your possible errata, please email it to our Customer Service Team at wileysupport@wiley.com with the subject line "Possible Book Errata Submission."

Assessment Test

1. What is Azure AD?
   - **A.** It's a cloud version of Windows Active Directory (AD).
   - **B.** It is a cloud-based identity management service.
   - **C.** It is used for enabling multifactor authentication (MFA).
   - **D.** It protects accounts from authentication-based attacks.

2. What is a managed identity?
   - **A.** A shared user account
   - **B.** A user account managed by another user
   - **C.** An identity that your Azure services can use for authentication
   - **D.** A tool for controlling access to a user account

3. What is Privileged Identity Management (PIM)?
   - **A.** Protection for highly valuable Azure resources
   - **B.** Protection of your organization's most privileged accounts
   - **C.** Protection for admin-level Azure accounts
   - **D.** A type of role-based access control (RBAC)

4. What is role-based access control (RBAC)?
   - **A.** Assigning individual permissions based on a user's jobs
   - **B.** Controlling assess based solely on an individual's job titles
   - **C.** An Azure tool for controlling access to resources in Azure
   - **D.** A method where you assign permissions to a job role/identity as needed, rather than assigning permissions to an individual

5. What is *not* a feature of Azure Firewall Manager?
   - **A.** DDoS protection
   - **B.** Azure Firewall deployment and configuration
   - **C.** Creation of global and local firewall policies
   - **D.** Integration with third-party security features

6. What is the function of an Azure Application Gateway?
   - **A.** It's a tool for building and operating scalable applications.
   - **B.** It's an application load balancer.
   - **C.** It filters web traffic to applications.
   - **D.** It's Azure's native web application firewall.

7. What is the function of Azure Front Door?

    A. DDoS protection

    B. Protection against web-based attacks on applications

    C. Filtering of web application attacks

    D. Launching and operating of scalable applications

8. Where can you configure basic Azure DDoS Protection?

    A. The Azure portal

    B. Under Target Resources settings

    C. It doesn't require configuration.

    D. The Azure command line

9. What is the purpose of an Azure policy?

    A. To enforce the standards of your organization and ensure compliance of your Azure resources

    B. To set parameters on what resources can be created

    C. To set parameters on who can access the resources

    D. To act as a documentation tool

10. What is *not* a feature of Microsoft Defender for Cloud?

    A. Real-time protection

    B. Automatic and manual scanning

    C. Detection and remediation

    D. Capture of logs

11. What is the purpose of threat modeling?

    A. Identifying threats currently on your network

    B. Mapping out potential threats and their mitigation

    C. Identifying vulnerabilities in upcoming applications

    D. Mapping out the secure architecture of a software product

12. What is the function of Microsoft Sentinel?

    A. It provides logging and monitoring for your Azure environment.

    B. It is an endpoint security tool for protecting network resources.

    C. It is the cloud-native security information and event management (SIEM) and security orchestration, automation, and response (SOAR) platform that performs threat detection and analytics.

    D. It allows you to manage Azure firewalls from a central location.

13. What is the purpose of an Azure storage account?

 A. It contains a list of usernames and passwords for authentication.

 B. It's a container for grouping databases.

 C. It's a type of user account.

 D. It stores data.

14. What is the function of Azure Cosmos Database (DB)?

 A. To store secrets in Azure

 B. To acts as a fully managed NoSQL database designed for modern application development

 C. To manage databases

 D. To manage virtual endpoints

15. What is Azure Key Vault used for?

 A. It's a cloud service for securely storing and accessing secrets.

 B. It's a cloud password manager.

 C. It provides physical protection for Azure servers.

 D. It stores data objects in Azure.

16. What is a threat vector?

 A. A nation-state threat actor

 B. A group or individual with malicious intent

 C. A type of malware

 D. A path or means for exploiting a vulnerability

17. Which of the following is a type of administrative security control?

 A. The separation of duties

 B. Security guards

 C. Security group policies

 D. Computer logging

18. Which of the following is a NoSQL store for structured data?

 A. Azure files

 B. Azure blobs

 C. Azure tables

 D. Azure disks

19. What are threat actors?

 A. A type of hacker group

 B. A group or individual with malicious intent

 C. A group with knowledge of company vulnerabilities

 D. Insider threats

20. What tool is best used for threat hunting?

   A. Microsoft's Threat Modeling Tool

   B. Azure Storage

   C. Microsoft Sentinel

   D. Azure Active Directory (AD)

Answers to Assessment Test

1. B. Azure AD allows employees (or anyone on an on-premises network) to access external resources with proper authentication.

2. C. Managed identities allow your Azure Services to authenticate.

3. B. Azure PIM has special features for managing, controlling, and monitoring access to your organization's most privileged accounts.

4. D. In RBAC, you assign permissions to a job role/identity, and then assign that role/identity to users as needed.

5. A. Azure has a dedicated tool for DDoS protection.

6. B. Azure Application Gateway is an application load balancer for managing traffic to back-end resources.

7. D. Azure Front Door is a tool for launching web applications.

8. C. Azure DDoS protection is enabled by default.

9. A. An Azure policy allows you check whether resources meet the standards you set and to correct those resources automatically.

10. D. Microsoft Defender for Cloud does log analytics but it doesn't capture logs.

11. B. Threat modeling is the process of identifying potential threats and mitigation of such threats.

12. C. Microsoft Sentinel provides SIEM and SOAR functionality in Azure.

13. D. Storage accounts contain all the different types of data objects in Azure.

14. B. Azure Cosmos DB is a service for creating NoSQL databases for application development.

15. A. Azure Key Vault is a service for securely storing secrets in Azure.

16. D. A threat vector is the path or means that a threat actor takes for exploiting a vulnerability.

17. A. The separation of duties is an admin security control where a company requires more than one person to complete a given task in order to prevent fraud.

18. C. Azure tables are a NoSQL store for the storage of structured data.

19. B. Threat actors are any group with a malicious intent that hacks into a company.

20. C. Microsoft Sentinel is Azure's premier threat-hunting solution as well as a SOAR and SIEM platform.

Chapter

1

Introduction to Microsoft Azure

THE MCA MICROSOFT CERTIFIED ASSOCIATE AZURE SECURITY ENGINEER ASSESSMENT TEST TOPICS COVERED IN THIS CHAPTER INCLUDE:

✓ **What Is Microsoft Azure?**

✓ **Cloud Environment Security Objectives**

- Confidentiality
- Integrity
- Availability
- Nonrepudiation

✓ **Common Security Issues**

- Principle of Least Privilege
- Zero-Trust Model
- Defense in Depth
- Avoid Security through Obscurity

✓ **The AAAs of Access Management**

✓ **Encryption**

- End-to-End Encryption
- Symmetric Key Encryption
- Asymmetric Key Encryption

✓ **Network Segmentation**

- Basic Network Configuration
- Unsegmented Network Example
- Internal and External Compliance

    - PCI-DSS
    - CCPA

- GDPR
- HIPAA
- PIPEDA

✓ Cybersecurity Considerations for the Cloud Environment

- Configuration Management
- Unauthorized Access
- Insecure Interfaces/APIs
- Hijacking of Accounts
- Compliance
- Lack of Visibility
- Accurate Logging
- Cloud Storage
- Vendor Contracts
- Link Sharing

✓ Major Cybersecurity Threats

- DDOS
- Social Engineering
- Password Attacks
- Malware

  - Adware
  - Ransomware
  - Spyware
  - Backdoors
  - Bots/Botnets
  - Cryptojacker
  - Keylogger
  - RAM Scraper
  - Browser Hijacking

In this chapter, I discuss Microsoft Azure as a platform and the common security issues for cloud computing. Security issues include common vulnerabilities, types of security threats, and their potential impact on a company. My goal is to outline the problems that the Azure Security Engineer certification is trying to teach you to solve.

What Is Microsoft Azure?

Microsoft Azure is a cloud platform consisting of more than 200 products and cloud services. It allows you to have your own contained IT infrastructure, which is entirely physically hosted at one or more of Microsoft's data centers. Azure allows you to develop and scale new applications or to run existing applications in the cloud. Its cloud services include the following:

Compute   These services allow you to deploy and manage virtual machines (VMs), Azure containers, and batch jobs. Compute resources created in Azure can be configured to use public IP addresses or private addresses, depending on whether or not they need to be accessible to the outside world.

Mobile   These products and services allow developers to build cloud applications for mobile devices and notification services, as well as support for backend tasks and tools for building application programming interfaces (APIs).

Analytics   These services provide analytics and storage for services across your Azure environment. They include features for real-time analytics, big data analytics, machine learning, and business intelligence.

Storage   Azure supports scalable cloud storage for structured and unstructured data. It also supports persistent storage and archival storage.

Security   These specialized products and services help identify, prevent, and respond to different cloud security threats. They include data security features such as encryption keys and data loss prevention solutions.

Networking   Azure allows you to create virtual networks, dedicated connections, and gateways, as well as services for traffic management and diagnostics, load balancing, DNS hosting, and security features.

Cloud Environment Security Objectives

When studying for the MCA Azure Security Engineer certification. you must first know the overall objectives of security and the common challenges involved in securing a cloud environment. Knowing the objectives and the challenges are important to understand the practical implications of the concepts that are taught in this book and for directly answering many exam questions. So, the first thing we must review is the *CIA triad* (see Figure 1.1).

FIGURE 1.1   The CIA triad

CIA stands for confidentiality, integrity, and availability, the three goals you are trying to accomplish.

Confidentiality

Confidentiality means that only people with the right access should be able to access any piece of information. In this section of the CIA triad, the focus is on implementing proper security controls that prevent unauthorized access to your company's resources. A common example of a control used to maintain confidentiality is requiring a login username and password, the idea being that only an authorized person will be able to provide the credentials and gain access to your resource.

Integrity

Integrity means that only people with the correct access are able to change or edit any piece of information within a company. It ensures that information is always accurate and can be trusted to be free of manipulation. A common example of a security control used to ensure integrity is the use of a *digital signature*. A digital signature is an encrypted hash value used to prove that a message has not been altered and to prove the identity of the sender. In a communication between two people, the digital signature leverages hashing algorithms and public key encryption to create a unique hash value of the original message or document, which can only be decrypted and read by the receiver. The message or document is then digitally signed and sent to the receiver. Once the receiver gets the message or document, they can generate their own hash value for the message or document, and if it matches the hash value that was shared by the sender along with the message, then they know the message has not been changed in transit (i.e., when moving from the sender to the receiver over the Internet).

Availability

Availability means that you want to ensure that your information and services are always available for use by the right user. Think about a company website, for example. As a business, you want to ensure that your company's website is always working and available for customer interactions. However, cyberattacks like distributed denial-of-service (DDoS) attacks make these services unavailable and can cost businesses thousands or even millions of dollars. Common examples of security controls that help maintain website availability are next-generation firewalls and specialized DDoS protection software.

Nonrepudiation

A fourth term, nonrepudiation, isn't included in the triad, but it is associated with the first three. *Nonrepudiation* simply means that no one should be able to perform an action online and then deny that they performed that action. For example, if I send an email or delete a file, there must be proof that I performed this action so that I can't deny it at a later date. One way that we prove it is by using the previously discussed digital signature.

Pretty much everything that you do within your cybersecurity operations is related to one or multiple elements of this triad; it's the most commonly used framework for understanding what you are trying to achieve as a cybersecurity professional.

Common Security Issues

Now that you have a basic understanding of what cybersecurity generally is trying to achieve, let's look at some of the common issues that cloud security professionals must deal with. Many of Azure's tools are built to address these issues, and it's very likely you have come across some of them in your daily work.

Principle of Least Privilege

The *principle of least privilege* simply means that you should only give users the amount of privilege they need to do their job and nothing more. Giving users anything more than what is necessary creates risk for the company without providing any benefit. For example, giving users more privilege than needed can be detrimental in a situation where an employee is being fired. Disgruntled employees are one of the biggest threats to a company because they have access to the internal network and have a motive to damage or steal information from it. Roughly 59 percent of employees steal information when they quit or are fired from their company. The amount of information that they have access to steal can be limited if you implement the principle of least privilege. Even if it's not a situation where the employee is leaving, if an employee's account has a high level of privilege and that account is misused or hacked by a cybercriminal, they will be able to access more information and perform more harmful actions using that account than with an account that has limited privileges. Think of what an admin-level account would be capable of accessing compared to a normal user account. The amount of damage a cybercriminal could do is staggering in such cases.

Zero-Trust Model

A *zero-trust model* is a security concept stating that an organization shouldn't automatically trust implicitly any device or entity inside or outside its perimeter and instead should verify everything before granting the device or entity access to anything. This model may contradict what some people assume—that if a device is inside the company network, then it should be okay to trust and it's not harmful. However, this is certainly *not* the case. Insider threats, advanced persistent threats (i.e., threat actors that sit on the network for extended periods of time), and legitimate accounts that have been compromised are all examples of cyberthreats that sit inside the company perimeter but shouldn't be trusted. Keep in mind the words of Charlie Gero, CTO of Enterprise and Advanced Projects Group at Akamai Technologies in Cambridge, Massachusetts:

> The strategy around Zero Trust boils down to don't trust anyone. We're talking about, "Let's cut off all access until the network knows who you are. Don't allow access to IP addresses, machines, etc. until you know who that user is and whether they're authorized. . ."
>
> www.csoonline.com/article/3247848/what-is-zero-trust-a-model-for-more-effective-security.html

Defense in Depth

Defense in depth is the idea that any important network resource should be protected by multiple layers of security (see Figure 1.2). This means that you should not have a single point of failure when it comes to the security controls that you use. It requires that you implement a variety of controls covering different aspects of security. The layers include the following:

   Policies, Procedures, and Awareness Training   While not technical controls, these documents and actions are part of overall security governance. They outline how the organization should approach their cybersecurity operations and mandate that certain actions must be taken to ensure the overall security of the company.

Physical Security   Even in a cloud environment, you should take time to audit how the cloud provider physically secures its servers and physical infrastructure. If someone is able to gain access to a machine physically, they can often bypass whatever security controls are in place on the machine itself. This can be as simple as disabling USB ports on a machine to prevent someone from plugging in a USB and uploading a virus. Also, in the event of a natural disaster, building fires, or other unforeseen circumstances, you must ensure that your systems are well protected.

Perimeter Security   Perimeter security is the first layer of security that sits between your digital network and outside attackers. It includes controls like perimeter firewalls, honeypots, and demilitarized zones (DMZs). Perimeter security is what separates your internal network from the outside world (the Internet). This area separates parts of your network so that only the resources that need to be exposed to the Internet will be exposed. For example, a DMZ is a separate part of the network, usually hosting only things like a web server that needs to be accessed by people outside the company network.

Network Security   Network security controls are located on the company network and are responsible for monitoring and controlling the company's internal network. These controls are not located on any one particular machine, but rather are attached to things such as a router, where they can monitor communications between different network devices and filter and block traffic accordingly. A common example of this is the network intrusion detection and prevention system (IDPS), which monitors all of the traffic on a network for signs of malicious activity. Once the IDPS locates such activity, it can provide alerts as well as take action to block that malicious activity from occurring.

Endpoint Security   Endpoint security controls are located on the actual endpoints on the network. An easy example to discuss is the antivirus software that you download to your computer. This antivirus software doesn't help to protect the network itself; it only scans files on your computer. The advantage is that it can do file-level detection as the software that operates on the network level cannot see the file or processes on any of the machines on the network. Endpoint security controls allow for more detailed detection and remediation.

Application Security   Application security is focused on securing the software applications that your business hosts. In the context of the cloud, many applications are hosted on cloud servers and are publicly available to anyone on the Internet. You need to know how to secure your applications so that people who visit the application and use it won't be able to exploit it. Application security begins during the creation of the application with source code reviews or dynamic application testing, where you try to find security bugs in the application. Once the application is completed, you need security like web application firewalls (WAFs) to protect the application from exploitation.

Data Security   The last element of defense in depth is data security—implementing controls that help you protect the data within your organization from being accessed by unauthorized people. A common security control is data encryption, which ensures that anyone who is eavesdropping will be unable to obtain information in a usable format. In a cloud environment, one of the biggest challenges is to control the access that people have so that only those who are supposed to have access to view information are able to.

FIGURE 1.2   Defense in depth

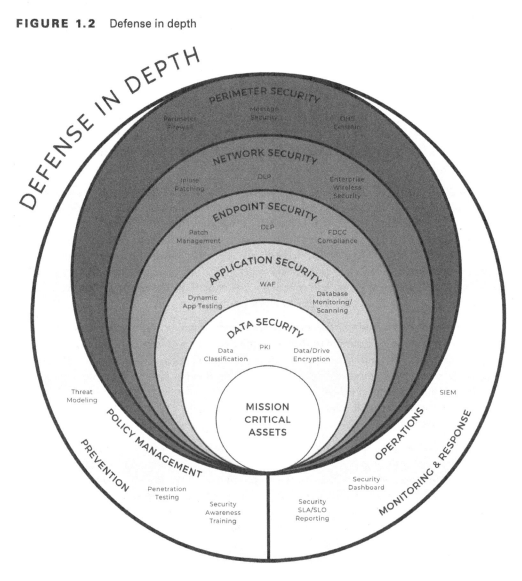

Avoid Security through Obscurity

Security through obscurity is the idea that you can keep a system secure by keeping it a secret, which isn't a good idea. Although keeping the system hidden does reduce the number of threats that might target it, it's typically only a matter of time before an attacker finds out about it. If you didn't take time to protect it, then it's relatively easy for the attacker to discover and exploit. A lot of interconnectivity exists among the systems in a cloud environment, so even if that system isn't connected to the Internet directly, it may be connected through numerous other systems to a device exposed to the Internet, and it can be discovered that way.

The AAAs of Access Management

Another part of cloud environment security that's heavily focused on throughout the exam is identity and access management (IAM). IAM is about ensuring that only authorized people have access to resources within a company. If people are able to gain unauthorized access, they may be able to plant malware on company systems, steal company information, or perform other damaging actions on company devices. There are three main components to IAM that you must understand: authentication, authorization, and accounting (AAA).

Authentication pertains to confirming that a user is who they claim to be. Each user has unique identification information that sets them apart from all other users, and that information can be used to prove their identity when needed. For example, when you log into a website, you provide a username and a password. That combination of information should only be known by you, the owner of the account, and it provides the website with a somewhat reliable method of authenticating their users.

There are three primary categories of authentication:

- Something you know (for example, a password)
- Something you have (for example, an access card)
- Something you are (for example, your fingerprint)

When you require a user to have at least two authentication methods across two categories, it's called *multifactor authentication,* which makes it much harder for attackers to authenticate themselves as someone else because they must steal two different sets of information.

The second A in AAA is *authorization,* which is the process of granting or denying a user access to system resources once the user is authenticated. Authorization determines the amount of information or services that a user can gain access to. If you've ever watched a military movie or worked in the military, you may have heard them use the phrase "classified information." Classified information means that only people who have a certain authorization level can access classified information. While your environmental resources may not be as important as classified military information, you should apply the same principle and work to limit user access to the least amount that they need in order to do their job (refer back to the principle of least privilege from earlier). On the system side, it means figuring out the privileges the user's account needs to work. For example, you must decide whether you are provisioning an account with guest access, regular user access, or administration-level privileges.

The final A in AAA stands for *accounting*, which is the ability to track a user's activity while accessing the company's resources and includes the amount of time spent on the network, the services accessed while there, and the amount of data transferred during their session. While this might seem invasive, it's an essential part of your organization's security policy. Accounting data is used for many things. First, this information enables you to perform a trends analysis and identify failed login attempts, which could indicate an attack. This information can also aid in detecting data breaches, forensics and computer investigations, billing, cost allocation, audits, and much more. It's important to be able to trace events back to specific user accounts during an investigation. For example, if you have a malware outbreak in the company, you want to know what account the malware originated from, how it could have spread, and if the situation has been contained. By tracing the events back to a specific user account, you can identify where it started from, whom it may have spread to, and therefore, if it has been contained based on the actions of that user account.

Properly enforcing the AAAs is your only reliable defense against insider threats. As stated previously, insider threats include disgruntled employees—people who feel like they've been mistreated by the company or perhaps are about to be fired. Having this accounting data can help you identify these bad actors ahead of time and prevent them from doing something malicious. Insider threats also can include employees who are committing fraud. By collecting this information on a regular basis, you will detect clues about those committing fraud and who are using their company position to hide it. Keep in mind that for IAM accounting to be effective, you should eliminate the use of generic or shared accounts. If an action on your system can't be tracked back to a single person, then it's not going to be very useful information to single out the bad actor in most cases.

Encryption

Encryption is an essential part of security in a cloud environment. Encryption is the process of encoding information so that it cannot be read by anyone other the intended recipient. This process begins with the original message (plaintext), which is encoded and converted into ciphertext, sent to the recipient, and then converted back into plaintext, where it can be read. Because a cloud environment can only be accessed over the Internet, a larger than normal opportunity exists for users to "eavesdrop" or gain unauthorized access to network resources. Therefore, you must encrypt your communications (e.g., email) whenever you are going to be sending sensitive data over the Internet.

Several types of encryption exist:

- End-to-end encryption
- Symmetric key encryption
- Asymmetric key encryption (public key cryptography)

End-to-End Encryption

End-to-end encryption is a system of communication where only the communicating users can read the messages. When the information is not being read by one of the users, it is always encrypted. As you read through this study guide, an emphasis is placed on trying to obtain end-to-end encryption wherever possible. This is important for preventing third parties from eavesdropping on your communications. You should have encryption through the entire communicating process with any sensitive information to avoid data leaks. The only time when sensitive information should be in plaintext, or unencrypted, is when it is in use.

Symmetric Key Encryption

In this form of encryption, the same or identical encryption keys are used to both encrypt and decrypt information (see Figure 1.3). An encryption key is a string of characters that is used to encode or decode data. Symmetric key encryption is divided into *stream ciphers* and *block ciphers*. Stream ciphers encrypt the message one bit at a time in a continuous flow, which is why it's called a stream cipher because it is a constant stream of bits being encrypted. A block cipher breaks the message up into a predetermined number of bits and encrypts them as a unit, one block at a time, until the entire message is encrypted. Symmetric encryption is typically less secure than asymmetric because it requires you to share the encryption key with everyone that you want to communicate with. However, it is much faster and best used in situations where you value speed over security.

Asymmetric Key Encryption

In asymmetric key encryption (see Figure 1.4), different keys are used for encryption and decryption of a message. First, the message is encrypted using a public key, which is shared between both users. Then the message is decrypted using a private key, which only the recipient of the message has. Asymmetric key encryption is arguably more secure than symmetric key encryption because you never have to send the decryption key over an insecure channel—your private key is kept on your personal workstation and is never emailed, thus reducing the risk of being read by attackers. Also known as public key encryption, this type of encryption is best suited for situations where you are processing smaller datasets and where speed isn't a huge concern.

FIGURE 1.3 Symmetric encryption

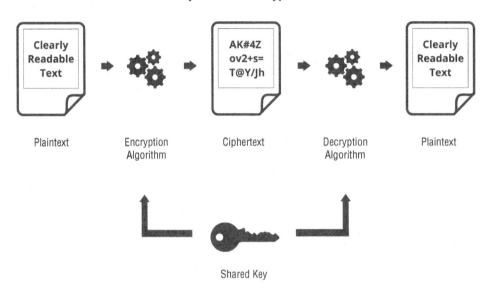

Symmetric Encryption

| Plaintext | Encryption Algorithm | Ciphertext | Decryption Algorithm | Plaintext |

Shared Key

FIGURE 1.4 Asymmetric encryption

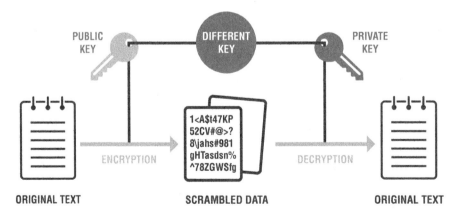

Asymmetric Encryption

PUBLIC KEY — DIFFERENT KEY — PRIVATE KEY

ORIGINAL TEXT — ENCRYPTION → SCRAMBLED DATA — DECRYPTION → ORIGINAL TEXT

Network Segmentation

The next element of cybersecurity we are going to discuss is *network segmentation,* which is all about dividing your computer network into smaller physical, or logical, components. Two devices on the same network segment can talk to each other directly, while separating a network into segments enables you to create some boundaries. Typically, each network segment will have data filtered by a router and a firewall (which is usually one device). Requiring data traffic to pass through a device allows for traffic to be inspected and security policies to be applied.

Network segmentation is a great way to limit the damage of data breaches. For example, the ability of ransomware or any other malware to spread is greatly reduced when a network is segmented properly and usually limits the malware to only the network segment where the infection began. Second, it helps to enforce the principle of least privilege by limiting an individual's access to certain network segments they need access to. Also, if you need to provide access to a third party, you can isolate the resource that they need to its own subnet and keep the third party isolated from the rest of your resources. Network segmentation can also boost the performance of a network because with fewer hosts on a subnet, local traffic is reduced. With less overall traffic on each subnet, it's also easier for you to identify potential suspicious behavior on each subnet because there is less noise to go through.

Basic Network Configuration

You always want to ensure that a firewall is located between you and the Internet to filter traffic that comes through to your internal network. In Figure 1.5, you see an example of simple but effective network segmentation for your organization. Called a *demilitarized zone (DMZ),* this is where you want to put your Internet-facing servers. You don't want application servers sitting on the same subnet as your internal servers. You also shouldn't have all of your Internet-facing servers on the same DMZ—only those that must communicate with one another regularly should be placed on the same DMZ. This way, if a hacker is able to compromise these Internet-facing servers, they'll be limited to its restricted zone.

Traffic from the DMZ1 zone is allowed to come in from the servers and workstations in the internal zone, but it cannot send information to the internal zone. Only traffic from DMZ2 is allowed to flow both ways. Because traffic from the Internet is routed to DMZ1, you'll want to prevent DMZ1 from sending traffic directly to the internal servers. Therefore, any traffic that needs to go to the internal servers must be routed to DMZ2, through the firewall, and then passed on to the internal zone. No traffic should go directly from the Internet to your internal zone, inbound or outbound.

Another important aspect is that typically Internet user access should be routed from an HTTP proxy server, which in Figure 1.5 is located on DMZ1. Again, you need to place a buffer between your internal network and the Internet because this is where most of your threats will be located.

FIGURE 1.5   A DMZ setup

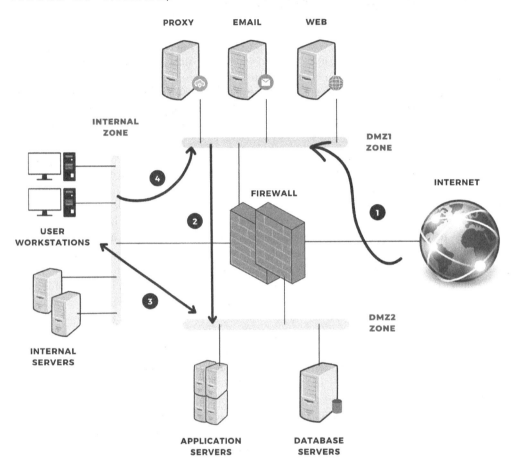

Finally, traffic for every subnet should be restricted to certain ports that are necessary for their job function and everything else should be closed. This restriction limits the number of attack options that a hacker has, because each open port on your machine represents a potential entry point to the machines on that subnet.

Unsegmented Network Example

To illustrate how important this is, let's use an example of a famous data breach that only occurred because the company's network was not segmented properly. In 2013, the department store Target had a data breach. This data breach began with a phishing email that was opened by an employee of a small HVAC company that did business with Target. The malware from this breach remained on the network of the HVAC company for two months before spreading to Target's network. Once inside Target's network, it was able to move laterally through the network and eventually installed itself on the point-of-sale (POS) terminals at many of the company's stores. The result: Over 110 million customers' data was compromised, resulting in over 100 lawsuits being filed and banks handing over $200 million to customers as a result. If Target had used proper network segmentation, this attack probably would have never happened, because the third party's network access would have been restricted to its own subnet. The cost of this data breach to Target itself was an estimated $61 million.

Internal and External Compliance

As a security engineer, you will be responsible for managing several network devices and ensuring that they are compliant with both internal and external standards. It will be at your company's discretion to determine the internal configuration standards to which your machines should adhere. External standards are less flexible and require that your environment have certain security measures in place to protect the data of your customers. The regulations you need to be aware of vary, depending on the type of business you work for. However, here's a summary of some of the most common ones.

PCI-DSS

The Payment Card Industry Data Security Standard (PCI DSS) is an information security standard for organizations that accept or process credit cards in any way. In September 2006, five major credit card brands (Visa International, MasterCard, American Express, Discover, and JCB) established the Payment Card Industry Security Standards Council (PCI SSC). PCI SSC was created for and continues to oversee PCI DSS. Failure to comply with the rules outlined in this standard can result in heavy penalties. For example, one Tennessee-based retailer was charged $13.2 million by Visa for failure to meet these standards. Typically, fines range from $5,000 to $10,000 per month until compliance is achieved, but these fines increase the longer a company doesn't meet compliance. Also, fines ranging from $50 to $90 can be charged per affected customer if a data breach occurs.

CCPA

The California Consumer Privacy Act (CCPA) gives California residents more control over the personal information that businesses collect on them. CCPA applies only to for-profit businesses that do business in California (regardless of where your headquarters are located) and that meet any of the following requirements:

- Have a gross annual revenue of over $25 million
- Buy, receive, or sell the personal information of 50,000 or more California residents, households, or devices
- Derive 50 percent or more of their annual revenue from selling California residents' personal information

The CCPA doesn't apply to nonprofit businesses or government agencies. It fines a maximum civil penalty of $2,500 for every unintentional violation and $7,500 for every intentional violation of the law.

GDPR

The General Data Protection Regulation (GDPR) is a privacy law set out by the European Union (EU). GDPR became effective as of May 25, 2018. Even though it was set in place by the EU, it affects all companies that collect information for citizens of the EU. Ernst & Young estimate that the world's 500 biggest corporations are on track to spend up to $7.8 billion on GDPR compliance (`www.securitymetrics.com/blog/how-much-does-gdpr-compliance-cost`). As of January 2020, GDPR has led to over $126 million in fines, with the biggest fine of €50 million paid out by Google. GDPR fines up to €20 million ($24.1 million), or 4 percent of annual global turnover, whichever is higher (`www.cnbc.com/2020/01/19/eu-gdpr-privacy-law-led-to-over-100-million-in-fines.html`).

HIPAA

The Health Insurance Portability and Accountability Act (HIPAA) was passed by Congress in 1996. The privacy aspect of HIPAA is overseen and enforced by the U.S. Department of Health and Human Services (HHS) office, starting in April 2003. From a compliance point of view, HIPAA is about mandating the protection of consumer health information, which is referred to as HIPAA privacy regulation. HIPAA privacy regulation requires healthcare providers and their business associates to develop and follow procedures to ensure the confidentiality and protection of protected health information (PHI).

PIPEDA

The Personal Information Protection and Electronic Documents Act (PIPEDA) is a regulatory requirement that applies to private sector organizations that collect personal information in Canada. It's designed to ensure the protection of personal information in the course of commercial business. Compliance requires that you follow 10 fair principles, which govern the collection, use, and disclosure of personal information, as well as provide access to personal information for customers. PIPEDA fines can reach up to $100,000 per violation.

Cybersecurity Considerations for the Cloud Environment

Roughly 94 percent of organizations are concerned about cloud security, according to a cloud security report (`www.checkpoint.com/cyber-hub/cloud-security/what-is-cloud-security/top-cloud-security-issues-threats-and-concerns`) conducted by `CheckPoint.com`. Among the top concerns are misconfiguration, unauthorized access, insecure interfaces, and hijacking of accounts. Next, we're going to review some of the main cybersecurity issues that occur in a cloud environment:

Configuration Management

In the Check Point survey, misconfiguration was ranked the highest, with 68 percent of respondents saying that it was a concern for their business (`www.checkpoint.com/cyber-hub/cloud-security/what-is-cloud-native-security/the-biggest-cloud-security-challenges-in-2021`). First, cloud infrastructure is designed to be easy to use and enable easy data sharing between parties, which makes it difficult to ensure that data is only accessible to authorized parties. Second, organizations do not have complete visibility or control over their cloud infrastructure. Typically, they will rely on the security controls that the cloud provider supplies to protect their environment, which is limiting. Third, many companies may not be familiar with securing a cloud environment and could end up with multiple deployments, each with different configurations, which makes it easy for a mistake to occur. Finally, unlike physical machines that are owned and maintained by your company, in a cloud environment you may have multiple users who have the ability to create new compute instances. Depending on how these instances are configured, you run the risk of people introducing vulnerabilities into your environment. To fix this issue, you need an effective way of knowing when people create new instances and the ability to ensure that all of these instances follow the proper configuration systems that you lay out for your business.

Unauthorized Access

Cloud-based deployments are typically accessible by the Internet. While this is convenient for employees and customers, it also makes it easier for an attacker to gain unauthorized access to an organization's cloud-based resources. An improperly configured security feature or compromised credentials could provide an attacker with access to your company's network, and because so many users connect remotely, the company often never knows.

Insecure Interfaces/APIs

Cloud service providers (CSPs) often provide customers with a lot of application programming interfaces (APIs) as well as interfaces for their customers. Many times these APIs are well documented and made available to the public to make them easier to use for CSPs' customers. However, because this information is readily available, it can also be found by potential hackers. If the company fails to properly secure these APIs, they can be found and exploited for accessing and stealing data from the company.

Hijacking of Accounts

About 50 percent of respondents claimed that the hijacking of accounts was a major concern in their cloud infrastructure. Many people use weak or commonly used passwords, and as a result, they can be easily guessed by cybercriminals. The problem only gets worse when you consider techniques such as *phishing*, which is when someone sends a fake message designed to trick someone into revealing sensitive information or installing malware. Phishing is commonly used to steal people's login information. As with any other network, gaining full access to someone's credentials can provide hackers with access to a lot of company information. In a cloud environment, companies usually have a diminished ability to identify and respond to these types of situations.

Compliance

Compliance refers to regulations that affect companies depending on their industry, size, and geographical location, and where their customers are. Your cloud environment holds information related to your company and its customers. You need to be sure that all of the data collection, storage, processing, and deletion in your cloud environment is happening in accordance with your company's compliance requirements. At first glance, this might seem straightforward, but there are some cloud-specific considerations that you must be aware of. First, you must understand how your servers are being physically stored and secured; then you need to understand how the data on the servers is being deleted and wiped when these instances are terminated. Forty-two percent of organizations surveyed by CheckPoint.com stated that they needed a specialized cloud compliance solution.

Lack of Visibility

Since an organization's cloud infrastructure is located outside the corporate network, many companies lack the security tools for properly monitoring the network. Also, whoever is responsible for security in that organization may not have the ability to monitor all of the systems in the cloud, and this limits the organization's ability to monitor their cloud-based resources.

Accurate Logging

You need to know what's going on in your environment, and the best way to do this is through accurate detection of errors and suspicious activities. One of the best ways to reliably accomplish this is through the logging of important events on the network. One of the complications with logging on a cloud environment is the synchronization of the time zones, because you may have servers operating out of different locations in different time zones, and correlating events to get an accurate depiction of what is happening can be difficult. In addition, you may have several machines existing on the network and many new instances being created on a regular basis, so you need a logging solution that is flexible enough to monitor and log all of the events of interest.

Cloud Storage

As with logging, you must have a good solution for storing your information on Microsoft Azure. This is important for storing company logs as well as other important company and customer information. This information needs to be easily accessible and configured so that only the right people can access that information. Such storage also includes backing up the data of your important files for later access if required.

Vendor Contracts

You should understand what your cloud provider (in this case, Microsoft) guarantees when it comes to their service level agreements (SLAs). An SLA is a commitment between a service provider and their client on the particulars of a service (e.g., quality, availability, and responsibilities). As mentioned previously, availability is one of the three important aspects of security. In the case of a cloud environment, you are affected by your provider's ability to provide you with good uptime for your cloud network. Understanding what your provider's SLA outlines in terms of availability and other aspects of your cloud environment will determine what additional steps you might need to take to ensure that your cloud environment is always available. It's vital that you and your company understand the provider's committed level of access because that will determine how much availability you can expect for your IT infrastructure.

Link Sharing

Cloud environments are designed for the easy sharing of information and invite collaborators via an email or link to a shared resource. The only problem with this method is that these invitations can be passed on to anyone, making it much more difficult to regulate exactly who has access to what on a network. Once the link is shared with a user, it's usually impossible to revoke access to just that single user without disabling the link entirely. In addition, revoking the link may not be feasible if it's been forwarded on to enough people and they've been given access via that method.

Major Cybersecurity Threats

Cybersecurity attacks consists of three elements. First is a *vulnerability*, which is a weakness found in a system or process that could lead to the compromise of that machine by a threat actor/agency. Second, a *threat actor* is someone or something that exploits a vulnerability to cause a compromise of that machine. Third is an *exploit*, which is the method that a threat actor uses to compromise a machine. In this chapter, we review some of the most common cyberattacks to an organization. This will help you to understand the remainder of this chapter and the book overall. As you read this book keep in mind that these are the attacks that you are trying to defend against when you implement the security controls highlighted in later chapters.

DDoS

Distributed denial of service (DDoS) occurs when a hacker makes a computer or console unable to respond, or at least much slower to respond (or lag). They do this by consistently sending traffic to that machine so that it becomes overwhelmed and cannot respond to legitimate traffic. In a cloud environment, hackers may send tons of traffic to your company's web servers (or another important part) in an attempt to make them unavailable. In a such an environment, companies might share hardware resources with other clients of the cloud provider via virtualization, which increases the risk of a DDoS attack affecting either company. Virtualization is the process of creating a virtual version of something rather than a physical one. In this situation, rather than having two physical hard drives for two different virtual machines, a cloud provider may use the same physical hard drive and simply divide its resources into two groups using virtualization. If a DDoS attack hits the physical machine, both VMs are affected.

Social Engineering

Social engineering is the practice of manipulating people into performing actions or giving up confidential manipulation. It's one of the most common attack vectors in security. One of the most common types of social engineering techniques used on companies are phishing attacks delivered through email. *Phishing* is the act of pretending to be a legitimate person in order to get someone to give up personal information such as their usernames, passwords, credit cards, and employee information. Eighty percent of all security incidents involve the use of a phishing attack (`https://spanning.com/blog/cyberattacks-2021-phishing-ransomware-data-breach-statistics/#:~:text=Phishing%20 attacks%20are%20responsible%20for,65%25%20of%20all%20phishing%20 attacks`). Figure 1.6 is a fine example of well-crafted phishing email.

FIGURE 1.6 Sample phishing email

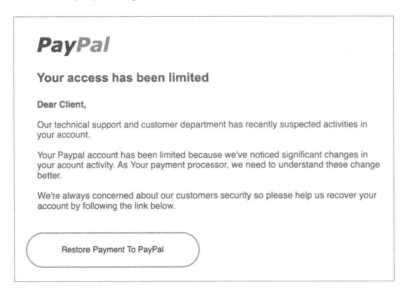

The goal of this email is to have the recipient click the login link, which then sends them to a replica of the PayPal site. Once the recipient enters their login information, it is then sent directly to the hacker to use however they wish.

Another way hackers use email in their attacks is to attach malware that looks like a real attachment in order to trick the user into downloading it. Many software packaging tools can be used to make programming scripts look like a PDF or Word document, with the correct file extension and icon. Additionally, hackers can write malware as macros, which can be attached to a legitimate Excel or Word file, and once it is downloaded and macros are enabled, the program can run automatically.

Lastly, we have *spear phishing*, which is the same as a phishing email but targeted for a specific individual. This attack type requires the hacker to do research beforehand in order to craft an email tailored to its recipient. Because these messages are so tailored, the hackers have a much higher chance of success than when using a regular phishing email. Spear phishing against high-level company executives like chief executive officers (CEOs), chief security officers (CSOs), or chief information officers (CIOs) is referred to as *whaling*.

Password Attacks

As mentioned previously, account hijacking is one of the big concerns when it comes to cloud computing. One way that this is often exploited is through password attacks. A *password attack* is any type of cyberattack that is used to guess/crack a user's passwords. The first and most basic type of attack is a *brute-force attack*, which is when a hacker tries random combinations in an attempt to correctly guess a user's password. This type of attack is extremely time consuming and is not very popular as a result. A more common method is *a dictionary attack*, which is where a hacker uses a preset list of passwords (possibly hundreds or thousands of them) to attempt to guess the user's correct password. Because many people use the same passwords or small variations thereof, this type of attack can be very effective and is how several accounts are compromised every year.

Malware

Malware, or malicious software, is any piece of code that is harmful to a computer system. Malware can do all sorts of harm to your machines, such as stealing information, stealing processing power, displaying malicious ads, or even using that machine to perform attacks on other machines. You should be aware of the following malware types.

Adware

Adware is a relatively harmless type of malware. After being installed, adware shows users advertisements meant to make profit for the hacker. Much of the software that is installed for legitimate applications is technically adware. Outside of being an annoyance, it doesn't do any harm to your computer except use up some of its resources.

Ransomware

One of the most popular and profitable types of malware is *ransomware*. This malware encrypts all of the information located on an infected system and demands payment from the system's owner in order to have the files restored to normal. It is consistently used against businesses and generates a large amount of revenue every year. In 2020 alone,

ransomware cost each victim on average $2.09 million in remediation costs (`www.forbes`
`.com/sites/forbestechcouncil/2021/07/13/with-ransomware-costs-on-the-`
`rise-organizations-must-be-more-proactive/?sh=2729af292dd5`).

Spyware

Spyware is a type of malware that sits on your computer, collecting information, and then
sends that information back to the attacker. This information can include the websites you
visited or your mobile phone's location. Spyware may even turn on your camera to view
your environment or to take pictures. This malware type is usually used to covertly steal
either customer information or business secrets that can be resold by a hacker for profit.

Backdoors

A *backdoor* is a piece of malware that enables an attacker to connect to your computer at
any time. Once a hacker gains access to your computer system, one of the first things they
do is set up a backdoor. Doing so provides them with repeated access—they won't have to
spend time hacking into your computer system again in the event that you fix the vulnerability that let them in, change your password, or otherwise improve the security of your
system.

Bots/Botnets

Bot/botnet malware are pieces of software that lie dormant on a computer until a hacker
gives it a command using a command-and-control (C&C) server. At that point, the bot malware becomes active and takes control of the computer to perform a certain task assigned to
it by the hacker (see Figure 1.7). One controlled computer is called a *bot*, and a collection of
controlled computers is known as a *botnet*.

Cryptojacker

A *cryptojacker* is a type of malware that uses your computer's processing power to mine
cryptocurrency and generate profit for a hacker. Usually, they target hundreds or thousands
of computers so that they can mine cryptocurrency very quickly and for a large profit.

Keylogger

Keyloggers are a type of malware that records the keystrokes on a computer and sends that
information back to the attacker. Generally, this information is used to discover people's
usernames, passwords, personal identification numbers (PINs), and other login information.
It can also be used to obtain other personal information, but that is less common.

FIGURE 1.7 How botnets work

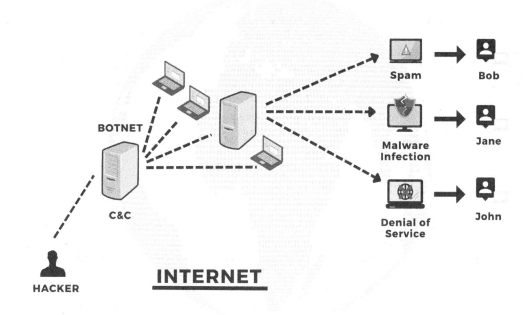

RAM Scraper

Remote access memory (RAM) is a type of temporary storage location on a computer. A *RAM scraper* collects information from the RAM and sends it back to the hacker. RAM scrapers can be very profitable for hackers gaining entrance into point-of-sale (POS) systems like cash registers, because for a brief period the systems store credit card numbers unencrypted. By collecting that information, a hacker gains access to credit card payment information that can be either reused or sold to other people for profit.

Browser Hijacking

Browser hijacking is when malware alters the way your web browser works to either redirect you to a website that the hacker wants you to visit, or to steal your information from the cookies that your web browser stores about your online activity. A *cookie* is a small piece of data that your web browser generates as you browse the Internet. Cookies are how websites are able to remember that you are logged in, save your shopping carts, recommend products to you based on your search history, and so forth.

Summary

Cloud computing continues to be a popular way for organizations to create scalable and convenient IT infrastructure at a fraction of the cost of creating an on-premises solution. However, cloud computing comes with many unique security challenges that must be addressed. Even in a cloud-computing environment, companies are still required to maintain the same level of security, and in some cases, even more so. In order for a cloud network to be accessible, it must be exposed to the Internet, which means that it can be seen by anyone located outside the network. Potential risk of exposure and attack is increased, thus making it even more important to have good security practices set in place.

Exam Essentials

Be able to define the CIA triad.   The CIA triad consists of three core principles for having a good cybersecurity program. First is confidentiality, which means that only people with the right access should be able to access any piece of information. Second is integrity, which means that only people with the correct access should be able to change or edit any piece of information; integrity seeks to make sure that the information is always accurate. Third is availability, which means that you must ensure that information and services are always available for use by the right user.

Know the purpose of a demilitarized zone (DMZ).   A DMZ is a subnetwork containing an organization's exposed, Internet-facing servers and acts as an exposed point to untrusted networks. For example, this is where companies typically place their web servers that need to be exposed to the Internet.

Be able to describe the principle of least privilege.   This principle states that you should give users the least amount of privilege that they need to perform their job and nothing more. Giving users anything more than what is necessary creates risk for the company without providing any benefit.

Know the AAAs of access management.   First is authentication, which is all about confirming that a user is who they claim to be. It's based on the idea that each user has unique information that sets them apart from all other users and can be used to prove their identity when needed. Next is authorization, which is the process of granting or denying a user access to system resources once the user has been authenticated. Authorization determines the amount of information or services to which the user can get access. The last A in AAA stands for accounting, which is the ability to track a user's activity while accessing the company's resources.

Be familiar with the two types of encryption.   The first is symmetric key encryption, where the same or identical encryption keys are used to both encrypt and decrypt information. The advantage of symmetric key encryption is that it's faster but typically less secure. The second type is asymmetric key encryption, where you use two different keys for the encryption and decryption of the message. This type of encryption is the more secure of the two, but it is much slower and is best suited for situations where you are processing smaller datasets and where speed isn't a huge concern.

Be able to define the zero-trust model. This is a security concept stating that an organization shouldn't automatically trust anything inside or outside its perimeter, and instead, should verify everything before granting it access to anything. Azure has many features that seek to authenticate users inside and outside the network before granting them privileged access.

Review Questions

1. Which of the following is not an element of the CIA triad?

    A. Confidentiality

    B. Integrity

    C. Availability

    D. Nonrepudiation

2. Which element relates to holding users accountable for their actions?

    A. Confidentiality

    B. Integrity

    C. Availability

    D. Nonrepudiation

3. Which element refers to protecting information from unauthorized access?

    A. Confidentiality

    B. Integrity

    C. Availability

    D. Nonrepudiation

4. Which element refers to protecting information from unauthorized changes, thus ensuring accuracy?

    A. Confidentiality

    B. Integrity

    C. Availability

    D. Nonrepudiation

5. Which element refers to ensuring that information is available when you need it?

    A. Confidentiality

    B. Integrity

    C. Availability

    D. Nonrepudiation

6. What does the principle of least privilege relate to?

    A. Limiting user accounts

    B. Limiting user access to what's needed

    C. Removing user access

    D. Removing access after terminating employees

7. What is the principle of a zero-trust model?

    A. Authenticate users who are outside a network.

    B. Authenticate all users with multifactor authentication (MFA).

    C. Authenticate users who are inside and outside the network.

    D. Do not allow anyone to authenticate to vital resources.

8. What is the core principle of defense in depth?

    A. Having multiple types of security features in place

    B. Having multiple layers of security features in place

    C. Having backups for each of your security features

    D. Investing heavily in security software for your company

9. Which of these is not a layer in defense in depth?

    A. Physical security

    B. Encryption security

    C. Application security

    D. Policies, procedures, and awareness training

10. What is security through obscurity?

    A. Hiding features of your security program

    B. Relying on hiding something to keep it secure

    C. Keeping information confidential

    D. Keeping your applications code a secret as a security practice

11. Which of these is not part of access management?

    A. Authentication

    B. Authorization

    C. Availability

    D. Accounting

12. Which type of encryption uses the same key for encryption and decryption?

    A. Public key encryption

    B. Asymmetric encryption

    C. Symmetric encryption

    D. End-to-end encryption

13. Which type of encryption uses a different key for encryption and decryption?

    A. Shared key encryption

    B. Asymmetric encryption

    C. Symmetric encryption

    D. End-to-end encryption

14. What is a DMZ used for?

   A. Segmenting a network

   B. Hosting network resources that are exposed to an untrusted network

   C. Hosting firewalls that are exposed to the Internet

   D. Serving as a type of network subnet

15. What is configuration management?

   A. How you set up company systems

   B. Ensuring that your systems are configured according to your company standards

   C. Ensuring that your systems don't have vulnerabilities

   D. A type of vulnerability management

16. What is a DDoS attack?

   A. It's a type of malware.

   B. It makes company resources unavailable.

   C. It's a type of web application attack.

   D. It mimics legitimate website traffic.

17. Which of these is not a major cybersecurity threat?

   A. DDoS

   B. Phishing

   C. Ransomware

   D. Adware

18. Which of the following doesn't determine your company's compliance requirements?

   A. Industry

   B. Company size

   C. Geographic location

   D. Type of software

19. What is an example of a security control used to maintain integrity?

   A. Username and password

   B. Proxy servers

   C. Digital signature

   D. Antivirus software

20. Which of these is not a type of malware?

   A. Ransomware

   B. Adware

   C. Rootkit

   D. Web cookies

Chapter

2

Managing Identity and Access in Microsoft Azure

THE MCA MICROSOFT CERTIFIED ASSOCIATE AZURE SECURITY ENGINEER ASSESSMENT TEST TOPICS COVERED IN THIS CHAPTER INCLUDE:

✓ **Manage Azure Active Directory (Azure AD) identities**

- Create and manage a managed identity for Azure resources
- Configure security for service principals
- Manage Azure AD directory groups
- Manage Azure AD users
- Manage external identities by using Azure AD
- Manage administrative units

✓ **Manage secure access by using Azure AD**

- Configure Azure AD Privileged Identity Management (PIM)
- Implement conditional access policies, including multifactor authentication
- Implement Azure AD Identity Protection
- Implement passwordless authentication
- Configure access reviews

✓ **Manage application access**

- Integrate single sign-on (SSO) and identity providers for authentication
- Create an app registration
- Configure app registration permission scopes
- Manage app registration permission consent

- Manage API permissions to Azure subscriptions and resources
- Configure an authentication method for a service principal

✓ **Manage access control**

- Configure Azure role permissions for management groups, subscriptions, resource groups, and resources
- Interpret role and resource permissions
- Assign built-in Azure AD roles
- Create and assign custom roles, including Azure roles and Azure AD roles

This chapter focuses on how to implement good identity and access management practices in Microsoft Azure. This includes topics like managing Azure Active Directory (AD) identities, securing access to resources, managing application access, and implementing role-based access.

Identity and Access Management

Identity and access management (IAM) covers roughly 30–35 percent of your exam. IAM is all about ensuring that only the correct users have access to technology resources and that no one else does. These resources include business processes, policies, and technologies that all come together to manage digital identities used in a computer environment. It's critical to ensure that only a select group has access to important resources on the network; IAM stems back to the principle of least privilege, in which only those who need access to a resource should have it. Fundamental IAM encompasses the following key points:

- How individuals are identified in a system
- How roles are identified and assigned in a system
- How levels of access are assigned to individuals or groups
- How individuals and their roles are added, removed, and updated in the system
- How a system's sensitive data is protected
- How accountability is ensured

Let's discuss these key points.

Identifying Individuals in a System

The first step in IAM is how individuals will be authenticated, or identified, on a system. Identification is typically performed by a user when they provide a username and a password—this combination should only be known by that user, and by providing this information they're proving to the system that they are who they say they are. In addition to a username and password, individuals can use the following types of identity to prove who they are to the system:

Temporary PINs or Hard Tokens   If you've ever used Google Authenticator or an RSA token, you are familiar with these forms of identity. You use an application or hardware token device, which generates a new code every minute, that can be used to log on to a system. Usually, this device is combined with a password for *two-factor authentication*. Two-factor authentication is a type of authentication where you use two authentication factors instead of one.

Facial Recognition   Facial recognition has become much more popular nowadays, especially since its adoption by Apple for its iPhone. This identification type uses the unique features of a user's face to identify the user. These features are much more difficult to impersonate than a password, but facial recognition is much harder to implement because it requires special software/hardware in order to operate.

Iris Scan   The iris is a thin circular structure located toward the front of the eye, and it controls how much light reaches the retina, a thin tissue at the back of the eye that translates images to the brain. An iris scan uses a camera to perform pattern-matching techniques on an individual's eye to find unique patterns. Whenever a user wants to be authenticated, the camera compares the patterns stored in the system's database to the patterns of the user trying to be authenticated. If those patterns match, the user is authenticated. Iris scans have an almost 0 percent false negative rate.

Retinal Scan   A retinal scan is performed by casting a beam of light on the human eye and mapping the unique blood vessel patterns within the retina. Retina scans have a low false negative rate, but its accuracy can be affected by disease. Additionally, retina scans must be performed at a close range and are considered to be invasive. They also tend to be more expensive than iris scans to implement because more sophisticated equipment is required.

Voice Matching   You can also use voice recognition as a means of identification. Voice recognition software measures unique biological factors that combine to create each person's unique voice. Although it isn't commonly used, voice recognition is still an option in certain situations, particularly for web apps or mobile phones. A common example of voice recognition is Siri on Apple's iPhones.

Identifying and Assigning Roles in a System and to an Individual

Early on, IT professionals assigned permissions on an individual basis, depending on the needs and rank of the person being assigned. However, you can imagine how inefficient and impractical that process quickly became, as company rosters began to grow into the hundreds or even thousands of employees. This approach also suffered from inconsistency because there was no guarantee that two people with the same job responsibilities would be given the same access. It was at this point that role-based access control (RBAC) came into play. Rather than assigning access to an individual, RBAC assigns roles for different job functions. Then when someone is hired, they are assigned a role that has all the access they need to do their job and nothing extra. One important aspect of IAM is how roles are defined and how they are assigned to an individual person.

Assigning Access Levels to Individuals or Groups

For role-based access to be effective, you must ensure that you assign the correct level of access to a role. Once the correct access level is assigned, then you can assign that access level to individuals or groups by assigning their account to that role. To do this, it's important to have a good understanding of what the role's job description is, which will ensure that the assigned individuals are given all of their access on time and won't be delayed in performing their work. If you have worked at a few different jobs, you may have noticed that many times you didn't have all the access that you needed right away. This is typically a sign that the company doesn't have good IAM set in place.

Adding, Removing, and Updating Individuals and Their Roles in a System

Next, IAM focuses on the addition, removal, and updating of individuals and their roles in a system. Picture the average corporation, where employees quit and/or are being fired, hired, or promoted on a regular basis. As a result, all of these people need to have their access increased or revoked, and in some cases, it needs to be done urgently. Disgruntled employees are the main culprits when it comes to stealing company information or corporate sabotage. People who feel they have been wronged by a business may try to get revenge by doing harm to the company, and they are able to do this due to the access their corporate accounts afford them. According to a (2009) article in *Infosec Magazine*, nearly 60 percent of fired workers steal company data before quitting (https://itbusiness.ca/news/ nearly-60-per-cent-of-fired-workers-steal-company-data-before- quitting/13115), and this is often because companies are too slow in removing an employee's access.

Protecting a System's Sensitive Data and Securing the System

IAM is designed to protect sensitive data by limiting the users who are given access to a particular resource. By default, all sensitive data should be inaccessible to everyone, and only those who have a verified business need for access to that resource should be given access to it. An *implicit deny* is a standard for security practices. You should, by default, deny/block all attempts to access or communicate with a system to limit your system's overall exposure to risk. Compromising legitimate accounts is one of the main ways that hackers gain access to a network, and doing so enables them to go undetected within the network for a long period of time. The protection of these accounts is vital to your company's security; without it, your company is open to exposure and lawsuits.

Enforcing Accountability

The last element of IAM is accountability, or holding all users accountable for their actions on a system. This means that admins should be able to see what actions are being performed on a user account and link all actions on the system back to an individual user. If you think back to the CIA triad in Chapter 1, "Introduction to Microsoft Azure," we discussed *nonrepudiation*, which means that security aims to ensure that no one can perform an action and then claim that they didn't perform it at a later date. This falls under the realm of IAM; through proper account monitoring, administration should be able to link every action to a user and therefore ensure that no one can deny having performed that action in the first place. It's one big reason why it's not a good idea to share a corporate account with someone, because you don't want to be held liable for anything someone else has done.

IAM in the Microsoft Azure Platform

Now that we have discussed IAM as a general security practice, let's delve into IAM in the Azure platform. In Azure, identity management seeks to provide four main capabilities to an organization's architecture:

- Provide a single sign-on capability to application users.
- Enhance the application to use modern authentication with minimal effort.
- Enforce multifactor authentication (MFA) for all sign-ins coming from outside the company's network.
- Develop an application to enable users to enroll and securely manage their account data.

   In Azure, you'll find *Azure Active Directory*, a service that creates and stores information on the network and that is easily accessible by authenticated users through a login process. Azure AD Authentication is the active process of users being verified in order to gain access to Azure AD. All of this user information is managed by network administrators.

Creating and Managing Azure AD Identities

Managed identities were created in response to a challenge that developers faced when it came to managing the secrets/credentials that were used to secure communications between different software components. Managed identities eliminate the need for developers to manually manage credentials. Managed identities are identities that applications can use to connect to any resource that supports Azure AD Authentication. Here are the two primary types of managed identities:

System-Assigned Managed Identities   Some services in Azure give you the option of enabling a managed identity directly on that service instance. As soon as you enable a system-assigned managed identity, another identity is created in AAD that's linked to the life cycle of the service instance. Only that Azure resource can use that particular identity to request tokens from AAD.

User-Assigned Managed Identities A user-assigned managed identity is managed separately from the resources that will use it. Because of this separation, this identity can be assigned to multiple instances of an Azure service.

Table 2.1 provides the details of the differences between the two types.

TABLE 2.1   Differences between system-assigned and user-assigned managed identities

Properties	System-assigned managed identity	User-assigned managed identity
Identity creation	This identity will be created as part of an Azure resource (e.g., an Azure virtual machine).	This identity will be created as a stand-alone Azure resource and will not be linked to any resource.
Identity life cycle	This identity will share a life cycle with the resource with which it was created. When the resource is deleted, the identity is deleted as well.	This identity will have an independent life cycle and will need to be deleted separately from any resource for which it is used.
Ability to be shared across Azure resources	This identity cannot be shared across resources and can only be associated with a single Azure resource.	This identity can be shared; the same identity can be associated with multiple Azure resources.
Standard-use cases	This identity is used for use cases that are contained in a single Azure resource or use cases that need independent identities.	This identity is used for use cases that run on multiple resources and can share a single identity or use cases where resources are recycled frequently but permissions are constant.

Enabling a System-Assigned Managed Identity When Creating a VM

A *virtual machine (VM)* is a virtual instance of a computer OS such as Windows 10. When creating a virtual machine and enabling a system-assigned managed identity, you need to ensure that you meet the following prerequisites:

- Ensure that your account has the VM contributor or a higher role assignment; this will give you the access needed to create a VM.
- Inside the create a virtual machine wizard, on the Management tab in the Identity section, turn Managed Service Identity on (see Figure 2.1).

FIGURE 2.1   Enabling a system-assigned managed identity on a VM

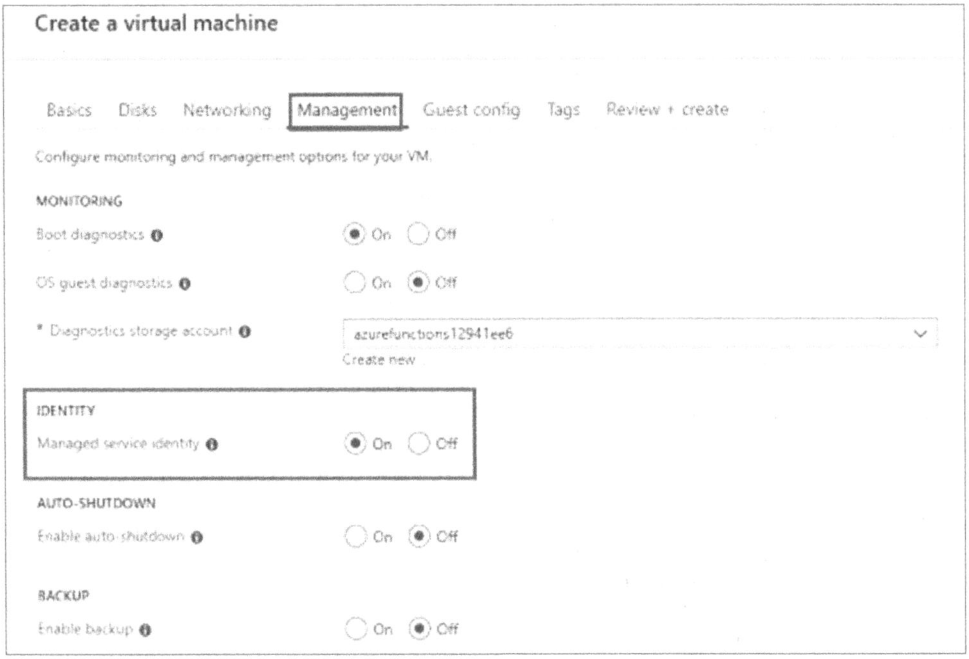

Enabling a System-Assigned Managed Identity on an Existing VM

What if your company has an existing VM? To enable a system-assigned managed identity on an existing VM, follow these steps:

1. Ensure that your account has the VM Contributor or a higher role assignment.

2. Navigate to the Azure portal on an account that is associated with the Azure subscription that contains the VM.

3. Navigate to the VM from the Azure portal and select Identity on the left side menu.

4. Under System Assigned Status, select On and then click Save.

Assigning a User-Assigned Managed Identity to an Existing Virtual Machine

Currently, the Azure portal doesn't support creating user-assigned managed identities during the creation of a VM, so we'll skip straight to existing VMs. The following steps show you how to assign a user-assisted managed identity to an existing VM. You must create the identity before performing these steps.

1. Go to the Azure portal on an account associated with the Azure subscription hosting the VM.

2. Navigate to the desired VM and click Identity, select User Assigned, and then click Add.

3. Select the user-assigned identity you want to add to the VM and click Add (see Figure 2.2).

FIGURE 2.2   Adding a user-assigned managed identity

Managing Azure AD Groups

Keep in mind that Azure AD is not a cloud version of the standard Windows service Active Directory. Nor is it a competitor of Active Directory. You take a Windows AD server, connect it to Azure AD, and extend your on-premises directory to Azure. This way, users can use the same credentials to access local and cloud-based resources. However, this integration isn't necessary. You may opt to use Azure AD as your *only* directory service to control access to your applications and services. Now that you understand what Azure AD is, let's explore Azure AD groups and why they are beneficial.

An Azure AD group aids you in organizing users by making it much easier to manage their permissions. It enables owners to assign a set of permissions to an entire group of users, rather than assigning permissions to users individually. Azure AD also allows you to set rules that will assign permission based on attributes such as a user's department and/or job title. This is facilitated through *dynamic groups* that can automatically add or remove users from groups based on certain characteristics.

Azure AD has two types of groups:

Security Groups   Security groups are the most common and are used to manage user and computer access to shared resources. For example, you may decide to create a security group for all your company's Human Resource (HR) analysts. This group provides them with access to the resources they need, and anyone with that job title designation is placed in that group upon being hired.

Microsoft 365 Groups   These groups are primarily used for collaboration among team members. This is commonly done by giving members access to a shared mailbox, calendar, files, SharePoint site, and so forth. A Microsoft 365 group is good for giving people outside your organization access to your company's group resources.

Creating Security Groups

To create a security group:

1. Navigate to the Azure portal.
2. Search for and select Azure Active Directory.
3. On the Active Directory page, select Group and New Group.
4. Select a group type, and then assign a group name, a group description, and the group's membership type.

   The membership type field can be one of three potential values:

   Assigned/Static   The group will contain users or groups that you manually select.

   Dynamic User   With this user type, you create rules based on the characteristics that enable attribute-based dynamic memberships for groups. A common example is when you assign membership to a group if a user is part of a certain department.

   Dynamic Device   For this group, you can create rules that will base the group's membership on the characteristics of a user's device (e.g., an iOS or Android device).

Creating Security Groups using Azure PowerShell

You can also create security groups using Azure PowerShell, which is a set of cmdlets for managing Azure resources directly, if you prefer to do your administration via the command line. Here is an example where a groups has been added using the `New-AzureADGroup` command:

```
New-AzureADGroup -Description "Marketing" -DisplayName "Marketing" -MailEnabled
$false -SecurityEnabled $true -MailNickName "Marketing"
```

Managing Azure Users

Every user who needs access to an Azure resource must have an Azure user account. A *user account* contains all the information necessary to authenticate the user. Once the user is authenticated, Azure AD builds an access token to authorize the user and determines what resources the user will have access to and what they can do with those resources.

Azure AD defines users according to categories:

Cloud Identities   Users in this category exist only within Azure AD and not on any other on-premises AD server. The source for these users will be your Azure AD.

Directory-Synchronized Identities   Users in this category originally existed in an on-premises AD that you want to bring into your Azure cloud environment. To do so, you use a synchronization activity utilizing Azure AD Connect that brings these users into your Azure AD, allowing them to exist on both the on-premises and the cloud instance of AD.

Guest Users   Users in this category exist outside Azure altogether and originate from a different cloud provider or separate Microsoft account. For example, they may be from an Xbox Live account. These types of accounts are useful when third parties need access to your Azure resources.

Adding Users to Your Azure AD

You can add users to your Azure AD in four ways:

- Syncing an on-premises Window Server AD
- Manually adding users via the Azure portal
- Using a command-line tool
- Selecting other options like Azure AD Graph API, Microsoft 365 Admin Center, and Microsoft Intune Admin Console

Let's break these down a little further.

Syncing an On-Premises Windows Server AD

Azure AD Connect enables you to synchronize a traditional on-premises AD with your Azure AD instance. It is the most common way that enterprise customers can add users to their Azure AD. The advantage to this approach is that users can use single sign-on (SSO) to access on-premises and cloud-based resources.

Using the Azure Portal

Using the Azure portal, you can manually add new users. The prerequisite is that you need to use an account that has the User Administrator role. To add a new user:

1. Open the Azure portal with the User Administrator role.
2. Search for and select Azure Active Directory.

3. Select Users and then select New Users.

4. Enter the required information and click Create.

Using a Command-Line Tool

If you have several users to add, a good option is to use a command-line tool, where you can run the `New-AzureADUser` PowerShell command. Check out the following example:

```
# First step is to create a password object
$PasswordProfile = New-Object -TypeName Microsoft.Open.AzureAD.Model
.PasswordProfile
# Next you assign the password
$PasswordProfile.Password = "<Your Password>"
# Creating the user
New-AzureADUser -AccountEnabled $True -DisplayName "Abby Brown"
-PasswordProfile
$PasswordProfile -MailNickName "AbbyB" -UserPrincipalName "AbbyB@contoso.com"
```

This returns the following output:

```
ObjectId                             DisplayName UserPrincipalName UserType
--------                             ----------- ----------------- --------
f36634c8-8a93-4909-9248-0845548bc515 Abby Brown  AbbyB@contoso.com Member
```

Another option is to use the Azure command-line interface (CLI):

```
az ad user create --display-name "Abby Brown" \
                  --password "<mypassword>" \
                  --user-principal-name "AbbyB@contoso.com" \
                  --force-change-password-next-login true \
                  --mail-nickname "AbbyB"
```

Other Options

The other options for adding users include Azure AD Graph API, Microsoft 365 Admin Center, and Microsoft Intune Admin Console if you are sharing the same directory.

Managing External Identities Using Azure AD

In Azure AD, you can use external identities to give people outside your organization access to your applications and resources via whatever identity they prefer. This allows groups like your business partners, customers, suppliers, third-party vendors, and any other guests to authenticate using their preferred identities. You may have seen this before if you've ever chosen to sign into an app using Facebook or Gmail. For example, the guest user's identity provider is responsible for managing their identity, and the app is responsible for managing access to its applications and resources using Azure AD. External identities are used to support the following use cases:

Business-to-Business (B2B) Collaboration   In this use case, you are inviting external users into your environment as a "guest user." Then you can assign permissions to that guest user while enabling them to use their existing credentials.

Business-to-Customer (B2C) Access to Consumer/Customer-Facing Apps   You can use Azure AD to enable your customers to sign in with an identity that they have already established.

Configuring External Collaboration

This following steps explain how to configure external collaboration using the Microsoft 365 groups:

1. Navigate to the Azure portal with the tenant Administrator role.

2. Select Azure AD.

3. Select External Identities ➤ External Collaboration Settings.

4. In the section Guest User Access Restrictions, select the level of access you want to give to guest users. You have three choices:

   - **Guest users have the same access as members (most inclusive):** Choosing this option grants guests the same level of access to Azure AD resources and directory data as member users.

   - **Guest users have limited access to properties and memberships of directory objects:** This is the default setting that provides limited access by blocking guests from certain directory tasks. For example, it blocks enumerating users, groups, or other directory resources.

   - **Guest user access is restricted to properties and memberships of their own directory objects:** This setting is the most restrictive—guests can only access their own profiles. Guests are not allowed to see other users' profiles, groups, or group memberships.

5. Under Guest Invite Settings (see Figure 2.3), choose how people can be invited to be a guest user. You can allow anyone to send invites or only assigned users or only admin users, and you can exclude everyone from within the company from sending an invite.

FIGURE 2.3   Guest Invite Settings

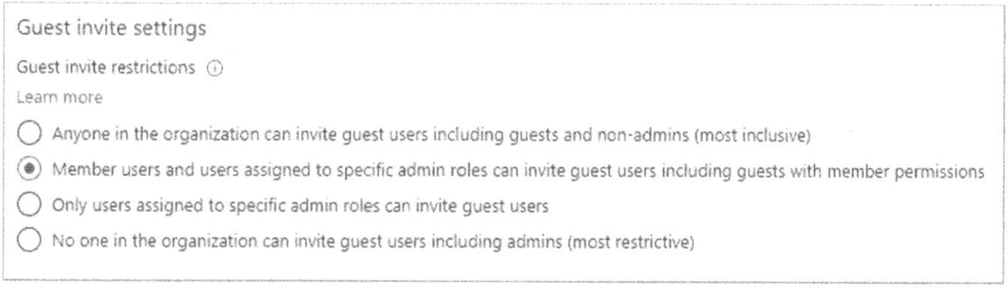

Guest invite settings

Guest invite restrictions ⓘ
Learn more

○ Anyone in the organization can invite guest users including guests and non-admins (most inclusive)

◉ Member users and users assigned to specific admin roles can invite guest users including guests with member permissions

○ Only users assigned to specific admin roles can invite guest users

○ No one in the organization can invite guest users including admins (most restrictive)

6. Enable guest self-service sign-up via user flows.

7. Choose whether you want to allow or deny invitations to the domains you specify.

Managing Administrative Units

Administrative units can restrict permissions in a role to any portion of the organization that you define. For example, you could limit someone's permissions to resources that are only in their region. In large companies, you may have similar job roles that are spread across multiple different regions, and you don't want someone having access to a region of resources that they aren't managing.

To ensure that the correct regions are managed by the correct users, you can create and manage administrative units by using the Azure portal, PowerShell cmdlets, scripts, or Microsoft Graph.

Managing Secure Access Using Azure Active Directory

In this section, we discuss how to secure access to Azure Resources using Azure AD, which is the primary IAM tool in Azure.

Configuring Azure AD Privileged Identity Management

Privileged Identity Management (PIM) is a service in Azure AD that enables you to manage, control, and monitor access to critical resources in your cloud environment. Its key features include:

- Providing just-in-time privileged access

- Assigning time-bound access to resources in Azure

- Enabling the approval requirement to activate privileged roles

- Enforcing MFA to activate a role

- Enabling the creation of notifications when privileged roles are activated

- Conducting access reviews to ensure that all user roles are needed and identifying opportunities to remove access

- Enabling you to download an audit history for internal or external audits

- Preventing the removal of the last active Global Administrator role assignment, which permanently prevents you from accessing some resources

Table 2.2 lists some terminology you must know to fully understand PIM.

TABLE 2.2 PIM terminology

Terms/ concepts	Role assignment category	Description
Eligible	Type	This is a role assignment where the user must perform actions to use the role. Being eligible means that they can activate the role as needed by performing the required actions.
Active	Type	This is a role assignment that doesn't require any actions to be used and remains activated, although it can be deactivated.
Activate	Type	To activate a role means a user must perform one or more actions to use the role for which they're already eligible.
Assigned	State	This describes when a user has an active role assignment.
Activated	State	This describes when a user who is eligible for a role assignment has performed the actions required to activate the role, and the role has been activated. The user can use this role only for a certain time period before they need to reactivate it.
Permanent eligible	Duration	This describes a role assignment where the user is always eligible to activate a role.
Permanent active	Duration	This describes a role where users can access it without needing to perform any actions to activate it.
Time-bound eligible	Duration	This describes when a user is only eligible to activate a role within particular start and end dates.
Time-bound active	Duration	This describes when a user can only use a role within particular start and end dates.
Just-in-time (JIT) access		This describes when users receive temporary access to perform privileged tasks only for the time that it is needed. Once the access is no longer needed, it is immediately removed, which prevents unauthorized users from gaining access to the permissions after they have expired.
Principle of least privilege access		This is a security best practice where every user is provided with only the privileges/access they need to perform their job and nothing more. It reduces the number of additional access points that exist in the environment and reduces the opportunities for misuse.

Setting Up PIM

To use PIM, you must have one of the two following licenses: Azure AD Premium P2 or Enterprise Mobility + Security (EMS) E5. To enable PIM for an organization, a user who has one of these licenses must go to the Roles and Administrators section in Azure AD. Once they select a role, they will automatically enable PIM for the entire organization and can either assign a "regular" role assignment or an eligible role assignment.

You must prepare PIM for the Azure AD roles to allow for automatic enrollment. To prepare, you should:

1. Configure the Azure AD role settings.

2. Give eligible assignments to your roles.

3. Allow eligible users to activate their Azure AD role just-in-time.

4. Discover Azure resources.

5. Configure Azure RBAC role settings.

6. Give eligible assignments.

7. Allow eligible users to activate their Azure roles just-in-time.

Implementing Conditional Access Policies, Including MFA

In this section, we discuss how to implement conditional access policies in Azure. Conditional access policies add extra limitations on user access to Azure resources so that you can have more fine-grained control of user access.

Multifactor Authentication

Multifactor authentication (MFA) provides an extra layer of security for your digital identities by requiring two or more different types of authentication for someone to log in. Here are some common types of authentication:

Something You Know   Examples include a password or a security question.

Something You Have   Examples include a code that is texted to you or a physical card that you carry to be scanned.

Something You Are   This includes biometrics—methods like a fingerprint scan or a retinal scan.

Something You Do   Examples include voice matching or the way you walk—anything that is unique to you.

MFA requires that you meet at least two of these criteria, which makes it much harder for an attacker to gain access to everything they need to hack your account. It's why so many companies are starting to adopt this model, especially in important industries such as financial institutions, healthcare institutions, or privileged user accounts. Azure AD has built-in MFA capabilities and can integrate with other MFA providers to help secure your accounts.

Conditional Access Policies

MFA isn't the only way to protect user accounts on Azure. Depending on different factors, conditional access policies also allow you to set conditions to block someone from logging in (see Figure 2.4) as well as other control features. One example is locking a login attempt from an unrecognized IP address or an unfamiliar device. Azure AD can provide conditional access policies based on the group, location, or device state. The location feature will allow your organization to differentiate between IP addresses that belong to the organization and those that don't. Logins from those locations should require MFA for enhanced security.

FIGURE 2.4   How conditional access policies work

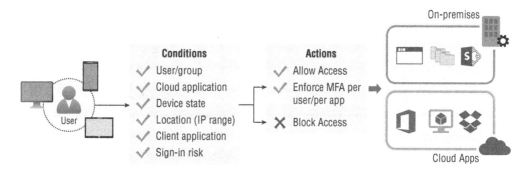

Implementing Azure AD Identity Protection

Identity Protection is a tool used to help organizations protect themselves from identity-based risks. To help with this, Microsoft analyzes roughly 6.5 trillion signals per day to identify and protect their customers from threats. It does this through three methods:

- Automated detection and the remediation of identity-based risks

- Investigating risks using data in the portal

- Exporting risk detection data to your security information and event management (SIEM) solution

To access Identity Protection, a user needs to be a security reader, security operator, security administrator, global reader, or global administrator. The breakdown of roles and their access is shown in Table 2.3.

TABLE 2.3 Breakdown of identity access roles

Roles	Features	Limitations
Global administrator	Has full access to Identity Protection	None
Security administrator	Has full access to Identity Protection	Cannot perform password resets
Security operator	Able to view all Identity Protection reports and overview blade	Unable to configure or change policies
		Cannot perform password resets
	Able to dismiss user risk, confirm safe sign-in, and confirm compromise	Unable to configure alerts
Security reader	Able to view all Identity Protection reports and overview blade	Unable to configure or change policies
		Cannot perform password resets
		Cannot configure alerts
		Unable to give feedback on detections

First, let's look at *automated detection* and *remediation*. This is performed through the creation and configuration of two types of risk policies: a sign-in risk policy and a user risk policy. Both of these policies allow for an automated response to risk detection in your environment and give users the option to self-remediate when a risk is detected.

Choosing a Risk Level

The first thing you must do is choose an acceptable risk level. Identity Protection places risk into one of three categories: low, medium, and high. While Microsoft does not give details on how the risk category is determined, each level shows a higher level of confidence that a user or sign-in has been compromised. You must select a level for Identity Protection to trigger an alert as the first step in creating a policy. Microsoft's recommendations are to set the user policy threshold to High, set the sign-in risk policy to Medium and above, and to enable self-remediation options.

Risk Remediation

Next, you need to decide how you are going to handle remediation when a violation is detected in your risk policy. You can choose to block access when a risk is detected, but this can prevent legitimate users from doing their job if the alert is a false positive. Microsoft suggests allowing self-remediation using Azure AD MFA and Self-Service Password Reset (SSPR). In this situation:

- When a user risk policy triggers, you can require a secure password reset. Doing so necessitates that Azure AD MFA be done *before* the user creates their new password with SSPR, thus resetting the user's risk.

- When a sign-in risk policy triggers, Azure AD MFA can be triggered. This will allow the user to prove it is them by using one of their preregistered authentication methods, thus resetting the sign-in risk.

Both options ensure that risk can be eliminated without providing any long-term interruptions to the user's access.

You can also manually exclude users in your organization, which may be necessary, depending on how the accounts are used.

Enabling the Policies

Risk policies can be enabled in two places, under conditional access and Identity Protection, with conditional access being the preferred method. The steps for enabling risk policies are as follows:

User Risk with Conditional Access:

1. Log into the Azure portal as a global administrator, security administrator, or conditional access administrator.

2. Choose Azure AD ➤ Security ➤ Conditional Access.

3. Select New Policy, then select Create New Policy.

4. Assign a name to your policy, ideally a name that suits what the policy will be used for.

5. Under Assignments, select Users And Workload Identities.

6. Under Include, select All Users.

7. Under Exclude, select Users And Groups and choose your organization's emergency access or in-case-of-emergency accounts. These are accounts that will be used in the event of an emergency.

8. Under Cloud Apps Or Actions ➤ Include, select All Cloud Apps.

9. Under Conditions ➤ User Risk, set Configure to Yes. Set Configure User Risk Levels Needed For Policy To Be Enforced to High, then select Done.

10. Under Access Controls ➤ Grant, select Grant Access and Require Password Change, and click Select.

11. Review your settings and set Enable Policy to On.

12. Once you are done, select Create to create and enable your policy.

Sign-in Risk with Conditional Access:

1. Log into the Azure portal as a global administrator, security administrator, or conditional access administrator.

2. Navigate to Azure AD ➤ Security ➤ Conditional Access.

3. Choose New Policy, then select Create New Policy.

4. Assign a name for your new policy.

5. Under Assignments, select Users And Workload Identities.

6. Under Include, select All Users.

7. Under Exclude, select Users And Groups, and choose your organization's emergency access or "break-glass" accounts.

8. Under Cloud Apps Or Actions ➤ Include, select All Cloud Apps.

9. Under Conditions ➤ Sign-in Risk, set Configure to Yes. Set the sign-in risk level this policy will apply to option to High and Medium.

10. Click Done.

11. Under Access Controls ➤ Grant, select Grant Access and Require Multi-Factor Authentication, and then click Select.

12. Review your settings and set Enable Policy to On.

13. Click Create to create and enable your policy.

Next we'll show you how to investigate risks using data in the Azure portal. Identity Protection provides three different reports that you can use to investigate data risks in your environment: *Risky Users*, *Risky Sign-ins,* and *Risk Detections*. You can find all three reports in the Azure portal by choosing Azure AD ➤ Security ➤ Report and downloading them in CSV format. Let's look at each of these reports and what actions can be taken based on the events.

Risky Users

Using the information in the Risky Users report, you can identify the following:

- Users who are at risk, who have had risk remediated, or who have had risk dismissed
- Details about detections
- History of all risky sign-ins
- Risk history
- Risky workload identities, which are workloads that have been flagged for risk

  You can then act in response to these events. Here are some common examples:

- Resetting the user's password
- Confirming if the user has been compromised
- Dismissing the user risk as a false positive

- Blocking a user from signing in
- Investigating further using Microsoft Defender for Identity

Risky Sign-ins

Azure creates the Risky Sign-ins report using data over the last 30 days. With the information in this report, you can identify the following:

- Sign-ins that were classified as one of the following:
  - At risk
  - Confirmed compromised
  - Confirmed safe
  - Dismissed
  - Remediated
- The real-time and aggregate risk levels of sign-in attempts
- The detection types that were triggered
- If conditional access policies have been applied
- The details of MFA
- Device information
- Application information
- Location information

You can then take the following actions in response to these events:

- Confirm if a sign-in indicates compromise
- Confirm if a sign-in is safe

Risk Detections

The Risk Detections report contains data for the last 90 days. With the information found in this report, you can locate the following:

- Information for every risk detection
- Other risks triggered at the same time as a risk detection
- The location of sign-in attempts
- A link to more details from Microsoft Cloud App Security (MCAS)

You can then decide to either return to the Risky Users or Risky Sign-ins report to act based on the information they gathered.

Risk Detection Data Export

Next you need to export risk detection data to your SIEM solution. You can use Azure service-to-service integration to export your risk detection data to the SIEM of your choice for further analysis.

Prerequisites:

- The account you use needs to have read and write permissions for the Log Analytics workspace.

- The account needs to have the Global Administrator or Security Administrator role for your Azure Sentinel workspace's tenant. Azure Sentinel is a cloud-native tool in Azure that is required as part of this process.

Instructions:

1. From the Azure Sentinel navigation menu, select Data Connectors.

2. Choose your desired service from the Data Connectors gallery. Select Open Connector Page from the preview pane.

3. Select the option to connect to start streaming events and alerts from your selected service into Azure Sentinel.

4. If there is a Create Incidents – Recommended section on the connector page, you can select Enable if you want to automatically create incidents from alerts.

Implement Passwordless Authentication

You implement passwordless authentication by replacing a password with another form of authentication, specifically something you have, something you are, or something you know. Passwordless authentication maintains a high level of security while being more convenient than using a password and two-factor authentication. See Figure 2.5 for the benefits of passwordless authentication.

FIGURE 2.5 Benefits of passwordless authentication

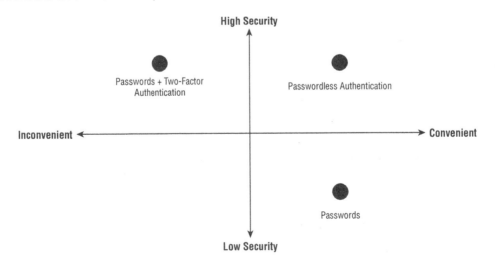

Azure AD offers three different passwordless authentication options: (`https://docs.microsoft.com/en-us/azure/active-directory/authentication/concept-authentication-passwordless`)

- Windows Hello for Business
- Microsoft Authenticator App
- FIDO2 Security Keys

Windows Hello for Business

This solution is for users who have their own Windows workstation. Their biometric and PIN credentials are linked to the user's PC, which prevents anyone other than the system's owner from logging into the system. Here are the steps:

1. The system owner signs into Windows using a biometric or PIN authentication, which unlocks the Windows Hello for Business private key. Next, the key is sent to the Cloud Authentication security support provider (Cloud AP provider).

2. The Cloud AP provider requests a nonce, which is a random number that will be used once from Azure AD.

3. Upon request, Azure AD will return a nonce that remains valid for 5 minutes.

4. The Cloud AP provider uses their private key to sign the nonce and returns it to Azure AD.

5. Upon receiving the signed nonce, Azure AD validates it using the user's registered public key. Once the signed nonce is validated, Azure AD creates a primary refresh token (PRT) with a session key that is encrypted to the device's transport key and returns the key to the Cloud AP provider.

6. The Cloud AP provider receives the encrypted PRT along with the session key. The Cloud AP provider can use the PRT to decrypt the session key and protect the session key using the device's Trusted Platform Module.

7. If everything goes correctly, the Cloud AP provider returns a successful authentication response to Windows. Then the user is able to access Windows, the cloud, and on-premises applications without the need to reauthenticate, which means you successfully implemented single sign-on (SSO).

Microsoft Authenticator

Although the Microsoft Authenticator app is typically used as part of MFA, it can also be used as a passwordless option. It allows users to sign into any platform or browser by using their phone application along with biometric authentication or a PIN to confirm. The process is as follows:

1. The user enters their username.

2. Azure AD detects that the user has passwordless login enabled and starts the authentication process.

3. A notification is sent to Microsoft Authenticator via Apple Push Notification Service for iOS devices or Firebase Cloud Messaging for Android devices.

4. The user receives the push notification on their phone.

5. The authenticator app calls Azure AD and receives a proof-of-presence challenge and nonce.

6. To complete the challenge, the user enters their biometric authentication or PIN to unlock their private key.

7. The nonce is signed with the private key and returned to Azure AD.

8. Azure AD then performs a private key validation using a public key and returns a token that allows the user to log in.

FIDO2 Security Keys

FIDO2 stands for Fast Identity Online version 2, and it promotes open authentication standards and reduces the use of passwords as a type of authentication. These security keys allow multiple types of authentication to be used but typically use USB devices. Using a hardware device to handle authentication means that this form of authentication cannot be phished and provides an overall increased level of security because there is no password that can be exposed or guessed. The process for authenticating using this method is as follows:

1. The user enters the FIDO2 security key. Windows then detects the use of a FIDO2 security key and sends an authentication request to Azure AD.

2. Azure AD sends back a nonce.

3. The user completes their portion of authentication to unlock the private key stored inside the FIDO2 security key's secure enclave.

4. The FIDO2 security key uses the private key to sign the nonce.

5. The primary refresh token (PRT) token request along with the signed nonce is then sent back to Azure AD.

6. Azure AD verifies the signed nonce using the FIDO2 public key.

7. Azure AD returns the PRT to enable access to on-premises resources.

Configuring an Access Review

Access reviews in Azure AD enable you to audit and manage group memberships and access company applications and role assignments. You can review user access consistently to ensure that only the correct people have access to company resources. Here are some of the key instances where you would want to use an access review:

To Prevent Too Many Users from Having Privileged Roles   You should keep track of which users have admin privileges, which of them are global admins, and if there are any guest users or business partners whose access has not been removed after it was no longer needed.

Whenever Automation Is Not Possible   In Microsoft, you can create rules that will automate membership for your security groups or your Microsoft 365 groups. However, there are situations where data is not in Azure AD or situations where users will need access after leaving a group. For example, let's say the data for the HR department is not in Azure AD and there's a situation where a user still needs access after leaving the HR department to train their new replacement. In such a situation, you could create an access review for that department to ensure that users who still need access have continued access.

When Changing the Purpose of an Existing Group   Whenever a group is going to be used for a different purpose, it's a good idea to perform an access review to ensure that everyone in that group needs the new access since the group is being used in a different risk content. This way, you can change the level of access that the group has to match their new business requirements.

To Review Business-Critical Data Access   For certain important company resources, it's a good practice to force people outside IT to regularly sign out and provide business justification on why they need continued access for auditing purposes.

To Maintain a Policy Exception List   While you can make policies that will fit the vast majority of users in your organization, there will always be unique situations that will require exceptions to the general policy. If the IT admin maintains a policy exception list, this will help you avoid oversight of policy exceptions and provide auditors with proof that all exceptions are being reviewed regularly.

To Gather Confirmation from Group Owners That Their Guests Still Need Access   An employee's access can be automated with some on-premises IAM, but most of the time invited guests are not. If a group grants a guest access to business-sensitive content, then you should request that group owners regularly confirm that the guests still have a business need for that access.

When Performing Reviews Periodically   You can configure access reviews to take place at set frequencies such as weekly, monthly, quarterly, or annually. You can also specify that reviewers be notified at the start of each review. Reviewers can approve or deny access easily within the Azure interface. Reviewers can make these decisions at their own discretion or with the help of recommendations from Azure.

Prerequisites for Creating an Access Review

Using access reviews requires an Azure AD Premium P2 license. Also, your account must be assigned to the Owner or User Access Administrator role for the Azure resources. To create access reviews for Azure AD roles, your account must be assigned the role of Administrator or Privileged Role Administrator.

To create an access review:

1. Sign into the Azure portal as a user who is assigned one of the prerequisite roles.

2. Select Identity Governance.

3. For Azure AD roles, select Azure AD Roles under Privileged Identity Management. For Azure resources, select Azure Resources under Privileged Identity Management.

4. For Azure AD roles, select Azure AD Roles again under Manage. For Azure resources, select the resources you want to manage, such as a subscription.

5. For Azure AD roles, under Manage, select Access Reviews, and then click New to create a new access review. This allows you to regularly check the access that you have assigned to users, roles, and groups in your environment.

6. Assign a name to the access review and give it a description if you would like (see Figure 2.6).

FIGURE 2.6   Naming your access review

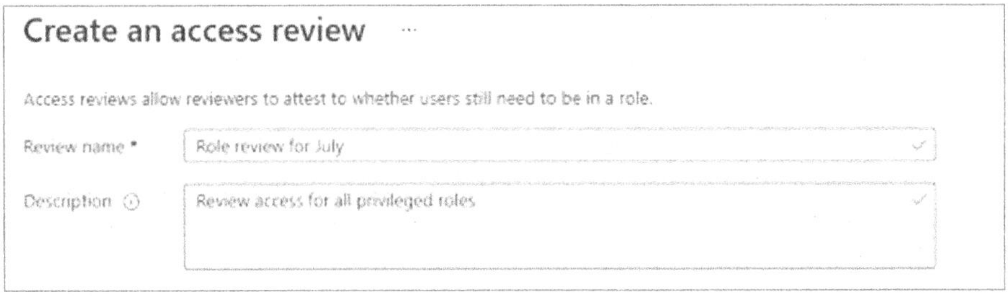

Create an access review   ···

Access reviews allow reviewers to attest to whether users still need to be in a role.

Review name *   Role review for July

Description ⓘ   Review access for all privileged roles

7. Choose the start date.

   By default, a new access review will occur once, start at the time it is created, and run for one month from its creation date. However, you can change any of these settings.

8. Set the access review frequency. If you would like to create a recurring access review, you can change the Frequency setting to anything from once to weekly, monthly, quarterly, semiannually, or annually. Define how many days each review will be open for input from reviewers using the Duration slider or text box.

9. Use the End setting to specify how you want to end the access review series.

   You have three ways that you can end an access review: you can have it run indefinitely, you can have a specific end date, or you can have it end after a predetermined number of occurrences have been completed (see Figure 2.7).

FIGURE 2.7   Selecting an end for your access review

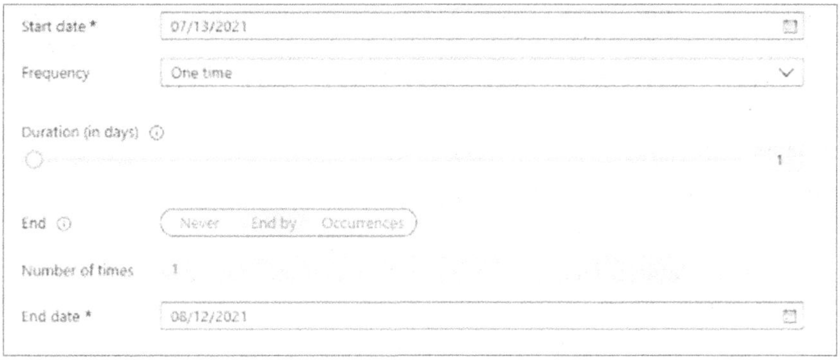

10. In the User Scope section, choose the option for your scope review. For Azure AD roles, the first scope option is All Users And Groups. This includes directly assigned users and role-assignable groups. For Azure resource roles, the first scope will be Users. You can also choose to review service principals if you want to review the machine accounts with direct access to Azure resources or the Azure AD role.

11. Under Role, select the privileged Azure resource or Azure AD role that you want to review.

12. In the Reviewers section, select one or more people to perform reviews for any users. You can select from the following:

   Selected Users   Use this option if you want to designate a specific user to complete the review. This option is available no matter what the scope of the review is, and the selected reviewers may review users, groups, and service principals.

   Members (Self)   This option allows users to review their own role assignments. The option will be made available only if the review is scoped to Users And Groups or Users. For Azure AD roles, role-assignable groups will not be included as part of the review when this option is selected.

   Manager   This option allows you to have the user's manager review their role assignments. This option will be available only if the review is scoped to Users And Groups or Users. Once you select the manager, you will also have the option to specify a fallback reviewer who can perform the review in their place. A fallback reviewer is asked to review a user when the user has no manager specified. For Azure AD roles, role-assignable groups will be reviewed by the fallback reviewer if one is selected.

Upon Completion Settings

Upon Completion Settings allows you to specify what happens when a review is completed, depending on what occurred during the access review. For example, if the reviewer didn't respond and failed to review someone's access, you can set it to any one of these options so that the system will apply that automatically:

- No Change: Leaves the user's access unchanged

- Remove Access: Removes the user's access

- Approve Access: Approves the user's access requests

- Take Recommendations: Defers to the system's recommendations on whether to deny or approve the user's access

   These options give you more flexibility so that you can have someone review and apply the changes yourself or have the system do it. In addition, you can select the option to send notifications to specific users or groups following the review. This allows you to keep stakeholders other than the review creator informed of the review process. You can enable this feature by clicking Select User(s) Or Group(s) (see Figure 2.8) and adding the users or groups that you want to be notified.

FIGURE 2.8   Enabling notification

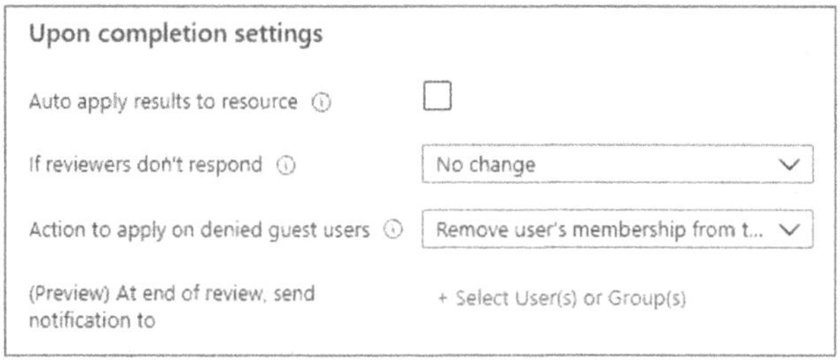

Advanced Settings

You can also specify additional settings such as the following:

- Showing recommendations based on the user's access information.

- Requiring reasons upon approval.

- Configuring Azure AD to send email notifications to reviewers when an access review starts and to administrators when a review is needed.

- Configuring Azure AD to send reminders of access reviews in progress to reviewers who have not yet completed their review.

- Additional content for reviewer email; while the content of the email sent to reviewers is autogenerated based on the review details, you have the option to add information via this option (see Figure 2.9).

FIGURE 2.9   Additional Content for Reviewer Email

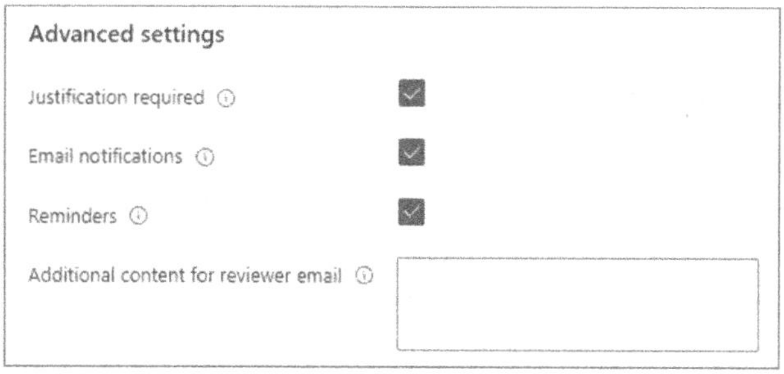

Managing Application Access

In this section, we will look at the importance of managing application access. This means having controls for preventing users from getting unauthorized access to applications in your Azure environment. The first control we are going to look at for doing this is single sign-on (SSO).

Integrating Single Sign-On and Identity Providers for Authentication

Single sign-on (SSO) is a feature that allows users to log in once and have access to all the resources they need. This is important because it prevents users from having to manage multiple accounts while still providing good security throughout the authentication process. First, let's look at how SSO works and why it's important.

Single Sign-On

Generally, the more accounts a user has to manage, the greater the risk of a credential-related security breach. In addition, it increases the strain on those who manage all those accounts. Help desk and other IT professionals will have to spend more time dealing with lockouts, password resets, and all the other administrative tasks associated with user accounts. Also, when a user leaves the company, rather than having to disable one account, they now must find and disable several different accounts. If just one account is left active by mistake, then they run the risk of having a security breach. SSO fixes this issue by making it so users only have to remember one ID and one password. This significantly reduces the likelihood of account mismanagement by either the user or the employees who manage these accounts.

Single Sign-On on Azure AD

As you know, Azure AD is a cloud-based identity service that has built-in support for synchronizing your on-premises AD, or it can be used as its own. This means that all your applications, whether in the cloud or on premises, can share the same login credentials. Azure AD lets you combine multiple data sources into a graph that you can use to give real-time identity protection to all your accounts in Azure AD.

Creating an App Registration

App registration allows you to get an application ID and redirect URI value that can be used to manage your application's authentication process. To add a new app registration, follow these steps:

1. The user asks to register an application—a request token is issued.
2. The authorization endpoint sends back an authentication.
3. The user consents to have the application registration.
4. A service principal is created from the application.
5. The token is returned to the user.

Configuring App Registration Permission Scopes

App registration is important for controlling access to applications in Azure. In this section, we focus on configuring permission scopes for our app registration.

App Registration Permission Scopes

The Microsoft identity platform uses OAuth2.0 authorization protocol to allow access to web-hosted resources for its users. Any web-hosted resource that integrates with the Microsoft Identity platform will have a resource identifier or application ID URL. Any of these resources can have a set of permissions defined that divide the functionality that users have when accessing that resource. The most common examples are read versus write permissions. By defining permissions for users, you have more fine-grained control on how resources data and API functionality is exposed on the web. Third-party applications can request these permissions from users and administrators, who will need to approve the request before the app can access data or act on the person's behalf.

Permission Types

By dividing permissions into smaller segments, you allow developers to request only specific permissions that they need to perform certain functions. Administrators are then able to see exactly what data a third-party application has access to, and you can be confident that it doesn't pose risks for your company and that it's not acting with malicious intent.

Permissions can be divided into the following:

Delegated Permissions   These are the permissions where there is a signed-in user present. In this case, either the user or an admin must consent to the permission that the app requests, and the app is delegated the permissions to act as the signed-in user.

Application Permissions   These are the permissions that run without having a signed-in user present. A common example is applications that run in the background. This type of permission can only be consented to by administrators.

Effective Permissions   These are the permissions that an application will have when attempting to make a request on a target resource. Effective permissions are a subset of delegated and applications permissions that defines what an application is able to do under each user. An effective permission is the intersection between the permission that has been granted to the application and the permissions of the user.

First, let's look at an effective permission as it relates to delegated permissions. Let's say an application is granted the user.readwrite.all delegated permission. While the name suggests that this would enable the application to read and update all user profiles, because the delegated permission is linked to a signed-in user, it is limited to only editing the user profile of the signed-in person. This is because the effective permissions of an application cannot exceed what the signed-in user is allowed to do and is therefore limited in its action.

Next let's look at application permissions. Because application permissions run without a signed-in user, in this case if it is assigned user.readwrite.all then the effective permissions of that application will be the ability to update any profile within the organization because no signed-in user account exists to limit its usage.

Managing App Registration Permission Consent

Before an application can access your organization's data, a user must grant that application permission to access that information. In this section, we explain how to grant permission consent to your applications in Azure.

Individuals

In an OAuth2.0 authorization request, an application can request the permissions it needs by using a scope query parameter. The scope parameter is a space-separated list of delegated permissions that the app is requesting. When a user first signs into an app, it sends a request for permission, which the user must accept for the application to have any permissions to operate. Each permission is indicated by appending the permission value to the resource identifier.

Entire Tenant

Simply put, a tenant represents your entire organization in Azure. If you're someone who works in a large company, you may need to give hundreds or thousands of people access when your company buys a license or subscription for an application. Many organizations want to proactively set up the application for use by all users in the organization. As part of the process, an administrator can provide consent for the application on behalf of the users in the tenant. If you choose to do this, then users won't need to provide consent to use the application.

Managing API Permission to Azure Subscriptions

An application programming interface (API) is a connection between computers or computer programs that allows them to communicate with each other. Azure can be used to host applications, so it's important that you understand how to configure APIs and to give applications access to your Azure subscriptions for all users.

API Access to Azure Subscriptions and Resources

Azure API Management is a tool that acts as a gateway between your web APIs and the public Internet. This is important if you want to provide API access to any Azure subscriptions or resources. It allows you to create API gateways that will provide controlled management access to your partners outside your cloud environment. Here are some of the key benefits to using API Management:

API Documentation   Having good API documentation will allow your clients or your on-premises teams to quickly and easily integrate their solutions. Azure API Management allows you to quickly expose the structure of your cloud APIs to clients through standards like OpenAPI. Additionally, you may have multiple versions of an API. With multiple versions, you can slowly phase in app updates because your apps don't have to use the new version right away.

Rate-Limiting Access   You'll want to provide quick and convenient access to your company's resources. If your API has the potential to access a large amount of data at one time, then you may want to limit the rate at which a single client can request that data. Rate limiting helps maintain good response times for every client by keeping one client from using up too much of the API's resources. API Management lets you set rate limits as a whole or for individual clients.

Health Monitoring   APIs are used by remote clients, which may make it difficult to identify problems or errors when they occur. With API Management, you can view error responses and log files while filtering by response type. This helps you easily identify errors, resolve them, and ensure that all your clients can access the information they need.

Support for Different Data Formats   API Management supports multiple data exchange formats, including formats like XML, CSV, and JSON.

Connections to Any API   APIs can be located across several different countries and use many formats. API Management allows you to centralize all of these into a single modern user interface.

Data Analytics   API Management allows you to visualize data related to your organization's API calls within the Azure portal, yielding a good overview of how your APIs are being used.

Security   Probably the most important feature, security is essential when you're talking about providing access to company resources for remote users. API Management uses OAuth2.0 user authorization and integrates with Azure AD to help limit the possibility of someone gaining unauthorized access to company resources.

API Permissions for Subscriptions

First, let's define some terms:

- An *organization* is any business entity or individual that uses Azure resources and is identified by one or more domain names.

- A *tenant* is a specific instance of Azure AD that is identified by its tenant ID. After registration, you are given the Azure AD tenant, which allows you to create your accounts. For every single organization, there can be one or multiple tenants.

- A *subscription* is simply a container that holds different resources in Azure. These resources are usually business related and are billed together. Each tenant can have one or multiple subscriptions.

Subscription keys are another tool for controlling access to Azure APIs. A subscription key is a unique, autogenerated string that must be passed in a client request to gain access to a resource. Every subscription has two keys, a primary and a secondary key; this way, if you need to change a key, you can still gain access to that resource while making the change. As a developer, you get access to a key by submitting a subscription request.

Configuring an Authentication Method for a Service Principal

A *service principal* is a type of account that can sign into Azure AD, but there is no human signing in for this process. Instead, it is identified by an application ID and a credential. Typically, the credential is a strong password, commonly referred to as a *client secret*. This is important because MFA can't be used due to the lack of a human user and therefore a strong password is required to protect the account. A service principal governs applications that are connecting to Azure AD. You can consider them the instance of the application in your company's directory. While any given application can have only one application object, applications can have multiple service principal objects.

The service principal can include:

- A reference back to an application object via an application ID property
- Records of a local user or group application's past role assignments
- Records of a local user and admin permissions that were granted to the application
- Past records of local policies like conditional access policies
- Records of the alternate local settings for a given application

You can create service principals in many ways. The most common is when users sign in to a third-party application integrated with Azure AD.

During sign-in, users will be asked by the application for permission to access their profile and other required permissions. Once the user gives their consent, Azure adds a service principal that represents that application to the directory.

Once you subscribe to Microsoft 365 or start a trial subscription, one or more service principals are created in the directory representing the different services used to deliver all the functionality of Microsoft 365. Some Microsoft 365 services, such as SharePoint, create service principals on a regular basis to facilitate secure communications between different components. This includes workflows such as the following:

- If an admin adds an application from the app gallery
- Configuring an application to use the Azure AD Application Proxy
- Connecting an application for single sign-on via Security Assertion Markup Language (SAML) or password SSO

Managing Access Control

In this section, we look at options for managing access control in the Azure environment. Access control simply means limiting the access that people are given to resources.

Interpret Role and Resource Permissions

Role-based access control (RBAC) is an authorization system built on the Azure Resource Manager that is designed to provide granular access management of Azure resources. Rather than assigning access individually, using Azure RBAC you can control access to resources by assigning Azure roles (https://docs.microsoft.com/en-us/azure/role-based-access-control/role-assignments-portal?tabs=current). A *role assignment* consists of three elements:

Security Principals   These are objects (see Figure 2.10) that represent users, groups, service principals, or a managed identity requesting access to an Azure resource. You will be assigning the role to this object.

FIGURE 2.10   Security principals

Role Definition   This is a group of permissions that identifies the list of actions that may be performed by the security principal who will be assigned this role. For example, read, write, and delete permissions are defined here.

Scope   This is the set of resources to which the access will apply. This way, the permissions you define in the role definition can be limited to specific resources. There are three levels that you can specify scope for: resource, resource group, and subscription, as shown in Figure 2.11.

FIGURE 2.11   Levels of scope

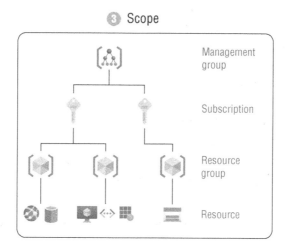

A *role assignment* is the process of taking the role that you created using these elements and attaching it to a user, group, service principal, or managed identity at a particular scope to grant access. In the event that you have multiple role assignments, the user's effective permissions will be the sum of all role assignments.

In addition to role assignments, Azure offers *deny assignments* that allow you to explicitly deny certain actions from a user, group, service principal, or managed identity. Role assignments allow you to define a set of actions that are allowed, whereas deny assignments define a set of actions that are not allowed. Deny assignments take precedence over role assignments.

Configuring Azure Role Permissions for Management Groups, Subscriptions, Resource Groups, and Resources

To configure an Azure role for RBAC, you must complete the following steps:

1. Identify the necessary scope. The scope is the set of resources that the access applies to, and it covers four levels. To begin, navigate to the Azure portal.

2. In the search box near the top of the screen, search for the scope you want to grant access to (e.g., subscriptions, resources, etc.).

3. Select the specific resource that you want.

4. Select the Add Role Assignment pane.

5. Select the Access Control (IAM) page to assign roles to grant access to specific Azure resources.

6. Select the Role Assignments tab to view the role assignments.

7. Click Add, then click Add Role Assignment.

8. In the role list, locate the role you want to assign and then select the role.

9. Next, select who will need access to this role.

10. From the Assign list, choose the type of security principal that you want to assign access to.

    If you choose a user-assigned managed identity or a system-assigned managed identity, then select the subscription where the managed identity is located.

11. In the Select section, search for the appropriate security principal.

12. Assign the role and click Save.

Assigning Built-In Azure AD Roles

Azure's role-based access control comes with several prebuilt roles that you can assign to users, groups, service principals, and managed identities. Assignments roles allow you to control access to Azure resources. Table 2.4 contains some examples of the built-in roles that Azure provides.

TABLE 2.4   Examples of built-in Azure roles

Built-in role	Description	ID
Contributor	This gives you full access to manage resources but doesn't give you the ability to assign roles in Azure RBAC, manage assignments, or share image galleries.	b24988ac-6180-42a0-ab88-20f7382dd24c
Owner	This provides the user with full access to manage all resources as well as assign roles in Azure RBAC.	8e3af657-a8ff-443c-a75c-2fe8c4bcb635
Reader	This role allows you to view all resources but doesn't allow you to make any changes to them.	acdd72a7-3385-48ef-bd42-f606fba81ae7
User Access Administrator	This role allows you to manage user access to your Azure resources.	18d7d88d-d35e-4fb5-a5c3-7773c020a72d9

Creating and Assigning Custom Roles, Including Azure Roles and Azure AD Roles

In the event that Azure's built-in roles don't give you the precise control that you want over user access, you will need to create *custom roles*. With custom roles (see Figure 2.12), you can define roles that meet your specific requirements and that you can assign to users, groups, and service principals at the scope of subscription, resource group, or resource.

FIGURE 2.12   Custom roles

```
[
  {
    "assignableScopes": [
      "/subscriptions/{subscriptionId1}",
      "/subscriptions/{subscriptionId2}",
      "/providers/Microsoft.Management/managementGroups/{groupId1}"
    ],
    "description": "Can monitor and restart virtual machines.",
    "id": "/subscriptions/{subscriptionId1}/providers/Microsoft.Authorization/roleDefin
    "name": "88888888-8888-8888-8888-888888888888",
    "permissions": [
      {
        "actions": [
          "Microsoft.Storage/*/read",
          "Microsoft.Network/*/read",
          "Microsoft.Compute/*/read",
          "Microsoft.Compute/virtualMachines/start/action",
          "Microsoft.Compute/virtualMachines/restart/action",
          "Microsoft.Authorization/*/read",
          "Microsoft.ResourceHealth/availabilityStatuses/read",
          "Microsoft.Resources/subscriptions/resourceGroups/read",
          "Microsoft.Insights/alertRules/*",
          "Microsoft.Insights/diagnosticSettings/*",
          "Microsoft.Support/*"
        ],
        "dataActions": [],
        "notActions": [],
        "notDataActions": []
      }
    ],
    "roleName": "Virtual Machine Operator",
    "roleType": "CustomRole",
    "type": "Microsoft.Authorization/roleDefinitions"
  }
]
```

You can create custom roles can be created in the Azure command-line interface (CLI), using a set of PowerShell commands to create and manage Azure resources. Table 2.5 contains a breakdown of the custom role properties used to create a custom role.

TABLE 2.5 Breakdown of the custom role properties

Property	Required	Type	Description
RoleName	Yes	String	This is the display name of the custom role. This display name must be unique at the scope of the Azure AD directory. It can include letters, numbers, spaces, and special characters. It has a maximum number limit of 128 characters.
Id Name	Yes	String	This is a unique ID for the custom role. This ID is automatically generated when you create a new role in Azure PowerShell or Azure CLI.
IsCustomRoleType	Yes	String	This field will indicate whether or not it is a custom role. It can be set to true or false.
Description	Yes	String	This is the description of a customer role. It can include several types of characters, with a maximum limit of 1,024.
Actions	Yes	String[]	This is a set of strings that outline the management operations that the role can allow to be performed.
NotActions	No	String[]	This is a set of strings that outline the management operations that the role can exclude from being allowed to be performed.
DataAction	No	String[]	This is a set of strings that specify the data operations that the role will allow to be performed within that particular object.
NotDataActions	No	String[]	This is a set of strings specifying the data operations that are excluded from the allowed DataActions.
AssignableScopes	Yes	String[]	This is a set of strings that specifies the scopes that the custom role is available for assignment.

Summary

This chapter focused on how identity and access management (IAM) is implemented on the Azure platform. IAM is all about ensuring that the correct people have access to resources in your cloud environment; this includes everything from authentication, to authorization, to accountability. You learned about Azure AD, which allows you to integrate your native

Windows Active Directory to use those users, groups, and policies on the Azure platform. In addition, we discussed several services for managing access to resources on your cloud platform.

Exam Essentials

Understand how to use access reviews for access management.   Azure AD access reviews enable your organization to efficiently manage group memberships and access to enterprise applications and role assignments. Access reviews allow you to review user access on a regular basis to ensure that only the right people have access to company resources.

Be able to define accountability as part of access management.   This simply means that administrators should be able to see all the actions that users are performing in a system.

Be able to explain what administrative units are used for.   Administrative units restrict permissions in a role to any portion of the organization that you define. For example, you could limit someone's permissions to resources only in their region. In large companies, you may have similar job roles that are spread across multiple different regions, and you don't want someone having access to resources that they aren't managing.

Be able to define authentication as part of access management.   Authentication is how users prove who they are to a system by providing a combination of information that should only be accessible by the owner of the account.

Be able to define authorization as part of access management.   This is how the system decides what access a person or group should have after authenticating them to the system.

Be able to explain how to implement Automated Detection and Remediation on Azure with risk policies.   This is performed through the creation and configuration of two types of risk policies: a sign-in risk policy and a user risk policy. Both policies allow for automated responses to risk detections in your environment and give users the option to self-remediate when a risk is detected.

Understand what Azure AD is compared to Windows Active Directory.   Azure AD is not a cloud version of Windows Server Active Directory. It's also not a competitor of Windows Active Directory; it simply allows you to take a Windows AD server and connect it to Azure AD to extend your directory to Azure. This allows users to use the same credentials to access both local and cloud-based resources. However, this integration isn't necessary; you can use Azure AD as your only directory service to control access to applications and services.

Understand the features of Azure AD Identity Protection.   Identity Protection is a tool used to help organizations protect themselves from identity-based risks. To help with this, Microsoft analyzes roughly 6.5 trillion signals per day to identify and protect their customers from threats. It does this through the following three methods:

- Automated detection and remediation of identity-based risks
- Investigate risks using data in the portal
- Export risk detection data to your SIEM

Be able to define what an Azure user is.   Every user who needs access to an Azure resource will need an Azure user account. This user account contains all the information that is needed to authenticate during the sign-in process. Once a user is authenticated, Azure AD builds an access token to authorize them and determines what resources they will have access to and what they can do with those resources.

Understand how conditional access policies are used for controlling access to resources.   Multifactor authentication isn't the only way to protect user accounts on Azure. Conditional access policies allow you to set conditions that can block someone from logging in, depending on different factors, such as blocking a login attempt from an unrecognized IP address or an unfamiliar device. Azure AD provides conditional access policies based on the group, location, or device state.

Be able to explain what managed identities are.   Managed identities are roles that essentially can be used to provide an identity for applications to use when connecting to resources that support Azure AD authentication.

Understand what Microsoft 365 groups are.   These groups are for collaboration by giving members access to a shared mailbox, calendar, files, SharePoint site, and so forth. This is good for giving access to group resources to people outside your organization.

Understand how passwordless authentication works.   This authentication is done by replacing a password with another form of authentication, specifically something you have, plus something you are or know. Passwordless authentication still maintains a high level of security while being more convenient than using a password plus two-factor authentication.

Understand what Privileged Identity Management (PIM) is.   This is a service in Azure AD that allows you to manage, control, and monitor access to important resources in your cloud environment.

Be able to define role-based access control (RBAC).   RBAC is where permissions are added to roles and roles are allotted to users to give them access. RBASC allows you to easily add access for new users without having to give access on an individual basis.

Understand the importance of security groups.   These groups are used to manage member and computer access to shared resources for a group of users. For example, you may create a security group for all Human Resource analysts that provides access to the resources they would need, in addition to anyone with that job title who is placed in that group upon being hired.

Be able to define what a service principal is.   A service principal is a type of account; it can sign into Azure AD, but there is no human signing in for this process. Instead, it is identified by an application ID and a credential. Service principals govern applications that are connecting to Azure AD and can be considered the instance of the application in your company's directory.

Understand what single sign-on (SSO) is and why it's valuable. Generally, the more accounts a user has to manage, the greater the risk of a credential-related security breach. It also creates a greater strain on the people required to manage all those accounts. SSO fixes this issue by making it so that users only have to remember one ID and one password, which significantly reduces the likelihood of account mismanagement by either the user or the employees who manage these accounts.

Review Questions

1. What is a managed identity?
   - **A.** An application identity
   - **B.** A user identity
   - **C.** An admin identity
   - **D.** A type of user account

2. What is Azure AD?
   - **A.** A cloud version of Windows AD
   - **B.** An integration of Windows AD in Azure
   - **C.** A distinct software application
   - **D.** Windows AD with a subdirectory in Azure cloud

3. How does role-based access control (RBAC) work?
   - **A.** You assign users individual roles.
   - **B.** Access is assigned to users individually.
   - **C.** Access is assigned to roles and users are assigned roles.
   - **D.** Access is assigned to users individually based on their job roles.

4. Which of the following is *not* an advantage of RBAC?
   - **A.** Less overhead
   - **B.** More consistent access control
   - **C.** Faster access for new employees
   - **D.** More authentication for users

5. Which of the following is *not* true of Azure AD Identity Protection?
   - **A.** Automated detection and remediation of identity-based risks
   - **B.** The ability to investigate risks using data in the portal
   - **C.** Multifactor authentication (MFA) for user accounts
   - **D.** Exporting risk data into your native SIEM

6. What is Azure AD Privileged Identity Management (PIM)?
   - **A.** A core feature of Azure AD
   - **B.** A tool for privileged account management
   - **C.** Azure AD for service accounts
   - **D.** Azure AD features for admin-level accounts

7. What is the benefit of conditional access policies?

A. Setting conditions on accessing Azure resources

B. Blocking access to outside users

C. Controlling the actions users can perform on a resource

D. Adding extra authentication for users

8. Which of the following is *not* a type of conditional access policy that you can create?

A. IP address

B. Geographic location

C. Device state

D. Type of resource being accessed

9. Which of the following is *not* a type of MFA authentication?

A. Something you know

B. Something you are

C. Something you have

D. Something you provide

10. Which of the following is *not* an automated response following an access review?

A. Removing access

B. Approving access

C. Taking recommendations

D. Rerunning the review

11. Which of the following is *not* a benefit of SSO?

A. Faster sign-ins

B. Fewer passwords to remember

C. Better security

D. More complex passwords

12. What app is used in Azure for SSO?

A. Authenticator

B. Azure Monitor

C. Azure AD

D. MFA

13. How are API permissions controlled in Azure?

A. RBAC

B. Authenticator app

C. Service principals

D. Azure API Manager

14. Which of the following describes Azure built-in AD roles?

   A. Any role created in Azure

   B. Premade Azure roles

   C. Roles created by Azure admins

   D. Azure roles that can be changed or edited

15. What are custom roles in Azure?

   A. Any role created in Azure by admins

   B. Premade Azure roles

   C. Roles created by Azure admins

   D. Azure roles that cannot be changed or edited

16. Which of the following is *not* a type of authentication method in Azure?

   A. Something you know

   B. Something you are

   C. Something you have

   D. Something you do

17. Which of the following is an example of something you know in MFA?

   A. PIN and password

   B. Hardware tokens

   C. Fingerprints

   D. Voice recognition

18. Which of the following is an example of something you are in MFA?

   A. PIN and password

   B. Hardware tokens

   C. Fingerprints

   D. Gender

19. Which is an example of something you have in MFA?

   A. PIN and password

   B. Hardware tokens

   C. Fingerprints

   D. Voice recognition

20. Which of the following is *not* a type of app permission in Azure?

   A. Delegated permissions

   B. Application permissions

   C. Effective permissions

   D. User permissions

Chapter 3

Implementing Platform Protections

THE MCA MICROSOFT CERTIFIED ASSOCIATE AZURE SECURITY ENGINEER ASSESSMENT TEST TOPICS COVERED IN THIS CHAPTER INCLUDE:

✓ **Implement advanced network security**

- Secure the connectivity of hybrid networks
- Secure the connectivity of virtual networks
- Create and configure Azure Firewall
- Create and configure Azure Firewall Manager
- Create and configure Azure Application Gateway
- Create and configure Azure Front Door
- Create and configure Web Application Firewall (WAF)
- Configure a resource firewall, including a storage account, Azure SQL, Azure Key Vault, or Azure App Service
- Configure network isolation for Web Apps and Azure Functions
- Implement Azure Service Endpoints
- Implement Azure Private Endpoints, including integrating with other services
- Implement Azure Private Links
- Implement Azure DDoS Protection

✓ **Configure advanced security for compute**

- Configure Endpoint Protection for virtual machines (VMs)
- Implement and manage security updates for VMs
- Configure security for container services
- Manage access to Azure Container Registry
- Configure security for serverless compute

- Configure security for an Azure App Service
- Configure encryption at rest
- Configure encryption in transit

In this chapter, we discuss how to implement good network security on the Azure platform. This includes components such as firewalls and their configuration, endpoint protection, network monitoring, and how to use the Azure-specific security tools to accomplish these tasks. We begin with a discussion of network security, including using network security groups, web application firewalls (WAFs), endpoint protection, and DDOS protection. Then a discussion follows about operational security, which includes vulnerability management, disk encryption, and Secure Sockets Layer/Transport Layer Security (SSL/TLS) certificates.

Implementing Advanced Network Security

All of your computer and information assets are stored on your company network. It's important to understand how to implement proper security controls to ensure that it's as difficult as possible for someone to gain unauthorized access to company resources. In this section, we will discuss how to secure communications and implement overall network security in Azure.

Securing Connectivity of Hybrid Networks

When securing the connectivity of hybrid networks, you must first understand that a hybrid network is when you have two or more different types of working networks connected in your setup. To keep these connected networks secure, you must be aware of your access control, the management of your resource groups, and the configuration of your network, among other considerations.

Access Control

The first recommendation for securing your hybrid networks is to use Azure role-based access control (Azure RBAC) for controlling access to your resources. Azure recommends that you create three custom roles to help facilitate this access control. The first custom role is the DevOps role, which has permission to administer the infrastructure for any applications, to deploy application components, and to monitor and restart virtual machines (VMs) in the environment. The second custom role is the general IT administrator role, which has permissions to manage and monitor all the network resources. Last is the security IT administrator role, which has permissions to secure network resources. This final role should have exclusive access to manage and configure your network's firewalls.

Resource Groups

The second recommendation for securing your hybrid networks is to assign your resources to resource groups according to their security needs. It's easier to manage your resources when you arrange them into resource groups. Then you can simply assign Azure RBAC roles to each resource group to restrict their access. Azure recommends creating the following resource groups for grouping your resources together:

> **Virtual Network Resource Group**   Azure recommends creating a separate resource group for the virtual network, excluding VMs, network security groups (NSGs), and any gateway resources used for connection to the on-premises network. The IT administrator role should be assigned to this group.

> **VMs and User-Defined Group**   Azure recommends creating a resource group for all the VMs used for the Azure firewall instance and user-defined routes in your gateway subnet. The security IT administrator role should be assigned to this group.

> **Application Tiers with Load Balancers and VMs Groups**   You should configure separate resource groups for every application tier that contains load balancers and VMs. The DevOps role should be assigned to this group.

Networking

We're now going to focus on how you can configure your network to properly filter out Internet traffic. You should add a Destination Network Address Translation (DNAT) rule to your Azure firewall for accepting inbound traffic. This addition allows you to have a single public IP address for your firewall instance, which will serve as the focal point for traffic to and from the Internet. When using this rule, you'll want to enable *forced tunneling* so that when you create a routing table, you can redirect all Internet-bound traffic back to your on-premises location using a site-to-site virtual private network (VPN) tunnel or ExpressRoute. This tunnel allows you to inspect and audit this Internet traffic as well as prevent it from going directly out to the Internet. Figure 3.1 demonstrates the difference; notice that the frontend subnet doesn't use forced tunneling—and, therefore, must go through the Internet to reach the on-premises network—but the backend and mid-tier subnets do not.

Other Security Considerations

You need to ensure that you route all on-premises user requests through the Azure firewall to ensure that the traffic is inspected and filtered out before passing it on. You want to use NSGs to block/pass traffic between different application layers as well.

FIGURE 3.1   How VPN tunneling works

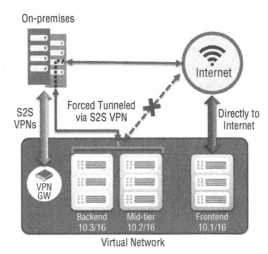

On-premises

Internet

S2S
VPNs

Forced Tunneled
via S2S VPN

Directly to
Internet

VPN
GW

Backend
10.3/16

Mid-tier
10.2/16

Frontend
10.1/16

Virtual Network

Securing Connectivity of Virtual Networks

In most modern networks, you'll need to connect to external networks from your cloud environment. Therefore, one of the most important items from a security point of view is to understand how to securely connect to those assets. If you fail to do so, people outside your network will be able to connect to resources within your computing environment and infiltrate your network. One of the first things you should do is provision the Azure Virtual Network (VNet), which is your computer network in your cloud environment. By default, no traffic is allowed between any two virtual networks, but you can enable it using *virtual network peering*, which is when you allow the next hop in a user-defined route to be a VM's IP address in a peered virtual network or a VPN gateway. The idea here is that your networks should be configured to allow traffic only where necessary.

Next, you need to look at securing the VMs on your VNet. All VMs have a network interface that allows them to communicate with other VMs, the Internet, and your on-premises networks. To control this traffic, you should make use of Azure's application security groups (ASGs) and ensure that they are correctly grouped. ASGs allow you to group VMs based on their workloads or functionality and to assign rules for allowing or blocking traffic to these group of VMs. You can then add these ASGs as a source or a destination while defining NSG rules.

For traffic between subnets, Azure recommends that you use NSGs. However, be sure that you don't confuse them with ASGs, which are used for traffic outside the Azure environment. NSGs are best suited for traffic to and from other Azure resources—otherwise, they function in a similar way to ASGs in that they filter traffic. NSGs are also capable of creating *NSG flow logs* that help you monitor the network flow and performance and address the security gaps. Log analysis can be easily done by enabling traffic analytics to gain quick insights into internal and external traffic flow from your applications.

Finally, you can use network virtual appliances (NVAs) such as a firewall to check inbound and outbound traffic as well. NVAs are good for more than just filtering traffic; they are also good at inspecting the traffic's contents. If you have a need to inspect traffic, then it's best to use user-defined routes (UDRs). UDRs allow you to control the next hop of traffic between Azure on-premises and Internet resources. Therefore, if you have a need to inspect traffic, you can place an NVA on a subnet and use the UDR to force traffic to route through that NVA.

Creating and Configuring Azure Firewalls

You've probably heard of and used a firewall, which is a network security system placed between a trusted network and an untrusted one. Firewalls monitor and control incoming and outgoing network traffic based on predetermined security rules. An *Azure firewall* is a managed, cloud-based firewall that's part of the Azure service (see Figure 3.2). Unlike the previously mentioned security groups that filter traffic based on simple criteria such as a source, destination IP, or port number, an Azure firewall is constantly being updated based on Microsoft's Threat Intelligence service on the latest Indicator of Compromises (IOCs) and Indicator of Attacks (IOAs) to help protect your network.

FIGURE 3.2   How an Azure firewall works

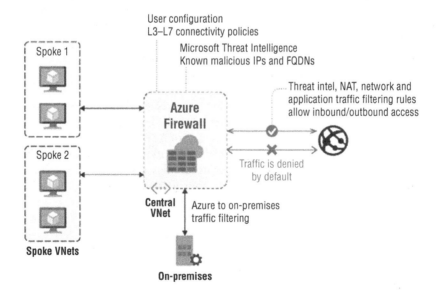

This firewall service integrates with Azure Monitor, which allows for logging and analytics and uses a static public IP address so that other firewalls can identify traffic coming from your network. Here are some of the notable features of an Azure firewall:

- Built-in high availability
- Availability zones
- Unrestricted cloud scalability
- Application fully qualified domain name (FQDN) filtering rules
- Network traffic-filtering rules
- FQDN tags
- Service tags
- Threat intelligence
- Outbound source network address translation (SNAT) support
- Inbound destination network address translation (DNAT) support
- Multiple public IP addresses
- Azure Monitor logging
- Forced tunneling
- Web categories
- Certifications

Azure Firewall Premium

The Azure firewall also has a premium version, which is a next-generation firewall that is useful for companies requiring very well-regulated cloud environments. Along with the features that come in the basic package, Azure Firewall Premium includes these additional features:

Transport Layer Security (TLS) Inspection   This feature decrypts outbound traffic, processes data in transit, and then re-encrypts the data and forwards it to its destination.

Intrusion Detection and Prevention System (IDPS)   This feature allows you to monitor network activities for malicious activity, log information about this activity, report it, and then configure IDPS to attempt to block malicious activity.

URL Filtering   This extends Azure Firewall's FQDN filtering so that it can evaluate an entire URL.

Web Categories   This feature gives administrators permissions to allow or deny users' access to certain website categories.

Creating an Azure Firewall

In order to create an Azure firewall, you must first have a VNet to deploy it to, and then you follow these steps:

1. Go to the Azure portal menu or home page and choose Create A Resource.

2. Type **firewall** in the search box and press Enter.

3. Select Firewall under Plan and click Create.

4. Choose your subscription, resource group (RG1), name (FW1), region, VNet, and public IP address, and then click Review + Create.

5. Review the summary and click Create.

Next, you must create rules for your firewall that will restrict the traffic that is allowed to pass through. There are two primary rules that you will use: application and network rules.

Application Rule

The following is an example of how to configure an application rule that allows outbound access to www.google.com.

1. Open RG1 and select the FW1 firewall.

2. On the FW1 page in the Settings section, select Rules (Classic).

3. Select the Application Rule Collection tab.

4. Select Add Application Rule Collection.

5. For Name, enter your desired name.

6. For Priority, enter **200**.

7. For Action, select Allow.

8. Under Rules, Target FQDNs, for Name enter **Allow-Google**.

9. For Source Type, choose IP Address.

10. For Source, enter **10.0.2.0/24**.

11. For Protocol: Port, type **http, https**.

12. For Target FQDNS, enter **www.google.com**.

13. Click Add.

FQDNs can be used to allow access to any domain. The Azure firewall comes with a rule collection for infrastructure FQDNs that are allowed by default.

Network Rule

A network rule is used to allow outbound access to any IP address. In the following example, there are two IP addresses on port 53 (DNS):

1. Select the Network Rule Collection tab.

2. Click Add Network Rule Collection.

3. For Name, enter a name for your network rule.

4. For Priority, enter 200.

5. For Action, select Allow.

6. Under Rules IP Addresses, for Name enter **Allow-DNS**.

7. For Protocol, select UDP.

8. For Source Type, select IP Address.

9. For Source, enter **10.0.2.0/24** (used for any internal IP address).

10. For Destination Type, select IP Address.

11. For Destination Address, enter the desired IP addresses, separated by commas.

12. For Destination Ports, enter 53.

13. Click Add.

After creating the firewall and its associated rules, you must also define a default route on your subnet that will route all outbound traffic through the firewall.

Create a Default Route

Follow these steps to create a default route on your subnet that will route all outbound traffic through your newly created firewall:

1. On the Azure portal menu, navigate to the search bar and search for **route tables**.

2. Click Create.

3. For Subscription, select your subscription.

4. For Resource Group, enter your resource group name.

5. For Region, select the same location that you used previously.

6. For Name, type your route name.

7. Click Review + Create.

8. Click Create.

Once the deployment is complete, click Go To Resource and open the route table that you just created. Then, follow these steps to configure your routing for the firewall:

1. Under Settings, choose Subnets > Associate.

2. Select Virtual Network, then enteryour desired VNet name.

3. For Subnet, select your desired subnet and then click OK.

4. Select Routes under Settings, then click Add.

5. For Route Name, enter **fw-dg**.

6. For Address Prefix Source, enter 0.0.0.0/0.

7. For Next Hop Type, select Virtual Appliance.

8. For Next Hop Address, enter the private IP address for the firewall that you selected in the previous step and click OK.

Creating and Configuring Azure Firewall Manager

Azure Firewall Manager is a security management service that allows you to control security policy and route management in your cloud environment. This means that you can use it to control inbound and outbound connections as well as routing on the network. It provides security management in two scenarios:

Secured Virtual Hubs: This is a Microsoft-managed resource that allows you to create hub and spoke network architecture.

Hub Virtual Network (VNet): This is the standard Azure virtual network that you will be creating and managing for your business.

Azure Firewall Manager Features

Let's explore the Azure Firewall Manager features:

Azure Firewall Deployment and Configuration   This feature allows you to deploy and configure Azure firewall instances across different regions and subscriptions.

Configuration of Global and Local Policies   Your IT team can create global policies that will enforce organization-wide firewall policies, as well as local firewall policies that will provide for more flexibility in firewall rules.

Integration with Third-Party Security-as-a-Service   You can integrate with other third-party security providers for additional network protection of your VNet.

Route Management   You can route traffic through your secured hubs for filtering or logging without needing to set up UDRs.

Creating and Configuring Azure Application Gateway

Azure Application Gateway is Azure's web traffic load balancer, which enables you to manage the amount of traffic going to your application and prevent it from becoming overloaded. The Application Gateway is more advanced than a traditional load balancer. Traditionally, load balancers operate at the Transport layer of the Open Systems Interconnection (OSI) model (Layer 4, TCP and UDP) and can only route traffic based on the source IP address and port to a destination IP address and port. However, Azure's Application Gateway operates at Layer 7 of the OSI model (the Presentation layer) and can make decisions based on additional attributes found in an HTTP request, such as URL-based routing. It comes with the following features:

Secure Sockets Layer (SSL/TLS) Termination   This means that the gateway handles the encryption and allows data to flow unencrypted to the backend servers. This can reduce encryption and decryption overhead on web servers. If required, it can be configured to do end-to-end encryption as well.

Autoscaling   Azure Application Gateway supports autoscaling, which means that it will scale out or scale in, based on the change in traffic loads, to optimize cost.

Zone Redundancy   The gateway can span multiple availability zones so there's no need to provision separate application gateways for different zones.

Static Virtual IP (VIP) Address   This means that the IP address connected to the application gateway will not change over its lifetime.

Web Application Firewall (WAF)   This feature provides centralized protection for your web application from publicly known exploits. For example, it will filter out Structured Query Language (SQL) injection attacks, cross-site scripting, directory traversals, and other attacks that come in through the web application itself. You can also configure the WAF solution to patch a known vulnerability once it is discovered.

Ingress Controller for Azure Kubernetes Service (AKS)   This means that you can use the application gateway as an ingress for an AKS.

URL-Based Routing   This feature allows you to route traffic to backend server pools based on the URL paths in the request.

Multiple-Site Hosting   This feature allows you to configure routing based on a hostname or domain name for multiple web applications on the same application gateway.

Redirection   This feature allows you to support automatic HTTP to HTTPs redirection, meaning that you can ensure that all communications between an application and its users will be encrypted.

Session Affinity   This means you are able to use gateway-managed cookies. This feature allows the application gateway to direct traffic from a user session to a server and to maintain user sessions on the same server.

WebSocket and HTTP/2 Traffic   Azure Application Gateway provides support for WebSocket and HTTP/2 protocols over ports 80 and 443.

Connection Draining   If you ever have a need to change the backend servers that your application uses (i.e., the backend pool), this ensures that all deregistering instances won't receive any new requests while allowing the existing requests to be sent to the appropriate servers for completion within the configured time limit. This includes instances that have been explicitly removed and those that have been reported as unhealthy by Azure's health probes.

Custom Error Pages   Azure Application Gateway lets you display custom error pages instead of the defaults, which allows you to prevent displaying information that should be kept confidential. Also, it gives you the chance to use your own branding and layout in the custom error page.

Rewrite HTTP Headers and URL   HTTP headers are used to allow the client and server to pass additional information with a request or response. By rewriting the HTTP headers, you can add security-related information HSTS/X-XSS protection, which is a feature that defends against cross-site scripting (XSS). You can remove header fields that may contain sensitive information and strip port information from the header. You can also rewrite URLs. When you combine this with URL path-based routing, you can route requests to your desired backend pool of servers.

Sizing   The standard application gateway is offered in three sizes: small, medium, and large.

Creating and Configurating the Azure Application Gateway

The easiest way to create an application gateway (see Figure 3.3) is to use the Azure portal as follows:

1. Go to the Azure portal menu and select Create a Resource.

2. Click Networking, and then select Application Gateway from the featured list.

3. On the Basics tab, enter these values for the following application gateway settings:

   - **Resource group:** Select your desired resource group, or click Create New if you need to create one.

   - **Application gateway name:** Enter the desired name of the application gateway.

At this point you can either select the VM you would like to use the Application Gateway with, or you can create one if you don't have one already.

4. On the Frontends tab, ensure that Frontend IP Address Type is set to Public.

5. For Public IP Address, click Add New, enter your desired name, and click OK (see Figure 3.4).

Now we move on to the Backend tab. In this section, we will be configuring how the application gateway will route requests using a collection of resources, which are known as a *backend pool*, to the backend servers that are responsible for serving route requests. A backend pool can consist of network interface cards (NICs), VM scale sets, public IP addresses, internal IP addresses, fully qualified domain names, and multi-tenant backends such as Azure App Service. To create a backend pool, follow these steps:

1. On the Backend tab, click Add A Backend Pool.

2. In the Add A Backend Pool window, fill in the following values to create the backend pool:

   - **Name:** Enter a name for the backend pool.

   - **Add Backend Pool Without Targets:** For this field, click Yes to create a backend pool with no targets by default. You will be able to add backend targets after the creation of the application gateway.

3. Click Add when you are ready to save the backend pool configuration, and then click Return on the Backends tab.

FIGURE 3.3   Creating an application gateway

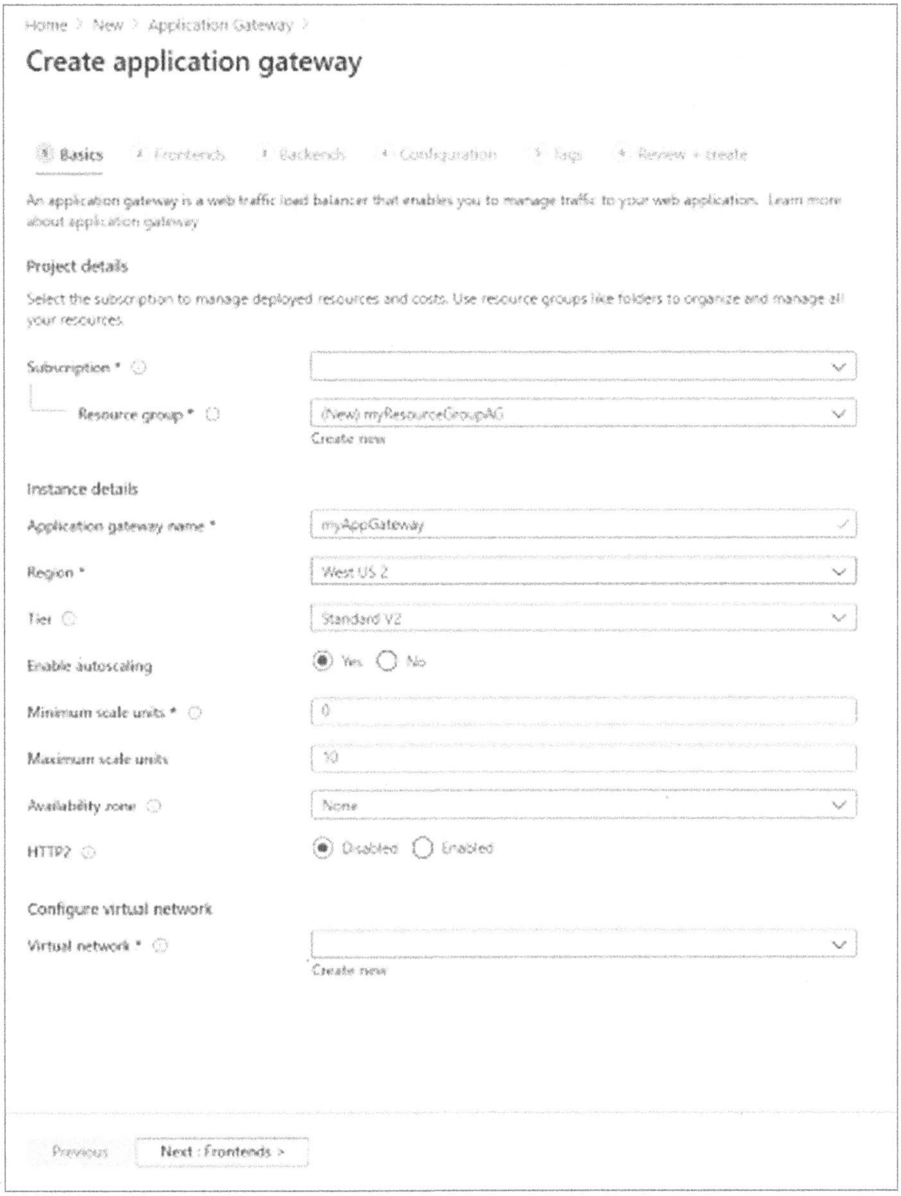

FIGURE 3.4   Adding a public IP address

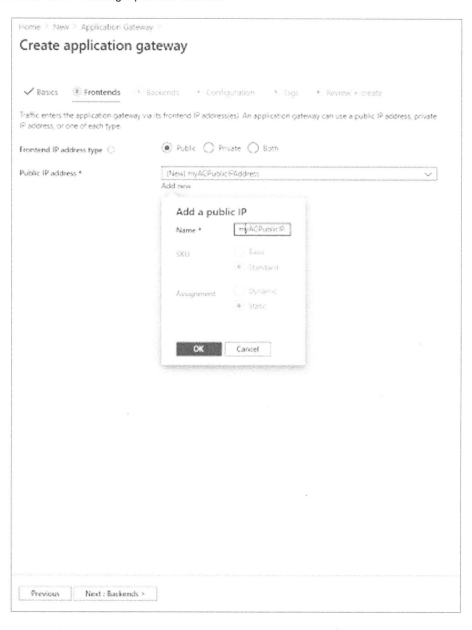

Configuration of the Backend Pool

Follow these steps to configure the backend pool:

1. Click Add A Rule in the Routing Rules section.

2. Enter a name for the routing rule that you will be creating.

3. Every routing rule requires a listener. On the Listener tab in the Add A Routing Rule window, add the following information:

   - **Listener Name:** Enter a name for your listener.
   - **Frontend IP:** Click Public and choose the public IP that you created for the frontend.

     You can leave the rest of the default values for the other settings on the Listener tab.

4. Select the Backend Targets tab to begin configuring the rest of the routing rule.

5. Select myBackendPool for Backend Target.

6. In the HTTP settings, click Add New to add a new HTTP setting. This HTTP setting determines how the routing rule behaves.

7. Enter a name for the HTTP setting and select 80 for Backend Port.

8. Accept the reminder of the default values for the other settings. Once you are done, click Add to return to the Add A Routing Rule window.

9. Click Add when you are ready to save the routing rule and return to the Configuration tab.

10. To complete the process, click Next: Tags and then click Next: Review + Create.

These steps will give you a basic application gateway that connects to a backend pool of resources. In this example, the backend pool is empty, but you can add to the pool any type of resource that you want and the application gateway will route the traffic to that resource.

Creating and Configuring Azure Front Door

Azure Front Door is great for building, operating, and scaling out your web applications. It is a global, scalable entry point used to create fast, secure, and widely scalable web applications using Microsoft's global network. It's not limited to just new applications, however. You can use Front Door with your existing enterprise applications to make them widely available on the web. Front Door providers have many options for traffic routing, and it has backend health monitoring so that you can identify any backend instances that may not be working correctly. While both Front Door and Azure Application Gateway are Layer 7 load balancers, the main difference is Application Gateway is a regional service whereas Front Door is a non-regional service. Here's some of the key features that come with Azure Front Door:

- Better application performance using the split TCP-based anycast protocol
- Intelligent health monitoring for all backend resources

- URL path-based routing for application requests
- Hosting of numerous websites via efficient application infrastructure
- Cookie-based session affinity
- SSL/TLS offloading and certificate management
- Ability to define a custom domain
- Application security via an integrated WAF
- The ability to redirect HTTP traffic to HTTPS seamlessly with URL redirect
- Custom forwarding path with URL rewrite
- Native support for end-to-end IPv6 connectivity and support for HTTP/2 protocol

Creating a Front Door for Your Application

To create an Azure Front Door for your application, follow these steps:

1. From the Azure portal menu, select Create A Resource. Then choose Networking ➤ See All ➤ Front Door And CDN Profiles.
2. Click Create and then select Azure Front Door in the Compare Offerings section.
3. Click Continue To Create A Front Door.
4. On the Basics tab of the Create A Front Door page, enter or select the following information in Table 3.1, and once you are done, click Next: Configuration.

TABLE 3.1 Setting options for your Front Door application

Setting	Value
Subscription	Select your desired subscription.
Resource Group	Enter the desired name in the text box.
Resource Group Location	Select your desired location.

5. In the Frontends/Domains section, click + to open the Add A Frontend Host dialog box.
6. For Host Name, enter a globally unique hostname. The example illustrated in Figure 3.5 uses *contoso-frontend*. Click Add.

Now that you have your frontend configured, you'll want to take your web applications that the traffic will be routed to and place them in a backend pool by following these steps.

1. While on the Create A Front Door page, in the Backend Pools section, click + to open the Add A Backend Pool dialog box.
2. For Name, enter the desired name, then click Add A Backend, as shown in Figure 3.6.

FIGURE 3.5 The contoso-frontend

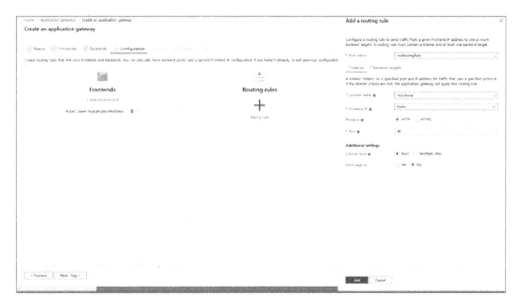

FIGURE 3.6 Adding a backend

3. In the Add A Backend section, enter the information in Table 3.2 and when you are done, click Add.

TABLE 3.2   Setting options for your backend pools

Setting	Value
Backend Host Type	Select App Service.
Subscription	Select Subscription.
Backend Host Name	Enter the name of your web app.
All other fields	Leave the defaults.

Repeat this process to add all the applications you want in this backend pool. When you're done, click Add at the bottom of the dialog box to complete the configuration (see Figure 3.7).

FIGURE 3.7   Click Add to complete the configuration.

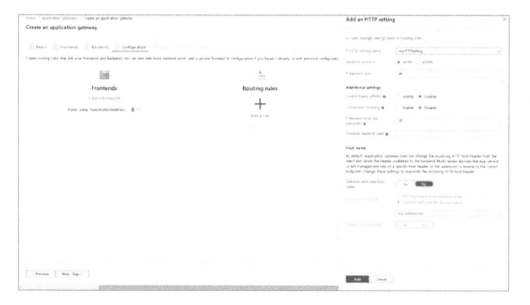

Routing Rules

The final step is to add a routing rule that maps your frontend host to the backend pool. Follow these steps:

1. On the Create A Front Door page, under Routing Rules, click + to configure a routing rule.

2. In the Add A Rule dialog box, for Name enter the desired name.

3. Accept all the default values, then click Add to add the routing rule.

4. From the Frontends/Domain dropdown list, select the domain that you want to route requests to. In Figure 3.8, it is *contoso-frontend.azurefd.net.*

FIGURE 3.8   Specify the domain to route requests to

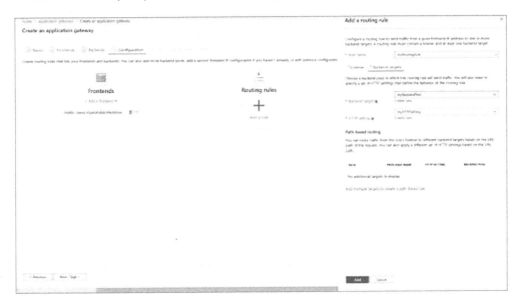

5. Click Review + Create (see Figure 3.9), then click Create.

Creating and Configuring a Web Application Firewall

A WAF is a specific type of application firewall that monitors, filters, and, if necessary, blocks HTTP traffic to and from a web application. Azure's WAF uses Open Web Application Security Project (OWASP) rules to protect applications against common web-based attacks such as SQL injection, cross-site scripting, and hijacking attacks. In Azure, WAFs are part of your application gateway, which you just learned how to configure in the previous section. All the customizations in a WAF are contained in a WAF policy that must be associated with your application gateway. A WAF policy can be attached to an application gateway at the global level, per-site level, and per-Uniform Resource Identifier (URI) level. The Global option allows you to associate the policy with every site behind your application gateway with the same managed rules, custom rules, exclusions, or any other rules you define. The Per-site option allows you to protect multiple sites with different security needs. Lastly, there is a path-based rule (Per URI), which allows you to set rules for specific website pages. It's also important to know that, in Azure, a more specific policy will always override a more general one. This means you can have a WAF policy at the global level that applies to all machines and have policies per-site that apply for specific instances. In that case, the per-site policies will override the policy at the global level. To create and configure a WAF, follow these steps:

FIGURE 3.9   Create the backend pool.

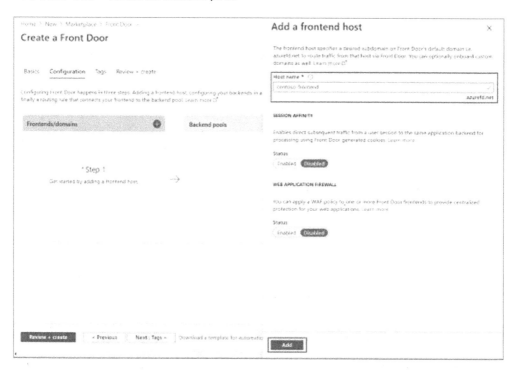

1. In the upper-left side of the Azure portal, click Create A Resource. Search for **WAF**, select Web Application Firewall, then click Create.

2. On the Create A WAF Policy page, on the Basics tab, enter the information in Table 3.3 in the appropriate fields. Then accept the defaults for the remaining settings and click Review + Create.

TABLE 3.3   Settings for creating a WAF

Setting	Value
Policy For	Regional WAF (Application Gateway).
Subscription	Select the desired subscription name.
Resource Group	Select your resource group.
Policy Name	Create a name for the WAF policy.

3. Click Managed Rules.

4. Define your rules, and then click Next: Policy Settings.

5. Define your policy, and then click Next: Custom Rules.

6. Leave this section empty and click Next: Association.

7. Click Add Association, and then select Application Gateway.

8. Select the Apply The Web Application Firewall Policy Configuration checkbox, even if it is different from the current configuration.

9. Click Add.

10. Click Review + Create, then click Create.

Configuring Network Isolation for Web Apps and Azure Functions

Azure App Service Environment (ASE) allows you to have an isolated and dedicated hosting environment to run your functions and web applications. There are two ways to deploy an ASE: you can use an external IP address (External ASE), or you can use an internal IP address (ILB ASE) because the internal endpoint is an internal load balancer.

Creating an External ASE

This method shows how to create an ASE and an App Service plan together:

1. From the Azure portal menu, choose Create A Resource ➢ Web ➢ Web App.

2. Select your subscription. The app and the ASE are created in the same subscriptions.

3. Select or create a resource group.

4. Select your OS (Windows, Linux, or Docker).

5. Select the App Service plan, and then click Create New. Linux web apps and Windows web apps cannot be in the same App Service plan but they can be in the same ASE.

6. From the Region drop-down list, select the region where you want to create the ASE.

7. Select Pricing Tier, and choose one of the isolated pricing SKUs.

8. Enter a name for your ASE. This name is used in the addressable name for your apps. For example, if the name of the ASE is *appsvcenvdemo*, the domain name is *.appsvcenvdemo.p.azurewebsites.net*.

9. Specify your Azure virtual networking details. Click Create New or select Existing.

10. Click Create to create the ASE. This process also creates the App Service plan and the app. The ASE, App Service plan, and app are all under the same subscription as well as the same resource group.

Creating an ILB ASE

Let's first create an ILB ASE:

1. From the Azure portal menu, select Create A Resource ➢ Web and then search for **App Service Environment v2**.

2. Select your desired subscription.

3. Select or create a resource group.

4. Enter the name of your ASE.

5. For Virtual IP Type, select Internal.

6. Select Networking.

7. Select or create a virtual network. If you choose to create a new VNet, it will be defined with an address range of 192.168.250.0/23. To create a VNet with a different address range, or in a different resource group than the ASE, you need to use the Azure Virtual Network creation portal.

8. Select or create an empty subnet. If you choose to select a subnet, it must be empty and not delegated. Also, the subnet size cannot be changed after the ASE is created. Microsoft recommends a size of /24; this will have 256 addresses, which is good for handling maximum-sized ASE and any scaling needs.

9. Once you are done making your selections, click Review + Create, then click Create.

Implementing Azure Service Endpoints

VNet service endpoints provide secure and direct connectivity to Azure services over an optimized route via the Azure backbone network. This way, you can have a more secure and efficient route for sending and receiving traffic (see Figure 3.10). Service endpoints allows private IP addresses on a VNet to reach the endpoint of an Azure service without needing a public IP address on the VNet.

FIGURE 3.10 Azure backbone explained

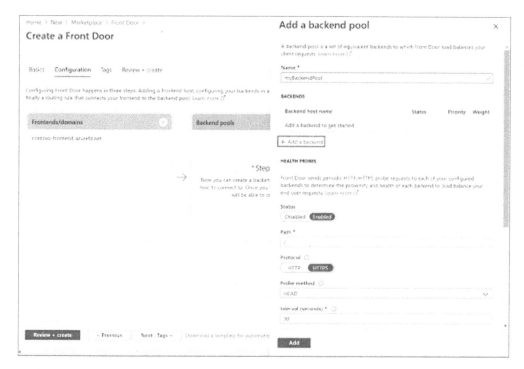

To implement a service endpoint, you need a user who has write access to the virtual network. Service endpoints are enabled per service, per subnet. The steps for creating a subnet and enabling a service endpoint are as follows:

1. To create the service endpoint policy, open the Azure portal.
2. Select Create A Resource in the top-left corner.
3. Type **service endpoint policy** and then click Create.
4. Enter or select information in the Basics tab: Subscription, Resource Group, Name, and Location.
5. Click Add under Resources and enter or select the following information: Service, Scope, Subscription, Resource Group, and Resource; then click Add.
6. (Optional) You can add information tabs if you like.
7. Click Review + Create.

Now that you have created the service endpoint, you can add it to resources like a subnet:

1. In the Azure portal, select Subnets under Settings, and then click Subnet.
2. On the Add Subnet page, select or enter the required information, and then click Save (see Figure 3.11).

FIGURE 3.11   Adding a service endpoint to your subnet

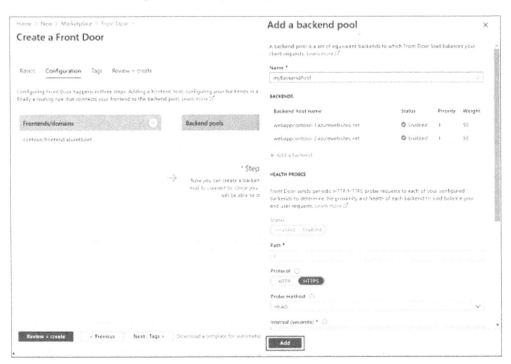

For more granular control over how the information flows, you can use a service endpoint policy. For example, you could use it with an Azure Storage account to only allow access to certain storage accounts (see Figure 3.12).

To configure a service endpoint policy, follow these steps:

1. Sign into the Azure portal.

2. Click Create A Resource in the upper-left corner.

3. In the search pane, type **service endpoint policy** and select Service Endpoint Policy; then click Create.

4. Enter, or select, the following information on the Basics tab: Subscription, Resource Group, Name, and Location.

5. Click Next: Policy Definitions and then click Add A Resource under Resources.

6. Enter the required information in the Add A Resource pane: Service, Scope, and Subscription.

7. (Optional) Enter or select any tag information on the Tags tab.

8. Click Review + Create. Validate the information and click Create. To make further edits, click Previous.

FIGURE 3.12   How service endpoints control information flow

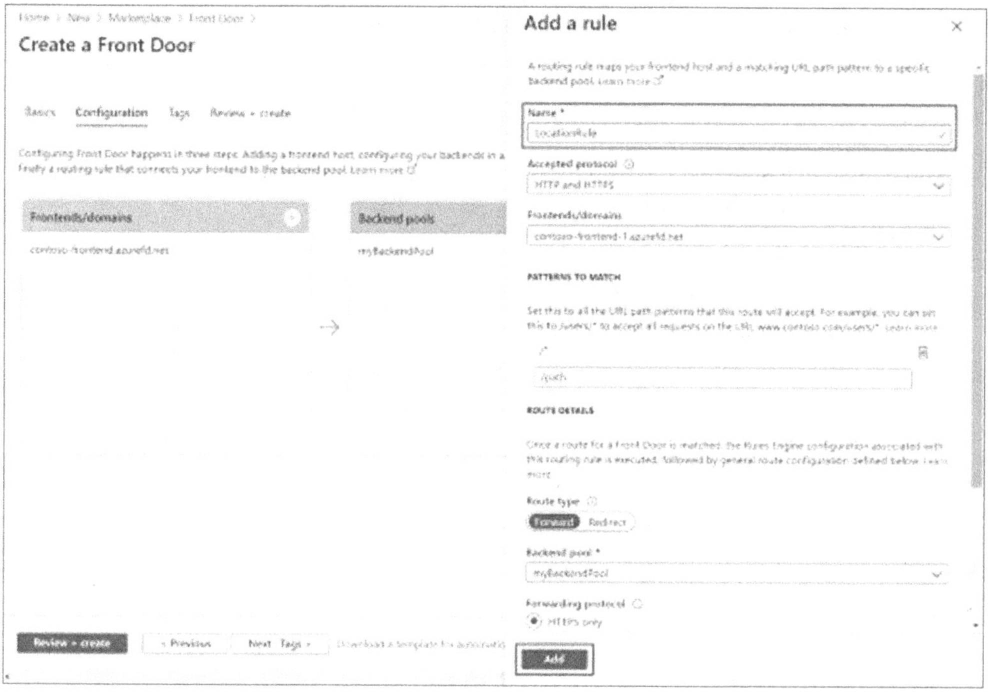

To attach the endpoint policies:

1. In the All Services field in the portal, type **service endpoint policies** and select Service Endpoint Policies.

2. Under Subscriptions, select your subscription and resource group.

3. Select the policy and click Policy Definitions to view or add more policy definitions.

4. Click Associated Subnets to view the subnets the policy is associated with. If there are no associations, then click edit Subnet Association to add one.

Implementing Azure Private Endpoints, Including Integrating with Other Services

A *private endpoint* is a network interface that uses a private IP address from your network. It connects you privately and securely to any service that is powered by Azure Private Link. Any service that is connected via a private endpoint is essentially a part of your virtual network. When using private endpoints, traffic to a private link resource is secure, and the platform will perform access control to validate that network connections are only reaching the specified resource. The difference between a service endpoint and a private endpoint is that a service endpoint is a publicly routable IP address whereas a private endpoint is a private IP in the address space of the virtual network. To create a private endpoint, follow these steps:

1. Sign into the Azure portal.

2. At the upper-left side of the screen in the portal, select Create A Resource ≻ Networking ≻ Private Link and then click Create.

3. In the Private Link Center, choose Private Endpoints from the menu on the left.

4. In Private Endpoints, click Create.

5. On the Basics tab of the Create A Private Endpoint page, fill in the required information.

6. Select the Resource tab or click the Next: Resource button at the bottom of the page.

7. On the Resources tab, fill in the required information.

8. Select the Configuration tab or click the Next: Configuration button at the bottom of the screen.

9. On the Configuration tab, fill in the required information.

10. Click Review + Create.

11. Click Create.

Implementing Azure Private Link

Azure Private Link allows you to access Azure platform-as-a-service (PaaS) services and Azure-hosted customer-owned/partner services over a private endpoint. Here are the key benefits of using Azure Private Link:

Privately Access Services on Azure   Using a private link ensures that traffic between your virtual network and the service will occur along Microsoft's backbone network, rather than exposing the service to the public Internet. Service providers can host their services in their own virtual network, and consumers will be able to access those services in their local virtual network.

On-premises and Peered Networks   You can also access services running in Azure from your on-premises network over ExpressRoute private peering, VPN tunnels, and peered virtual networks. This gives you a secure way to migrate workloads from on-premises to Azure without needing to traverse the Internet to reach that service.

Prevent Data Leakage   When using a private endpoint with a private link, consumers will be mapped to an instance of the PaaS resource instead of the whole service. Access to any other resource is blocked and, therefore, data leakage is prevented by providing only the access that is needed by the customer.

Global Reach   Using private links, you can connect to services running in other regions.

Creating a Private Link Service

To create a private link, you will need to have a virtual network with a NAT gateway and a load balancer associated with it. Once you have both, you can follow these steps to create the private link service:

1. In the Azure portal, click Create A Resource.

2. Enter **Private Link** in the Search The Marketplace box. Click Create.

3. On the Overview page, under Private Link Center, click the blue Create Private Link Service button.

4. On the Basics tab under Create Private Link Service, enter or select the information in Table 3.4.

TABLE 3.4   Basic settings for creating a private link service

Setting	Value
Project Details	
Subscription	Choose your subscription.
Resource Group	Select your resource group.
Instance Details	
Name	Enter your private link name.
Region	Enter your region.

5. Select the Outbound Settings tab or click Next: Outbound Settings at the bottom of the page.

6. On the Outbound Settings tab, enter or select the information in Table 3.5.

TABLE 3.5   Outbound settings for a private link service

Setting	Value
Load Balancer	Select your load balancer.
Load Balancer Frontend IP Address	Select your frontend load balancer.
Source NAT Subnet	Select your subnet.
Enable TCP Proxy V2	Leave the default of No. If your application expects a TCP proxy v2 header, click Yes.
Private IP address settings	Leave the default settings.

7. Select the Access Security tab or click Next: Access Security at the bottom of the page.

8. Leave the default of Role-Based Access Control Only on the Access Security tab.

9. Select the Tags tab or click Next: Tags.

10. Select the Review + Create tab or click Next: Review + Create.

11. Click Create on the Review + Create tab. Below are the settings for linking to a private endpoint (Table 3.6).

TABLE 3.6   Settings for linking to a private endpoint

Setting	Value
Project Details	
Subscription	Select your desired subscription.
Resource Group	Choose the name of your resource group.
Instance Details	
Name	Enter your endpoint name.
Region	Enter your region.

12. Select the Resource tab or click the Next: Resource button.

13. On the Resource tab, enter the information shown in Table 3.7.

TABLE 3.7   Settings for the Resource values in a private endpoint

Setting	Value
Connection Method	Select Connect To An Azure Resource In My Directory.
Subscription	Select your subscription.
Resource Type	Select Microsoft.Network/privateLinkServices.
Resource	Select the name of your private link service.

14. Select the Configuration tab or click the Next: Configuration button.

15. On the Configuration tab, enter the information shown in Table 3.8.

TABLE 3.8   Configuration settings for a private endpoint

Setting	Value
Virtual Network	Select your virtual network.
Subnet	Select your subnet.

16. Select the Review + Create tab or click the Review + Create button.

17. Click Create.

Implementing Azure DDoS Protection

Distributed denial-of-service (DDoS) is the biggest concern when it comes to availability in a cloud environment. Unlike attacks like ransomware, which normally require access to a company's internal network, a DDoS attack can be performed once a hacker can find the IP address of the target server(s). A DDoS attack attempts to exhaust an application's resources by sending a large number of requests, resulting in the application being overloaded and unavailable to legitimate users. Any endpoint that is publicly accessible from the Internet can be targeted by a DDoS attack. Every endpoint in Azure is protected by Azure's infrastructure DDoS Protection Basic free of cost and requires no user configuration or application changes. This protection comes with two primary features:

Always-On Traffic Monitoring   Your application traffic patterns are monitored 24 hours a day, 7 days a week, looking for indicators of DDoS attacks. DDoS Protection Standard instantly and automatically mitigates the attack once it is detected.

Extensive Mitigation Scale   Over 60 different attack types can be mitigated, with global capacity, to protect against the largest known DDoS attacks.

However, the Basic plan is significantly less effective than the DDOS Protection Standard plan. Azure's DDoS Protection Standard combined with the application design best practices we discussed previously provide enhanced DDoS mitigation features. The Standard plan is automatically tuned to protect your specific Azure resources and, once enabled, requires no application or resource changes. The Standard plan comes with these additional features:

Native Platform Integration   Azure DDOS protection is natively integrated into Azure, including being able to apply configurations through the Azure portal. DDoS Protection Standard has the ability to understand your resources and resource configurations.

Turnkey Protection   As soon as DDoS protection is enabled, it will automatically protect all resources on a virtual network without any need for intervention or user definition.

Adaptive Tuning   This allows Azure DDoS protection to learn your application's traffic profile over time and to choose the profile that best suits your service. It then continues to observe your traffic and change the profile accordingly over time.

Multilayered Protection   Whenever you deploy a WAF, DDoS Protection Standard provides protection at Layers 3, 4, and 7 (i.e., the Network, Transport, and Application layers) of the OSI model.

Attack Analytics   This feature provides you with a detailed report every 5 minutes during an attack and a complete summary of the attack once it has finished. You can stream the flow logs into Azure Sentinel or an offline security information and event management (SIEM) system for near-real-time monitoring of attacks against your systems.

Attack Metrics   These metrics allow you to view summarized metrics for every attack via Azure Monitor.

Attack Alerting   You can configure alerts at the start and stop of an attack as well as during an attack using built-in metrics. These alerts can be integrated into an operational software of your choosing such as Azure Monitor logs or Splunk.

DDoS Rapid Response   You have the option of engaging the DDoS Rapid Response (DRR) team to aid you with an attack investigation if the standard features aren't sufficient.

Cost Guarantee   You can receive data transfer and application scale-out service credits for resource costs incurred due to documented DDoS attacks.

Configuring Enhanced Security for Compute

Compute in cloud computing describes the concepts and objects related to software computation. It is a term used to reference elements like processing power, memory, networking, storage, and other resources that are required for computation. In this section, you'll learn how to secure these processes in Azure.

Configuring Azure Endpoint Protection for VMs

Microsoft Endpoint Protection for Azure provides antimalware protection to Azure VMs. It does this in three primary ways:

Real-Time Protection   In this way, Endpoint Protection acts similar to any other antimalware solution that will give you alerts when you attempt to download a piece of software that may be malware, or when you attempt to change important Windows security settings.

Automatic and Manual Scanning   Endpoint Protection comes with an automatic scanning feature that will alert you of any detected malware on your VMs. This feature can be turned on or off at your discretion.

Detection/Remediation   For severe threats, some actions will automatically be taken in an attempt to remove the malware and protect your VM from a potential or further infection. It can reset some Windows settings to more secure settings.

Table 3.9 lists the steps to configure Microsoft Endpoint Protection (`https://docs.microsoft.com/en-us/mem/configmgr/protect/deploy-use/endpoint-protection-configure`).

TABLE 3.9   Steps to configure Microsoft Endpoint Protection

Steps	Details
Create an Endpoint Protection point site system role.	The first step is to install the Endpoint Protection point site system role. It must be installed on only one system server, and it must be installed at the top of the hierarchy for the servers, meaning the central admin site.
Configure alerts for Endpoint Protection.	Alerts are important for informing an admin when certain events have occurred. Alerts can either be displayed in the alerts node of the monitoring workspace or be emailed to users.
Configure definition update sources for Endpoint Protection clients.	You can use Endpoint Protection to download definition updates. A definition is used in threat intelligence to detect potential threats.
Configure the default antimalware policy and create custom antimalware.	As soon as you download the Endpoint Protection client, the default antimalware policy will be applied. Any custom policies that you have deployed will be applied by default within 60 minutes of the client being downloaded.
Configure custom client settings for Endpoint Protection.	You can use custom client settings for several computers in your hierarchy all at once.

Implementing and Managing Security Updates for VMs

Implementing security updates quickly and regularly is an important part of good security in the cloud. By applying security updates, we get rid of security vulnerabilities that can be used to cause security incidents. In this section, you'll learn how to push security updates to virtual machines.

Updating Management in Azure Automation

Azure system updates are managed by Update Management (`https://docs.microsoft.com/en-us/azure/automation/update-management/overview`) in Azure Automation. Using this platform, you can see the compliance of machines in your environment, view the status of available updates, and facilitate the process of installing these updates on your machines (see Figure 3.13).

FIGURE 3.13   How Update Management works in Azure

Update Management also integrates with Azure Monitor logs to store update assessments and to update deployment results as log data so that you can review that information later.

Enabling Update Management in Azure Portal

Follow these steps to enable Update Management in the Azure portal:

1. Go to the Azure portal and navigate to Virtual Machines.
2. On the Virtual Machines page, select the VMs you want to add to Update Management.
3. Select Services, and then click Update Management to open the Update Management feature.

The list of VMs is filtered to show only those that are in the same subscription and location. If your VMs are in more than three resource groups, the first three resource groups are selected.

4. An existing Log Analytics workspace and Automation account are selected by default. If you want to use a different Log Analytics workspace and Automation account, click CUSTOM and select them from the Custom Configuration page. When you choose a Log Analytics workspace, a check is made to determine if it is linked with an Automation account. If a linked Automation account is found, you will see confirmation; click OK. If the workspace selected is not linked to an Automation account, you see no confirmation. Select an Automation account and click OK when finished.

5. Deselect any VM that you don't want to enable. VMs that can't be enabled are already deselected.

6. Click Enable to enable the feature. After you've enabled Update Management, it might take about 15 minutes before you can view the update assessment.

Implementing and Managing Security Updates

In this section, we will look at steps for implementing security updates in Azure. The first step will be defining your scope.

Defining Your Scope

First, you must limit the scope of the assessment to a select group of target computers to receive the update. To do so, follow these steps:

1. Go to the Azure portal.

2. Go to the Log Analytics workspace where Update Management was enabled.

3. Select Scope Configurations under Workspace Data Sources.

4. Click the ellipsis next to MicrosoftDefaultScopeConfig-Updates Scope Configuration and click Edit.

5. In the editing pane, expand the Select Computer Groups portion to show the saved searches that will be added to the scope configurations.

6. Create your custom group that defines the scope of computers that you want.

7. Save your changes.

Compliance Assessment

The next step to implementing a security update is to review the update compliance results for all machines in your environment.

To view an update assessment across all machines from your Automation account, navigate to Automation Accounts and select from the list your Automation account with Update Management enabled. In your Automation account, choose Update Management from the left menu. You will then be presented with the latest health assessment report (Figure 3.14).

FIGURE 3.14   Results from the latest update assessment

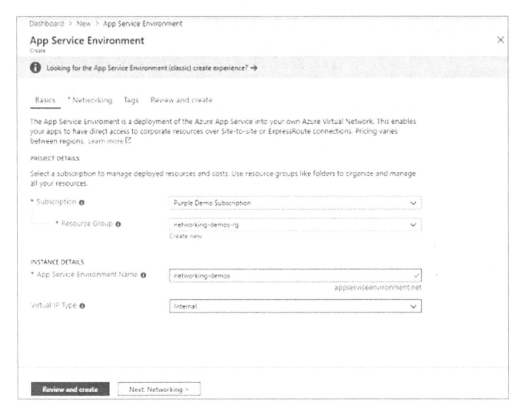

Here you can find information such as the last time a machine was assessed. Typically, compliance scans run every 12 hours by default.

You can also find the health of the update agent, and if there is an issue with the agent, select the link to go to the troubleshooting documentation, which can help you correct the problem.

Lastly, under the Information link, you can find a support article that gives you important information about any available updates.

Deploying Updates

Once you've narrowed your scope and reviewed the assessment results, it's time to deploy the updates to the machines on your network. To do this, you schedule a deployment that fits into your schedule and service window. You can also choose to deploy updates based on type, such as only security updates. This allows you to exclude updates that you don't want to do. To deploy an update, sign into the Azure portal and follow these steps:

1. Go to Automation Accounts and select your Automation accounts with Update Management enabled.

2. Go to Update Management and select Schedule Update Deployment.

3. Under New Update Deployment, type a unique name for the deployment.

4. Select the operating system you want to target for the update.

5. In Groups To Update, select the group of machines that you want to update; this can be a combination of subscription, resource groups, locations, and tags.

6. In the Machines To Update section, select the specific machines you want to update. If you want to update the entire group of machines, leave the default.

7. In the Update Classifications region, choose the updates that you want to be included in this update (see Figure 3.15).

FIGURE 3.15   Choosing update deployments

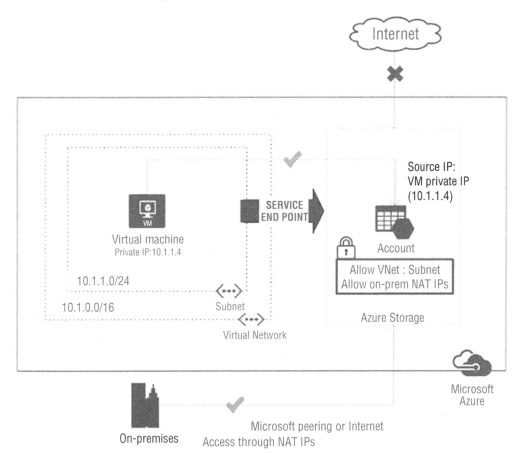

8. Use Include/Exclude Updates to include or exclude updates based on KB article ID numbers. A KB article ID is a knowledgebase article that is used to reference a specific update uniquely.

9. Click Schedule Settings and choose the time you want to run the update.

10. Use Recurrence to specify if this is a onetime deployment or a recurring schedule.

11. In the Pre-scripts + Post-scripts section, you can select scripts to run before or after the deployment.

12. Use the Maintenance window to specify the amount of time allotted to install updates. If the window closes while the updates are still processing, the current update will be installed and the rest will *not* be attempted—it will not stop installing updates halfway through.

13. Use the following reboot options to specify how you want to handle reboots during deployment:
    - Reboot If Necessary (default)
    - Always Reboot
    - Never Reboot
    - Only Reboot (don't install updates)

14. Click Create once you are done. You can find the schedule you created under Deployment Schedules located on the Status dashboard.

Configuring Security for Container Services

The Microsoft Defender for Cloud is the Azure-native solution for securing containers. It offers three main solutions for securing containers (see Table 3.10):

Vulnerability Scanning You can enable Microsoft Defender for Cloud for container registries, and the Security Center will scan any images pulled, pushed to your registry, or imported within the last 30 days. The scanner is integrated with the vulnerability scanner Qualys. If any issues are found, you will be notified in the Azure Defender Dashboard, which will provide actionable recommendations on how to resolve the issue.

Monitoring of Your Docker Configuration A docker container is a software package that includes everything needed to run an application. Azure Security Center will continuously assess the configuration of your docker containers and compare them with the Center for Internet Security (CIS) Docker Benchmark to ensure that they are sufficiently hardened. If the containers don't meet the necessary requirements, you will be notified and the Azure Security Center will generate security recommendations for remediating the issues.

Continuous Monitoring of Kubernetes Clusters Kubernetes clusters are a set of nodes that run containerized applications. The Azure Security Center works with Azure Kubernetes Service (AKS), which is a Microsoft-managed container orchestration service. AKS provides you with security controls for your Kubernetes clusters, and also provides visibility into the security posture of your Kubernetes clusters. The Azure Security Center allows you to constantly monitor the configuration of your AKS clusters and will automatically generate recommendations based on the latest industry standards for security.

TABLE 3.10   Microsoft Defender for Cloud features

Resource type	Protections provided by Azure Security Center
Kubernetes Clusters	Security Center provides continuous monitoring and assessment of your clusters to find and identify misconfigurations and potential threats.
Container Hosts	Security Center continuously assesses your docker environments to identify misconfigurations and to provide recommendations on how to mitigate threats.
Azure Container Registry (ACR)	Security Center provides vulnerability assessments and management tools to assess the security of ACRs.

Managing Access to the Azure Container Registry

The Azure Container Registry is an Azure service for building, storing, and managing container images and their related artifacts. When it comes to security, the Azure Container Registry supports a set of built-in Azure roles that allow you to assign various permission levels to an ACR. This allows you to use RBAC to assign specific permissions to users, service principals, or other identities that may need to interact with a registry. You can also create custom roles with a unique set of permissions.

Configuring Security for Serverless Compute

Azure has created a whitepaper, Functions and Serverless Platform Security | Microsoft Azure (`https://azure.microsoft.com/en-us/resources/azure-functions-serverless-platform-security`), dedicated to highlighting the security issues in serverless computing, and it will be the main source of material for this section. Serverless computing is a method of providing backend services for computing on an as-use basis. This way, you can run your applications without having any dedicated servers that you must pay for, you only pay when you need to use the service. Here are some of the main issues that Azure identified when securing serverless compute:

Shared Responsibility Model   Using a serverless compute service relieves you from managing servers and security updates, but you still have many responsibilities, such as creating secure application code, data encryption, identity management, and more. It's up to you as the security engineer to ensure that the proper security controls are in place (see Figure 3.16).

FIGURE 3.16   Azure's shared responsibility matrix

Increased Attack Surface and Complexity   Events such as HTTPs, application programming interfaces (APIs), message queues, cloud storage, and Internet of Things (IoT) device communications are a big source of data consumption for serverless functions. These messages introduce complex protocols and messages that increase the chances of an attack. Standard application layer protections can't inspect this type of traffic and, therefore, can't filter out malicious attacks.

Debugging Chaos   Difficulties occur when debugging a nested service call that has failed. Third-party services and data in transit make debugging code very difficult, and unfortunately there's currently no mitigation for this.

Telemetry and Insights Everywhere   Serverless computing increases application fragmentation because of the number of moving functions and services. This fragmentation and the creation of new services can lead to situations where you are unable to identify patterns and insights that are important for identifying potential security events or indicators of compromise/attack.

Microsoft Recommendations

Here are some of Microsoft's key recommendations (`https://azure.microsoft.com/ mediahandler/files/resourcefiles/azure-functions-serverless-platform- security/Microsoft%20Serverless%20Platform.pdf`; `https://azure .microsoft.com/en-us/resources/azure-functions-serverless-platform- security`) for securing serverless compute on the Azure platform:

- Ensure your applications/code do not explicitly trust input; all input should be validated.

- Use safe APIs to authorize user input or APIs.

- Always validate and authorize a user's input before passing it to an interpreter.

- Be sure that your code runs with the least privileges needed to perform its intended task.

- Be aware that inputs can come from expected and unexpected event triggers.

- When performing threat modeling, consider all potential event types and entry points into a system.

- Use a WAF to inspect HTTPS traffic that is coming into your serverless application.

- Avoid building custom authentication schemes. Use the built-in authentication facilities that the serverless environment provides. For example, Azure App Service provides built-in authentication and authorization support, which allows you to authenticate and sign in users without having to write any code or minimal code in your Azure function.

- Use mobile authentication using a provider software development kit (SDK).

- Provide security capabilities, such as good cloud storage configurations, multifactor authentication (MFA), and encryption of data at rest and in transit to avoid sensitive data leakages.

- Be familiar with the storage security controls that can be used to secure the data you store in the cloud.

- Implement the identity and access management (IAM) capabilities that are relevant to your platform and ensure that each function has its own designated user role that runs with the least privileges.

- Use Privileged Access Management (PAM) combined with RBAC to manage, control, and monitor access to important Azure resources.

Configuring Security for an Azure App Service

By default, the apps that are hosted in Azure App Service are accessible directly through the Internet and can reach only Internet-hosted endpoints. However, from a security point of view this isn't ideal, as you want to have more control of the outbound/inbound network traffic going to/from your application. Fortunately, several features in Azure can help you control access to your web applications. First, you need to understand how Azure processes communication to/from your applications. The roles that handle incoming requests are called *frontends* and the roles that host the customer workload are referred to as *workers*. All of the roles in an App Service deployment exist in a multi-tenant deployment and can't connect directly to your network. Rather than connecting the networks, you need features that can handle the different aspects of application communication. Table 3.11 lists the features that will handle requests *to* your application exclusively, in addition to features that will handle requests *from* your applications exclusively.

TABLE 3.11   Features that handle inbound and outbound requests to your application

Inbound features	Outbound features
App-Assigned Address	Hybrid Connections
Access Restrictions	Gateway-Required Vnet Integration
Service Endpoints	Vnet Integration
Private Endpoints	

App-Assigned Address This feature is used for IP-based SSL calls and can be used to give your app an address unique to that application. When using an app-assigned address, the application's traffic will still go through the same frontend roles that handle traffic coming into the App Service (see Figure 3.17).

FIGURE 3.17   How app-assigned addressing works

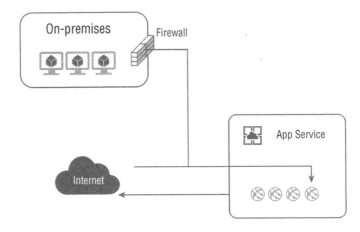

Access Restrictions   This feature allows you to filter inbound requests. You can build a list of allow and deny rules (similar to those used in a firewall or security groups) that are evaluated in the priority order that you identify (see Figure 3.18). You can restrict access based on many different factors.

FIGURE 3.18   Inbound access restrictions

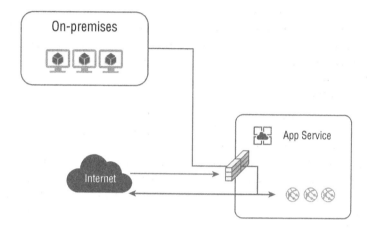

First, you create IP-based access restrictions rules that will allow you to restrict access to your application to a specific set of IP addresses, which can be IPv4 or IPv6. Next, you can filter based on *service endpoints*, which allow you to restrict inbound access to your application so that traffic is only allowed if it comes from a certain set of subsets that you selected. It works alongside IP-based access restrictions. It's important to note that service endpoints aren't compatible with remote debugging. If you want to use remote debugging with your application, your client can't be in the same subnet that has service endpoints enabled.

Next, you can configure access restriction rules based on service tags. Service tags are defined sets of IP addresses for use by Azure services. They allow you to filter inbound traffic from the Azure services that you specify.

For every access restriction rule, you have the option to add additional *HTTP header filtering*, which allows you to further inspect any incoming requests and filter based on their HTTP header values. One common use case for HTTP header filtering is using it to restrict access to traffic from proxy servers. Another common use case is using it to restrict access to a specific Azure Front Door instance via a service tag rule. Each header may have up to eight values per rule. Azure currently supports these HTTP headers:

- X-Forwarded-For
- X-Forwarded-Host
- X-Azure-FDID
- X-FD-HealthProbe

Private Endpoints

As discussed previously, a private endpoint is a network interface that connects you securely to your web app via an Azure private link. Private endpoints use a private IP address from your virtual network, which effectively makes your web app part of your virtual network. It's important to note that this feature can *only* be used with inbound data flows to your web app. Private endpoints help prevent data exfiltration, because the only thing you can reach using a private endpoint is the app that it is connected to and nothing else on the private network. Some common use cases for private endpoints are to restrict access to your web app and to isolate it from resources in a virtual network, exposing an application on a private IP in your virtual network and protecting your web app with a WAF.

Hybrid Connections

App Service hybrid connections allow your applications to make outbound calls to specific Transmission Control Protocol (TCP) endpoints. For this to work, the endpoint must be located on-premises, in a virtual network, or anywhere that allows outbound traffic to Azure on port 443. To enable this feature on web apps, you need to install a relay agency called *Hybrid Connection Manager* on a machine that is running Windows Server 2012 or later. Once the app in App Service performs a DNS lookup on the host and port defined in the hybrid connection, the traffic will automatically redirect through the hybrid connection and out of the Connection Manager. This feature is popular with developers because it enables access to on-premises resources without needing to create an inbound firewall hole.

Common use cases for hybrid connections are to:

- Access resources hosted in a private network that aren't connected to Azure using a VPN or ExpressRoute.

- Support a migration of an on-premises application to an App Service without needing to move the supporting databases.

- Provide access to a single host and port with improved security.

- Provide security in scenarios that aren't covered by other outbound connectivity methods.

- Perform development in App Service in a way that allows the apps to easily use on-premises resources. You can develop applications in App Service in a way that will make it easy to use on-premises resources.

Gateway-Required VNet Integration

Gateway-required VNet integration enables your app to make outbound requests into an Azure VNet (see Figure 3.19). This feature connects the host your application is running on to a virtual network gateway on your network by using a point-to-site VPN, which allows for secure communication to and from the network. Once you configure this feature, your application will receive a point-to-site address assigned to each instance. This feature solves the common problem of accessing resources in other virtual networks. This feature can be used to connect through a virtual network to other virtual networks or on-premises resources.

FIGURE 3.19   Gateway-required VNet integration

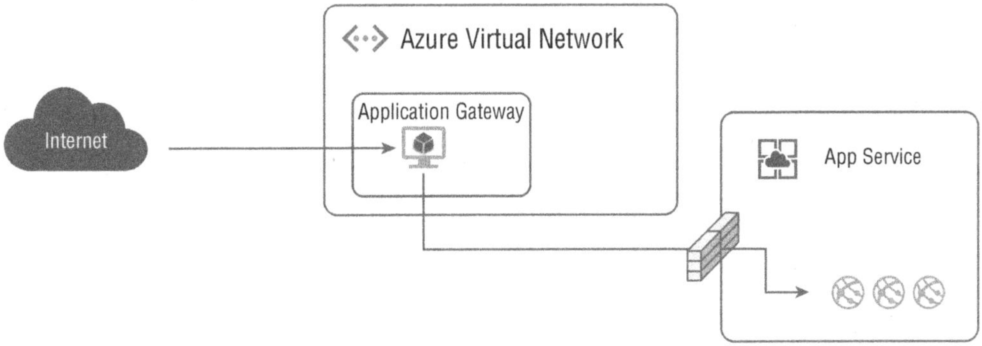

Common use cases for this feature include:

- Accessing resources that are using private IPs in your classic virtual networks
- Accessing resources that are on-premises when there is a site-to-site VPN
- Accessing resources in a cross-region VNet that have not been peered to a VNet in your region

Regional VNet Integration

Regional VNet integration addresses some of the shortcomings of a gateway-required VNet integration. Gateway-required VNet integration can't access resources across Azure's ExpressRoute, and it can't make calls to services that are secured using a service endpoint. Azure's ExpressRoute is a service that allows you to extend your on-premises network into the cloud. To integrate with resources in these scenarios, you need to use a regional VNet integration. This feature enables you to place the backend of your application in a subnet in a Resource Manager VNet in the same region as your application. Here are some common use cases for this feature (see Figure 3.20):

- Accessing resources in Resource Manager VNets that are in the same region
- Accessing resources in peered VNets
- Accessing resources that have been secured using service endpoints
- Accessing resources that are accessible via ExpressRoute or VPN connections
- Accessing resources in a private network without having to set up a virtual network gateway
- Securing all outbound traffic
- Enabling forced tunneling for all outbound traffic

FIGURE 3.20   Azure ExpressRoute

Common Use Cases and Their Corresponding Features

For any given use case, there are multiple features that you can use to achieve your goals. Microsoft offers a few recommendations, shown in Table 3.12 and Table 3.13.

TABLE 3.12   Microsoft inbound use case recommendations

Inbound use case	Feature
Supporting IP-based SSL	App-assigned address
Supporting unshared and dedicated inbound IP addresses	App-assigned address
Restricting access to your app from a set of defined IP addresses	Access restrictions
Restricting access to your applications from resources inside your virtual networks	Service endpoints Internal Load Balancer (ILB) ASE Private endpoints
Exposing your application using a private IP on your virtual network	ILB ASE Private endpoints Private IP for inbound traffic on an application gateway instance with service endpoints

Inbound use case	Feature
Protecting your applications using a WAF	Application gateway and ILB ASE Application gateway with private endpoints Application gateway with service endpoints Azure Front Door with access restrictions
Performing load balancing for traffic in different regions	Azure Front Door with access restrictions
Performing load balancing for traffic in the same region	Application gateway with service endpoints

TABLE 3.13   Microsoft outbound use case recommendations

Outbound use cases	Feature
Accessing resources in another Azure VNet in the same region	VNet integration ASE
Accessing resources in another Azure VNet in a different region	VNet integration and virtual network peering Gateway-required VNet integration ASE and virtual network peering
Accessing resources that are secured with service endpoints	VNet integration ASE
Accessing resources in a private network that isn't connected to Azure	Hybrid connections
Accessing resources across Azure ExpressRoute circuits	VNet integration ASE
Securing outbound traffic leaving your web application	VNet Integration and Network Security Groups ASE
Routing outbound traffic leaving your web application	VNet integration and route tables ASE

Configuring Encryption at Rest

In Azure, encryption at rest is implemented as transparent data encryption (TDE), which protects data at rest from authorized access. It performs real-time encryption and decryption of a database, its associated backups, and the transaction log files for that database while they are at rest, without requiring any changes to the application. TDE is enabled for all newly deployed Azure SQL databases, and the database encryption key is protected via a built-in server certificate. Certificate maintenance and rotation of the encryption and decryption keys are managed by Azure and require no user action.

TDE also supports Bring Your Own Key (BYOK) for encryption through the use of Azure Key Vault. Key Vault provides a central key management platform, leverages hardware security modules, and enables the separation of duties between the management of keys and data, which can be important for meeting security compliance requirements.

Configuring Encryption in Transit

SQL Database and SQL Managed Instance help secure customer data by encrypting data in transit using TLS. Azure SQL products enforce encryption at all times for all connections, which helps ensure that all data in transit is secure. As administrator, when you're configuring a connection string used by an application, you should specify an encrypted connection and not trust the server certificate. Doing so forces your application to verify the server certificate and protects your application from man-in-the-middle attacks.

Exam Essentials

Be able to explain how to secure your hybrid networks with Azure RBAC.   The first recommendation for securing your hybrid networks is to use Azure role-based access control (Azure RBAC) to control access to your resources. Azure recommends that you create three custom roles to help facilitate this. First is a DevOps role that has permission to administer the infrastructure for any applications, deploy different application components, and monitor and restart VMs on the environment. Second is a general IT administrator role that is used to manage and monitor all of the network resources. Last is a security IT administrator role that is used to secure network resources; this role should have exclusive access to manage and configure the firewalls.

Be able to explain how to use resource groups to group resources efficiently.   It's easier to manage your resources when you group them together into resource groups. Then you can simply assign Azure roles to each group to restrict their access all at once. In a hybrid network, Azure recommends creating these resource groups: First, a resource group for the virtual network (excluding the Virtual Machines), NSGs, and the gateway resources for connecting to the on-premises network. The IT administrator role should be assigned to this group. Next is a resource group for the VMs for the Azure firewall instance and user-defined routes for the gateway subnet. The security IT administrator role should be assigned to this group. Lastly, you should configure separate resource groups for each application tier that contains a load balancer and VMs. The DevOps role should be assigned to this group.

Be able to explain how DNAT works. For accepting inbound traffic, you should add a Destination Network Address Translation (DNAT) rule to your Azure firewall. This will allow you to have a single public IP address for your firewall instance to serve as the focal point for traffic to/from the Internet. In using DNAT, you want to enable *forced tunneling*, which allows you to redirect all Internet-bound traffic back to your on-premises location using a site-to-site VPN tunnel. This tunnel allows you to inspect the traffic and audit the traffic, as well as prevent the traffic from going directly out to the Internet.

Be able to explain the function of NSGs. For traffic between subnets, Azure recommends that you use network security groups (NSGs). Be sure not to confuse them with ASGs, which are used for traffic outside the Azure environment. NSGs are best suited for traffic to/from other Azure resources; otherwise they function similar to ASGs in that they filter traffic. NSGs are also capable of creating NSG flow logs to help you monitor performance and security. The logs can be created easily by enabling traffic analytics to gain quick insights into internal and external traffic flow from your applications.

Be able to explain the function of ASGs. To control this traffic, you want to make use of Azure's application security groups (ASGs). These groups allow you to create specific rules for allowing or blocking traffic and to assign them to a group of VMs easily.

Be able to define what Azure Firewall is. This is a managed, cloud-based, stateful firewall as a service. Unlike the security groups above, which filter based on simple criteria such as source and destination IP or port number, Azure Firewall is constantly being updated, based on Microsoft's threat intelligence service on the latest IOCs and IOAs that help protect your network.

Be able to explain the function of Azure Application Gateway. This gateway is Azure's web traffic load balancer, which enables you to manage the amount of traffic going to your application and prevent it from getting overloaded. Azure's Application Gateway is more advanced than a traditional load balancer. Normally, load balancers operate at the transport layer of the OSI model (layer 4 TCP and UDP) and can only route traffic based on source IP address and port, to a destination IP address and port. However, Azure's Application Gateway operates at layer 7 of the OSI model and can make decisions based on additional attributes found in an HTTP request, such as URL-based routing.

Be able to explain the function of Azure Front Door. This tool is great for building, operating, and scaling out your web applications. Azure Front Door is a global and scalable entry point used to create fast, secure, and widely scalable web applications using Microsoft's global network. It's not limited to just new applications; you can use Front Door with your existing enterprise applications to make them widely available on the web. Front Door providers have many options for traffic routing and backend health monitoring so that you can identify any backend instances when they aren't working correctly.

Know how Azure Web Application Firewall (WAF) protects against cyberattacks.   A WAF is a specific type of application firewall that monitors, filters, and if necessary, blocks HTTP traffic to/from a web application. Azure's WAF uses OWASP rules to protect applications against common web-based attacks, such as SQL injection, cross-site scripting, and hijacking attacks.

Be able to explain what an Azure service endpoint does.   VNet service endpoints provide secure and direct connectivity to Azure services over an optimized route via the Azure backbone network. This way you can have a more secure and efficient route for sending and receiving traffic. It allows private IP addresses on a VNet to reach the endpoint of an Azure service without needing a public IP address on the VNet.

Be able to define what an Azure private endpoint does.   A *private endpoint* is a network interface that uses a private IP address from your network. It connects you privately and securely to any service powered by an Azure private link. Any service that is connected via a private endpoint then is essentially a part of your virtual network. When using private endpoints, traffic to a private link resource is secured, and the platform will perform access control to validate that network connections are only reaching the specified resource.

Define what an Azure private link does.   Azure private links allow you to access Azure PaaS services and Azure-hosted customer-owned/partner services over a private endpoint.

Explain the function of Azure DDoS Protection.   Every endpoint in Azure is protected by Azure's infrastructure DDoS Protection (basic) free of cost and requires no user configuration or application changes. It comes with two primary features:

1. **Always-on traffic monitoring:** All of your application's traffic patterns will be monitored 24/7 and analyzed for any indicators of DDoS attacks.

2. **Extensive mitigation scale:** It can mitigate over 60 different attack types and specializes in protecting against even the largest known DDoS attacks.

Be able to explain the features of Azure Endpoint Protection for VMs.   Microsoft Endpoint Protection for Azure provides antimalware protection to Azure VMs in three primary ways:

1. **Real-Time Protection:** In this way, endpoint protection acts similar to any other antimalware solution that will provide you with you alerts when you attempt to download software that may be malware, or when you attempt to change important Windows security settings.

2. **Automatic and Manual Scanning:** Endpoint protection comes with an automatic scanning feature that will alert you of any detected malware on your VMs. This feature can be turned on or off at your discretion.

3. **Detection/Remediation:** For severe threats, some actions will automatically be taken to remove the malicious software and protect your VM from potential infection or further infection. It can also reset some Windows settings to more secure settings.

Define what Azure Container Registry is. The Azure Container Registry is a service for building, storing, and managing Azure container images and their related artifacts. When it comes to security, the Azure Container Registry supports several built-in Azure roles that allow you to assign various permissions levels to an Azure Container Registry. You use RBAC to assign specific permissions to users, service principals, or other identities that may need to interact with a registry. You can also create custom roles with a unique set of permissions.

Review Questions

1. What is Azure Front Door used for?
    A. Traffic routing to backend resources
    B. DDoS protection
    C. Added scalability for web applications
    D. Malware protection

2. What is Azure Web Application Firewall used for?
    A. Filtering network traffic
    B. Providing protection for your web application from known exploits
    C. Encrypting and decrypting traffic to your web app
    D. Routing traffic from your web application

3. What is not a feature of Azure DDoS Protection?
    A. DDoS mitigation at scale
    B. Blocking of IP addresses
    C. 24/7 traffic monitoring
    D. Reimbursement due to excessive downtime

4. What is not a feature of Azure DDoS Protection Premium?
    A. Attack analytics
    B. Tracking an IP address's origin
    C. Adaptive tuning
    D. Attack alerting

5. What are Azure service endpoints used for?
    A. Communicating between different subnets on the Azure network
    B. Hosting web applications
    C. Connecting to Azure services over the Azure backbone network
    D. Communicating with systems outside the network

6. What are Azure private endpoints used for?
    A. Hosting network services
    B. Creating forced tunneling
    C. Encrypting traffic
    D. Connecting you securely to any service that has an Azure private link

7. What is encryption at rest?

    A. Encrypting data that is sitting in memory

    B. Encryption when data is in use

    C. Encryption when data is not being used or moved

    D. Encryption when data is being transported

8. What is encryption in transit?

    A. Encrypting data that is sitting in memory

    B. Encryption when data is in use

    C. Encryption when data is not being used or moved

    D. Encryption when data is being transported

9. Which is not a recommended type of custom role for access control?

    A. A DevOps role

    B. An IT administrator role

    C. A database administrator role

    D. A security IT administrator role

10. How are resource groups used for access control?

    A. They allow you to filter traffic to resources in the group.

    B. By grouping resources together, you can assign roles to all resources in the group.

    C. They are required for assigning roles to resources.

    D. You can attach NSGs to resource groups.

11. What is DNAT used for?

    A. Translating private IP addresses to public IP addresses

    B. Filtering inbound traffic

    C. Having a single public IP address for your firewall

    D. Having public IP addresses for subnets

12. What is the difference between ASGs and NSGs?

    A. There is no difference.

    B. ASGs filter traffic outside the network, whereas NSGs filter internal traffic.

    C. ASGs allow for more advanced filtering than NSGs.

    D. ASGs only allow you to filter application traffic.

13. How do NSGs allow you to monitor performance and security?

    A. Through automated reports

    B. Via NSG flow logs

    C. Through real-time dashboards

    D. By examining traffic between NSGs

14. What can you use to control how traffic moves throughout the network?

    A. An NVA

    B. A UDR

    C. NSGs

    D. ASGs

15. Which of the following is not a feature of Azure Firewall?

    A. Threat intelligence

    B. Network traffic filtering

    C. Forced tunneling

    D. DDoS Protection

16. What is the purpose of an Azure Application Gateway?

    A. Web traffic load balancing

    B. Subnet traffic routing

    C. Zone redundancy

    D. Protecting against web application attacks

17. Which of the following is not a feature of Azure Application Gateway?

    A. Web traffic load balancing

    B. Autoscaling

    C. SSL/TLS termination

    D. Web application protection

18. What attacks will a WAF not protect you from?

    A. SQL injection

    B. Cross-site scripting

    C. Hijacking attacks

    D. Unauthorized access

19. Which of the following is not a common web application attack?

    A. SQL injection

    B. Cross-site scripting

    C. DDoS attacks

    D. Web app hijacking

20. Which feature helps in creating new backend resources on demand?

    A. Web traffic load balancing

    B. Autoscaling

    C. SSL/TLS termination

    D. Web application protection

Chapter

4

Managing Security Operations

THE MCA MICROSOFT CERTIFIED ASSOCIATE AZURE SECURITY ENGINEER ASSESSMENT TEST TOPICS COVERED IN THIS CHAPTER INCLUDE:

- Configure centralized policy management.
- Configure a custom security policy
- Create a policy initiative
- Configure security settings and auditing by using Azure Policy

✓ **Configure and manage threat protection.**

- Configure Microsoft Defender for Servers (not including Microsoft Defender for Endpoint)
- Evaluate vulnerability scans from Azure Defender
- Configure Microsoft Defender for SQL
- Use the Microsoft Threat Modeling Tool

✓ **Configure and manage security monitoring solutions.**

- Create and customize alert rules by using Azure Monitor
- Configure diagnostic logging and log retention by using Azure Monitor
- Monitor security logs by using Azure Monitor
- Create and customize alert rules in Microsoft Sentinel
- Configure connectors in Microsoft Sentinel
- Evaluate alerts and incidents in Microsoft Sentinel

Many large companies have a security operations center (SOC), a central unit in the organization that deals with the security issues arising within the company. Typically, a SOC is responsible for monitoring an entire company's network and dealing with any security alerts that come from the security software monitoring that network. This security monitoring includes the three levels of building blocks within the company: people, processes, and technology. Managing security operations within Azure means being able to effectively monitor your cloud environment, receive actionable information and alerts based on the activities occurring on the network, and taking action to remediate any issues as soon as possible. As we go through this chapter, keep those items in mind. First, you must have an effective means of monitoring your company's cloud environment. Next, you must be able to identify what activities on your network represent potential security threats. Lastly, you must be able to remediate those issues and bring your organization back to a state of security and compliance.

Configure Centralized Policy Management

The SOC must set up and centralize the operation, management, and creation of the company's security policy. Not only must they define who manages and enforces, but they must create the rules and regulations that make up that policy as well. First, let's look at defining the security policy.

Configure a Custom Security Policy

Azure policies help to enforce your organization's standards and its compliance in accessing cloud resources. An Azure policy gives you the ability to define a set of properties that your cloud resources should have, and then it compares that defined list of properties to the actual properties of your resources to find those that are noncompliant. These business rules, which are described using JavaScript Object Notation (JSON) format, are called *policy definitions*. You can assign policy definitions to any set of resources that Azure supports. These rules can use functions, parameters, logical operators, conditions, and property aliases to match the exact scenario that you want for your organization.

You can also control the response to a noncompliant evaluation of a resource with the policy definitions. For example, if a user wants to make a change to a resource that will result in it being noncompliant, you have multiple options. You can deny the requested change, you can log the attempted/successful change to that resource, you can alter the resource *before/after* the change occurs, and so on. All of these options are possible by adding what's called an *effect* in the policies that you create.

You can create policies from scratch, or you can use some of Azure's prebuilt policies that are created and available by default:

- **Allowed Storage Account SKUs (Deny):** This policy will determine if a storage account being deployed is within a predetermined set of stock keeping unit (SKU) sizes that's defined by your organization. It will deny all storage accounts that don't meet the set of defined SKU sizes.

- **Allowed Resource Type (Deny):** This policy defines the resource types that you are allowed to deploy. Any resources that aren't on this list will be denied.

- **Allowed Locations (Deny):** This policy allows you to restrict the location that your organization can select when deploying new resources and allows you to enforce geo-compliance for all new resources.

- **Allowed Virtual Machine (VM) SKUs (Deny):** This policy allows you to specify a set of VM SKUs that you are able to deploy in your organization (`https://docs .microsoft.com/en-us/learn/modules/build-cloud-governance-strategy-azure/6-control-audit-resources-azure-policy`). All others will be blocked.

- **Add a Tag to Resources (Modify):** This policy will add a required tag and its value to any resource that's created.

- **Not Allowed Resource Types (Deny):** This policy will prevent a specified list of resource types from being deployed.

Create Custom Security Policies

To create individual policies, the easiest method is to use Azure Policy. Azure Policy is a service that allows you to create, assign, and manage the policies that will control or audit your cloud resources. You can use Azure Policy to create individual policies, or you can create initiatives, which are combinations of individual policies. There are three steps to implementing a policy in Azure Policy:

1. Create a policy definition.   A *policy definition* defines what you want your policy to evaluate and what actions it should take on each resource to which it is assigned. For example, say you want to prevent VMs from being deployed in certain Azure regions, so you create a policy preventing VM deployment in that region. Here are some other examples of Azure Policy definitions:

- **Enable Multifactor Authentication (MFA) on accounts with write permissions on your subscription:** This policy requires that MFA be enabled on all accounts with write permissions on your subscription, to help prevent a breach of an account or resources.

- **Cross-Origin Resource Sharing (CORS) should not allow every resource to access your web applications:** CORS is an HTTP feature that allows a web application running under one domain to access resources in a different domain. To protect against cross-site scripting attacks, modern web browsers prevent cross-site scripting by default, but this policy allows only the required domains to interact with the web applications.

- **System updates should be installed on your machines:** This policy allows Microsoft Defender for Cloud to recommend any missing security patches for your servers, making it easy to apply them as needed.

2. Assign the definition to resources.   Next, you need to assign the policy definition to the resources that you want them to affect. Referred to as a *policy assignment*, this involves assigning a policy definition to a specified scope. For example, you may want the policy to affect all VMs in a certain geographical region. Policy assignments are inherited by all child resources within the scope by default. That way, any new resources created within that scope will automatically be assigned that policy assignment.

3. Review the evaluation results.   Once a condition is evaluated against a resource, the resource is marked as either compliant or noncompliant. You then have the option to review the results and decide what action needs to be taken. Policy evaluations occur approximately once per hour.

4. Implement a custom policy.   To implement your custom security policy, you must follow these steps:

1. Go to the Azure portal, select All Services, and search for **policy**.
2. Select Definitions under Authoring on the left side of the Azure Policy page.
3. Select Policy Definition at the top of the page.
4. Fill in the following information:
   - **Definition Location:** Enter the management group or subscription.
   - **Name:** Assign a name to your policy definition.
   - **Description:** Provide a description of what the policy definition is supposed to do.
   - **Category:** Choose an existing category or create one for the policy definition.
5. Create JSON code that will outline the policy parameters, the policy rules/conditions, and the policy effect.
6. Finally, save the policy.

Creating a Policy Initiative

You're able to create custom initiatives using Microsoft Defender for Cloud by following these steps:
1. From the Microsoft Defender for Cloud menu, select Security Policy.

2. Select the subscription or management group for which you want to create a custom initiative.

3. On the Security Policy page, under Custom Initiative select Add A Custom Initiative.

4. On the Add Custom Initiatives page, review the list of custom policies that you have created in your organization. If you haven't already created the policy you want to apply, click Create New.

5. Enter the following details for your custom initiative:

    -   Enter the definition's location and name.

    -   Select the policies to include and click Add.

    -   Enter any other parameters you want and click Save.

    -   Return to the Add Custom Initiatives page and add the initiatives that you want.

    Once your initiative is applied, you are able to see the results in two ways:

-   In the Defender for Cloud menu, select Regulatory Compliance and a compliance dashboard will open to show your new custom initiative alongside the built-in initiatives.

-   You will receive notifications containing recommendations if your environment doesn't follow the policies you've defined.

Configuring Security Settings and Auditing by Using Azure Policy

Every policy definition that you create in Azure Policy will have a determination evaluation called an *effect*. The effect determines what will happen when a policy rule is evaluated for matching. This effect can be applied whether it's the creation of a new resource, an updated resource, or an existing resource. Here are the different types of effects that you can create in Azure:

Append: This effect is used to add extra fields to a resource during its creation or update. For example, let's say that you have a policy for all the storage resources in your environment. You can add an append effect that will specify what IP addresses are allowed to communicate with your storage resources and it will be applied during the creation of any storage resource.

Audit: This effect is used to create a warning event, which is stored in the activity logs when your policy evaluates a noncompliant resource; however, it will not stop the request. For example, if you have a policy that states all VMs must have the latest software patch applied, and a VM exists that doesn't have that patch applied when the policy is evaluated, then it will create an event in the activity log that details this information.

AuditIfNotExists: This effect takes it a step further by allowing the effect to have if and then conditions. If you've programmed before, it works similar to an if-then statement. This effect allows you to audit resources related to the resource that matches the *if* condition but fails to match the *then* condition. For example, you can use this effect if you want to determine whether VMs have an antimalware extension installed and then audit the VMs for a separate condition if the antimalware extension is missing.

Deny: As the name suggests, this effect allows you to prevent a resource create/update request from being fulfilled if it doesn't match the standards outlined in the policy definition you created.

DeployIfNotExists: This effect executes a template deployment when a condition is met. Typically, that condition is the absence of a property. For example, you may have a policy that evaluates a Structured Query Language (SQL) server database to see whether or not TransparentDataEncryption is enabled. If it isn't, then a deployment is executed based on a predetermined template.

Disabled: This effect allows you to disable individual assignments when a policy is evaluated. Whereas deny would prevent a resource create/update request from being fulfilled in its entirety, disable allows you to remove individual assignments that may be causing the noncompliance.

Modify: This effect is used to add, update, or remove properties/tags on a subscription or resource during its creation or update. Existing resources can be remediated with a remediation task. For example, you may want to add a tag with the value `test` to all VMs that are created for testing purposes so that they don't get confused with production VMs.

Order of Evaluation

If you have multiple effects attached to a policy definition, there is a certain order in which the effects will be evaluated. This order of evaluation (`https://docs.microsoft.com/en-us/learn/modules/build-cloud-governance-strategy-azure/6-control-audit-resources-azure-policy`) is as follows:

- **Disabled:** This is checked first to determine if a policy rule should be evaluated.

- **Append and Modify:** This is evaluated next. Because either one of these can cause a change in the request, it's possible that neither Deny or Audit will be evaluated at all.

- **Deny:** Next evaluated is Deny. This is important because by evaluating Deny first, double-logging of an undesired resources is prevented.

- **Audit:** Audit is *always* evaluated last.

Configuring and Managing Threat Protection

Like any computer network, your cloud environment will be subject to attacks from a number of different cyberthreats. In addition to your third-party security solutions, Azure comes with several security features to help you protect your network from these attacks. In this section, we'll go over some of the main tools for defending against threats in Azure and how to configure and manage them effectively.

Configuring Microsoft Defender for Cloud for Servers (Not Including Microsoft Defender for Endpoint)

Microsoft Defender for Cloud is one of the primary tools used for cloud workload protection (CWP), which is a procedure for keeping cloud-based services secure. When you enable Microsoft Defender, you get several additional security features that help you better protect your company. Defender comes with three main categories of protection: endpoint detection and response, advanced protection capabilities, and vulnerability management.

Endpoint Detection and Response

The first thing Microsoft Defender for Cloud affords you is endpoint detection and response (EDR) capabilities through an integration with Microsoft Defender for Endpoint. Using this integration, Defender can consistently scan your environment and generates security alerts detailing the affected resources, suggests remediation steps, and in some situations, gives you the option to trigger an automated response. It also gives you the ability to export these alerts to Microsoft Sentinel or any third-party SIEM that is compatible with the tool, if you would rather perform analysis on that platform.

Advanced Protection Capabilities

Defender also provides the following advanced protection capabilities:

Just-in-time virtual machine access (JIT): This feature locks down inbound traffic to your VMs up until the point where access is needed to provide cloud services. This simply means that users will be denied access at all times, except when it is needed for your cloud services, and users will be required to request the opening of ports when needed. This limits threat actors' opportunities to probe machines via open management ports like Remote Desk Protocol (RDP) or Secure Shell (SSH) and makes your VMs less likely to be targeted for attacks.

Adaptive Application Controls (AAC): These controls are an intelligent and automated solution for whitelisting known-safe applications for your machines. Whitelisting is where you allow certain identified applications access. When you have this feature enabled, you will get alerts if any applications are running on your machines other than the ones that you've whitelisted yourself. This is very useful for servers with a specific function like a web server or a SQL server, where you will know in great detail what applications should be run on those servers.

Adaptive Network Hardening (ANH): As discussed in earlier chapters, network security groups (NSGs) are used to filter traffic to and from resources. However, sometimes the actual traffic that is flowing is just a subset of the rules that are created; those extra rules that are allowing traffic only add extra risk without serving any purpose. ANH can provide recommendations for modifying NSG rules based on actual traffic patterns, known trusted configuration, threat intelligence, and other indicators of compromise.

Docker Host Hardening: Defender can identify unmanaged containers and continuously assess the configuration of Docker containers, then compare it to the Center for Internet Security (CIS) Docker Benchmark. Defender for Cloud incorporates the entire ruleset of the CIS Benchmark and will alert you if your containers don't satisfy any of the controls.

Fileless Attack Detection: A *fileless attack* is a type of cyberattack that injects malicious payloads into computer memory to avoid detection by disk-based scanning techniques. The payload exists in the computer's memory and compromises processes that will perform different malicious activities. Typically, this type of attack can be very difficult to detect. With fileless attack detection, Defender provides automated memory forensic techniques to identify attack toolkits, techniques, and behaviors. This feature scans your machine at runtime and extracts insights from memory for computer processes. Ultimately, Defender will generate detailed security alerts, which include descriptions with process metadata that can be used for investigation.

File Integrity Monitoring (FIM): FIM allows Defender to examine files and registries of an operating system, application software, and other items in your environment for any change that might indicate an attack. Defender uses a comparison method to determine if the current state of a file is different from the previous file scan. You can then view these comparisons to determine if it is valid or a suspicious change.

Linux Auditd Alerts and Log Analytics Agent Integration (Linux Only): The Auditd system consists of a kernel-level subsystem that is responsible for monitoring system calls. It filters them using a specified ruleset and then writes messages for them to a socket. Defender integrates these elements with the Log Analytics agents. The agents then collect the Auditd records, enriches them by correlating different events across the environment, and aggregates them into events that can be used to detect malicious behaviors on cloud and on-premises Linux machines.

Vulnerability Management

Last on this list is vulnerability scanning for your VMs and SQL databases:

Microsoft Threat and Vulnerability Management: You can discover vulnerabilities and misconfiguration in real time with Microsoft Defender for Endpoint without needing to deploy software agents or perform periodic scans. The threat and vulnerability management tool will prioritize vulnerabilities based on the most current threat landscape, detections that are found in your organization, sensitive information held on vulnerable devices, and your specific business context.

Qualys vulnerability scanner integration: If you haven't heard of it before, Qualys is one of the most popular and well-respected vulnerability scanners in the cybersecurity industry. In Azure, you can run vulnerability scans on your resources, powered by the popular tool Qualys. However, unlike commercial products, you can gain access to the tool without needing a Qualys license or even a Qualys account at no additional cost. You can use Qualys to review the findings from these scans and to respond to them all from the Microsoft Defender for Cloud dashboard.

Setting Up Defender on Your Server

Onboarding one or more machines to threat and vulnerability management can be done at the Microsoft Defender for Cloud dashboard. First, select your security recommendation; for this example, choose this:

A vulnerability assessment solution should be enabled on your virtual machines.

To automatically identify vulnerabilities on existing and new machines, follow these steps:

1. From the Defender for Cloud menu, choose Environment Settings under Management.

2. Select the appropriate management group and subscription.

3. Navigate to the Auto Provisioning page under Settings.

4. Set the option Auto Provisioning to On for the vulnerability assessment and then select Microsoft Threat And Vulnerability Management.

5. Click Save.

To view the findings for all supported vulnerability assessments, go to Defender for Cloud's menu and open the Recommendations page.

You can deploy the Qualys integrated scanner to Azure and Hybrid Machines by following these steps:

1. Go to the Azure portal and open Microsoft Defender for Cloud.

2. Use the Microsoft Defender for Cloud menu to open the Recommendations page.

3. On the Recommendations page, select this recommendation:

A vulnerability assessment solution should be enabled on your virtual machines.

Note that once you make this selection, all of your machines will be placed in one or more of the following security groups:

- **Healthy resources:** This group includes machines where Microsoft Defender for Cloud has detected a vulnerability assessment solution running on them.

- **Unhealthy resources:** This group contains machines that can have a vulnerability scanner extension deployed, but it hasn't been as of yet.

- **Not applicable resources:** This group includes machines that can't have a vulnerability scanner extension deployed, and therefore, cannot be scanned.

4. Take the list of unhealthy machines and select the ones that you want to receive a vulnerability assessment solution for, and then click Remediate.

5. Select the Recommend option, which is to deploy an integrated vulnerability scanner.

6. You will be asked to confirm, so click Remediate.

Configuring Microsoft Defender for SQL

Microsoft Defender for SQL is an add-on to the traditional Microsoft Defender package that adds a data security package to help secure your databases and their data. It comes with two primary features: a vulnerability assessment for SQL servers on machines and a vulnerability assessment for SQL databases.

Vulnerability Assessment for Azure SQL Servers on Machines

Microsoft Defender for SQL includes a threat detection feature that helps you identify and mitigate potential database vulnerabilities based on unusual activities that may indicate threats to your database. The Threat Protection Service constantly monitors your SQL servers for common threats, such as SQL injection, brute-force attacks, and privilege abuse. This vulnerability assessment service will scan your database every 12 hours. The dashboard will provide you with an overview of your assessment results across all your databases. It provides a summary of the healthy and unhealthy databases and an overall summary of the failed checks sorted by risk.

You can set up Microsoft Defender for SQL on your machines by following these steps:

1. Install the agent extension. There are two versions of Defender agents that you can install, depending on your machines:

    SQL Server on Azure VM: You'll need to register your SQL Server VM with the SQL Infrastructure as a Service (IaaS) Agent extension.

    SQL Server on Azure Arc–enabled servers: You'll need to install the Azure Arc agent by following the installation methods described in the Azure Arc documentation.

2. You must provision the Log Analytics agent on your SQL server's host (https://docs.microsoft.com/en-us/azure/defender-for-cloud/ defender-for-sql-usage):

    SQL Server on Azure VM: For your SQL machines that are hosted on an Azure VM, you can enable autoprovisioning of the Log Analytics agent. You can also choose to follow the manual procedure for onboarding your Azure Stack Hub VMs. This can be done by going to the Defender for Cloud dashboard and choosing Auto Provisioning under Settings.

    SQL Server on Azure Arc–enabled servers: If you have a SQL server that is managed through Azure Arc, you can choose to deploy the Log Analytics agent using the Defender for Cloud recommendation "Log Analytics agent should be installed on your Windows-based Azure Arc-enabled machines."

    SQL Server on-prem: For your SQL server that is hosted on an on-premises Windows machine without Azure Arc, there are two options for connecting to Azure:

    > **Deploy Azure Arc:** You can connect any Windows machine to Defender for Cloud. However, there are benefits to using Azure Arc. For example, it provides deeper integration across your entire Azure environment. If you set up Azure Arc, you'll be able to see the SQL Server Azure Arc page in the Azure portal, and your security alerts will appear on a dedicated Security tab on that page. Microsoft recommends setting up Azure Arc on the host and following the instructions for SQL Server on Azure Arc detailed earlier.

Connect the Windows machine without Azure Arc: If you decide to connect a SQL server running on a Windows machine without using Azure Arc, then you will need to connect it to the Log Analytics workspace.

3. Enable the optional plan on Defender for Cloud's Environment Settings page (https://docs.microsoft.com/en-us/azure/defender-for-cloud/ defender-for-sql-usage).

4. Using the Defender for Cloud menu, open the Environment Settings page.

   ▪ If you're using the default workspace for Microsoft Defender for Cloud (named defaultworkspace-[*your subscription ID*]-[*region*]), then select the relevant subscription.

   ▪ If you're not using the default workspace, select the relevant workspace (enter the workspace's name in the filter if necessary).

5. Select the option SQL Servers On Machines. The plan will be enabled on all SQL servers connected to the selected workspace. The protection will be fully active after the first restart of the SQL Server instance.

   Optionally, you can create email notifications for security alerts. You can create a list of recipients that will receive email notifications when Defender for Cloud alerts are generated. The email will contain a direct link to the alert in Defender for Cloud with all the relevant details.

Finding and Investigating Security Alerts

You can find the alerts from Defender for SQL in the Microsoft Defender for Cloud Alerts page, on the host machine's security page, on the Workload Protections dashboard, or through the direct link provided in an alert notification.

To access the security alerts, from the Defender for Cloud menu, select Security Alerts, and then select the alert you want to investigate. Alerts are designed to list all the information you need to remediate them in their details. They contain detailed remediation steps and information to assist investigations in each alert.

Vulnerability Assessment for Azure SQL Database

Now that we've discussed the first feature, the vulnerability assessment for SQL servers on machines, let's cover the second feature: Azure's SQL vulnerability assessment service for SQL databases. This feature helps you in discovering, tracking, and remediating potential vulnerabilities affecting your databases. This service monitors your SQL servers for cyberthreats, such as SQL injection, brute-force attacks, and abuses of privilege. Once it detects suspicious activities, it provides action-oriented security alerts in the Microsoft Defender for Cloud, with the details surrounding the suspicious activity, recommendations on how to mitigate the threats, and recommended options for continuing the investigations with Microsoft Sentinel. You can also customize the assessment report by setting up an acceptable baseline for:

▪ Permission configurations

▪ Feature configurations

▪ Database settings

This vulnerability assessment service is built into Azure SQL databases and comes with a knowledge base of rules that flag security vulnerabilities. Some things that it looks for are deviations from security best practices, misconfigurations, excessive permissions, and unprotected sensitive information, among others. These rules are based on Microsoft's best practices for secure databases and focus on security issues that would pose the greatest risk to your database and the information held in it.

Configuring Vulnerability Assessment for Azure SQL Databases

To configure your vulnerability assessment for your SQL databases, follow these steps:

1. Go to the Azure portal, and open the appropriate resources in Azure SQL Database, SQL Managed Instances, or Azure Synapse Analytics.

2. Under the Security heading, select Microsoft Defender For Cloud.

3. Click Configure to open the Microsoft Defender For SQL pane.

4. On the Server Settings page, configure these SQL settings:

    a. You need to configure a storage account to store scan results for all the databases on your server or managed instances.

    b. Here you can configure vulnerability assessments to be run automatically on a weekly basis for detecting security misconfigurations. To do this, set Periodic Recurring Scans to On. You can also define where those results will be sent by setting email addresses in Send Scan Reports To. Additionally, you can configure email notifications to be sent to admins and subscription owners by enabling "Also send email notifications to admins and subscription owners."

5. You can also run SQL vulnerability assessments on demand by following these steps:

    a. Go to the selected resource's Defender for Cloud page and select View Additional Findings In Vulnerability Assessment (see Figure 4.1), and you will be able to view the scan results from past scans.

    b. To run an on-demand scan, click Scan in the Vulnerability Assessment tool. See Figure 4.2.

Remediating Vulnerabilities on Microsoft Defender for SQL

Once a vulnerability scan has been completed, the report will be displayed in the Azure portal (see Figure 4.3). In this report, you will find the following information:

- An overview of your organization's security state
- The number of issues found
- An organized list of risks by severity
- A list of the findings for further investigations

FIGURE 4.1   Vulnerability Assessment findings

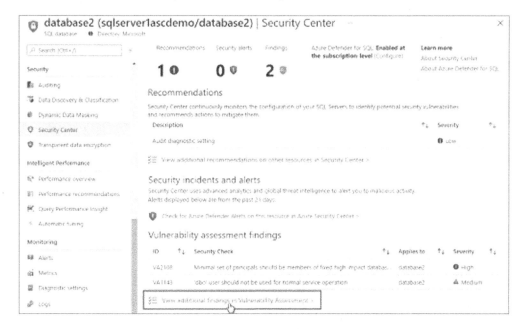

FIGURE 4.2   Clicking Scan in the Vulnerability Assessment tool

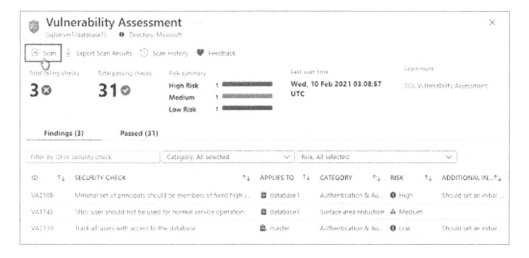

FIGURE 4.3   Vulnerability Scan report findings

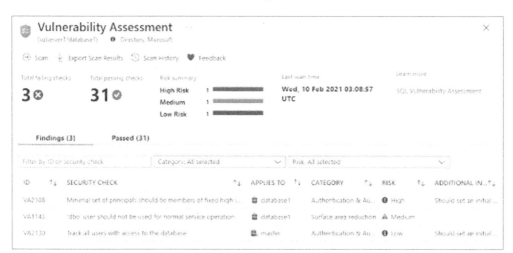

Remediating Discovered Vulnerabilities

First, you should review your results and identify which areas of the report findings are genuine security issues. It's important that you filter out the false positives as early on as possible so that you do not waste time investigating alerts that are not important. You may also want to organize the alerts that are legitimate issues, according to your business's priorities. While Azure does give risk ratings depending on your security team's priorities, they may not properly align with your organization's security objectives.

Select each failed result to see the severity of the failure and why the security check failed. Simply click the Security check to obtain a detailed explanation, as well as actionable remediation information for resolving the issue.

As you review the results of the vulnerability assessment, you can mark certain results as an acceptable baseline for your environment, which will allow Defender to recognize that the item is normal so that Defender no longer creates alerts when the item is found. It's a great way to reduce the number of false positives that occur on future reports. To confirm that it works, click the Scan button to run an on-demand scan, and you will notice that any findings that you've added to the baseline are now in the Passed column.

Now that you have removed the false positives, you can review all the security checks for legitimate security issues and follow the security recommendations to resolve any remaining issues. Doing so will ensure that your organization maintains a high level of security for your SQL servers and databases.

Exporting an Assessment Report

If you would prefer to have your report in a different format, Microsoft Defender for Cloud allows you to export your scan results in a downloadable Excel report. This report's Summary tab displays an overall summary of the assessment, which includes all the failed checks.

The report also includes a Results tab that contains the full set of scan results. This results scan is useful for reporting purposes, as you may need to send the reports to a manager or your team, or keep a record of all the scans performed for auditing purposes. If you want a report of all the scans you've run, you'll find it by selecting Scan History in the Vulnerability Assessment pane, where you can select any individual scan to view the detailed results.

Using the Microsoft Threat Modeling Tool

Threat modeling is the process of identifying risks and threats that are likely to affect an organization. This tool helps you appropriately plan your countermeasures and security controls to mitigate threats. When you are threat modeling, you need to take into account multiple elements in order to get a good overview of your company's threat landscape, which consists of all threats pertaining to your organization.

Elements of Threat Modeling

Let's delve deeper into threat modeling by breaking down threat elements.

Threat Actors

The first thing you need to identify is the threat actors who will be targeting your organization. A *threat actor* is a state, group, or individual who has malicious intent. In the cybersecurity field, this usually means they are seeking to target private corporations or governments with cyberattacks for financial, military, or political gain. Threat actors are most commonly categorized by their motivations, and to some extent, their level of sophistication. Here are some of the most common types of threat actors:

Nation-State   Nation-state threat actors are groups that have government backing. Nation-state actors are typically the most advanced, with large amounts of resources provided by their governments; they have relationships with private sector companies and may leverage organized crime groups to accomplish their goals. They are likely to target companies that provide services to the government or that provide critical services like financial institutions or critical infrastructure businesses do. Their goal can be to obtain information on behalf of the government/crime syndicate backing them, to disable infrastructure of the target, and in some cases, to seek financial gain.

Organized Crime Groups/Cybercriminals   These are organized crime groups and hackers who are working together or individually to commit cybercrimes for financial gain. One of the most common attack examples that this group performs are ransomware attacks, where they hope to get a big payout from the company. Generally, they will target any company with data that can be stolen or resold, as well as companies that have enough money to pay a high ransom.

Hacktivist   A hacktivist is someone who breaks into a computer system with a political or socially motivated purpose. They disrupt services to bring attention to their cause, and typically don't target individual civilians or businesses for financial gain. Their main goal is to cause some type of social change, and they will target companies whose actions go against what they believe is correct conduct.

Thrill Seekers   This type of threat actor simply hacks for the thrill of the hack. While they don't intend to do any damage, they will hack into any business that piques their interest with the goal of testing themselves or gaining notoriety.

Script Kiddies   These individuals are the lowest level of hackers—they don't have much technical expertise and rely primarily on using prewritten hacking tools to perform attacks. Because they cannot target companies with customized exploits, they typically only target companies with vulnerabilities that can be easily detected by outside scans. Due to their inability to customize or create hacking tools of their own, script kiddies can be defended against by simply being up to date with patching and standard information security best practices.

Insider Threats   These are individuals who work for a legitimate company and are usually disgruntled employees seeking revenge or a profit. They can also be associated with any of the groups mentioned earlier and work as an insider by providing them with company information and getting them access to the company's network from within.

Threat Vectors

A *threat vector* is the path or means by which a threat actor gains access to a computer by exploiting a certain vulnerability. The total number of attack vectors that an attacker can use to compromise a network or computer system or to extract data is called the *attack surface* of your company. Your goal when threat modeling is to identify as many of your threat vectors as possible and to implement security controls to prevent attackers from being able to exploit these threat vectors. Here are some common examples of threat vectors:

Compromised Credentials   These are stolen or lost usernames, passwords, access keys, and so on. Once these credentials are obtained by attackers, they can be used to gain access to company accounts, and therefore, the company network.

Weak Credentials   Typically, these credentials are easily guessable or weak passwords that can be obtained using brute force or that can be cracked with software.

Malicious Insiders   These are disgruntled or malicious employees who may expose information about a company's specific vulnerabilities.

Missing or Poor Encryption   A lack of encryption can allow attackers to eavesdrop on electronic communications and gain unauthorized access to sensitive information.

Misconfiguration   Having incorrect configurations gives users access that they should not have, or it creates security vulnerabilities that shouldn't exist. For example, if you have insecure services running on your Internet-facing machines, someone may be able to exploit that vulnerability by scanning the machine.

Phishing Emails   Most malware is spread via email attachments in phishing emails. Such emails continue to be one of the most popular threat vectors used by hackers to get malware onto corporate machines.

Unpatched Systems   Unpatched systems are one of the biggest entry points for attackers to gain entry into an organization. Most cyberattacks do not exploit zero-day vulnerabilities, which means most vulnerabilities are old and known. Most often, hackers exploit machines with vulnerabilities that haven't had patches applied yet.

Poor Input Validation   Having poor input validations allows attackers to perform many injection-based attacks, such as cross-site scripting (XSS), SQL injection attacks, and so on. This type of vulnerability is commonly exploited on web applications and websites.

Third- and Fourth-Party Vendors   Third- and fourth-party vendors play a big part in your company's security posture. Vendors typically have trusted relationships with your company where you open up aspects of your network, share information and client data, and use products in your business. Attackers can take then advantage of this trust relationship to gain access to your company's internal environment. SolarWinds's attack in December 2020 is an example. Hackers were able to hack into SolarWinds and place malware into the software update they were pushing out to their clients. Because the clients already trusted SolarWinds, they downloaded the software update without performing any checks. It resulted in hundreds of clients becoming infected with malware.

Cyberthreat Surface

Your *cyberthreat surface* consists of all the endpoints that can be exploited that give an attacker access to your company's network. Any devices that are connected to the Internet, such as phones, laptops, workstations, and even printers, are potential entry points to your network and are part of your threat surface. It's important to have your threat surface mapped out so that you understand what needs to be protected to prevent your business from being hacked.

Countermeasures

Now that you have identified your threat surface, the most relevant threat actors for your business, and the threat vectors they will likely use, you can start planning your appropriate *countermeasures*. Countermeasures are a wide range of redundant security controls you can use to ensure that you have *defense-in-depth* coverage. Defense in depth simply means that every important network resource is protected by multiple controls so that no single control failure leaves the resource exposed. The key here is not only to have multiple layers of controls but to also ensure that you use all the appropriate categories and types of security controls to defend your company.

Control Categories

You must ensure that you have coverage for all of the following control categories so that your company is properly protected:

Physical Controls   These include all tangible/physical devices used to prevent or detect unauthorized access to company assets. They include fences, surveillance cameras, guard dogs, and physical locks and doors.

Technical Controls   These include hardware and software mechanisms used to protect assets from nontangible threats. They include the use of encryption, firewalls, antivirus software, and intrusion detection systems (IDSs).

Administrative Controls   These refer to the policies, procedures, and guidelines that outline company practices in accordance with the company's security objectives. Some common examples of administration controls are employee hiring and termination procedures, equipment and Internet usage, physical access to facilities, and separation of duties.

Control Types

In addition to having coverage for all the control categories to protect your company, you must ensure that you have coverage for all the following control types:

Preventive Controls   A preventive security control is what you use to prevent a malicious action from happening. It typically is the first type of control you want, and when working correctly, it provides the most effective overall protection. Preventive controls are part of all the control categories. Here are some examples along with their control category:

>   **Computer Firewalls (Technical)**   A firewall is a hardware or software device that filters computer traffic and prevents unauthorized access to your computer systems.

>   **Antivirus (Technical)**   Antivirus software is a software program that prevents, detects, and removes malware from computer systems.

>   **Security Guards (Physical)**   Security guards are typically assigned to specific areas and are responsible for ensuring that people do not go into restricted areas unless they can prove they have a right to be there.

>   **Locks (Physical)**   This refers to any physical lock on a door that prevents people from entering without having the proper key.

>   **Hiring and Termination Policies (Administrative)**   During the hiring process, items like background checks help to prevent people with a history of bad behavior (e.g., sexual violence) from being hired by the company. Termination policies allow managers to get rid of people who are causing problems for the company.

Separation of Duties (Administrative)   Separation of duties means a company requires more than one person to complete any given task. This policy prevents people from committing fraud, because every process requires multiple people, and any individuals trying to commit fraud would be noticeable by those responsible for carrying out the processes.

Detective Controls   Detective controls are meant to find any malicious activities in your environment that snuck past the preventive measures. Realistically, you're not going to stop all the attacks against your company before they happen, so you must have a way to find out when something has failed so you can correct it. Here are some examples:

Intrusion Detection Systems (Technical)   Intrusion detection systems monitor a company's network for any signs of malicious activities and send alerts whenever an abnormal activity is found.

Logs and Audit Trails (Technical)   Logs and audit trails are records of activity on a network or computer system. By reviewing these logs, you can discover if malicious activity occurred on the network or computer system.

Video Surveillance (Physical)   Video surveillance includes setting up cameras to video important areas of a company, and then having people monitor those video feeds to see if anyone who isn't supposed to be there is able to gain access.

Enforced Staff Vacations (Administrative)   Enforced vacations help to detect fraud by forcing individuals to leave their work and have someone else pick up that process in their absence. If someone has been doing fraudulent activity, it will become apparent to the new person performing their work.

Review Access Rights Policies (Administrative)   By reviewing an individual's access rights, you can see who has access to resources they shouldn't, and you can review who has been accessing those resources.

Deterrent Controls   These controls attempt to discourage people from doing activities that are harmful to your company. By incorporating deterrent controls, you will have fewer threats to deal with, because it becomes harder to perform the fraudulent action or makes the consequences for getting caught well-known. Here are some examples and their control types:

Guard Dogs (Physical)   Having guard dogs can intimidate potential trespassers and help deter crime.

Warning Signs (Physical)   By advertising that your property is under video surveillance and has security alarms, people are deterred from trying to break in.

Pop-up Messages (Technical)   By displaying messages on users' computers or corporate homepages, your company can warn people of certain bad behaviors (e.g., no watching porn on a company laptop).

Firewalls (Technical)   You may have experienced a firewall when you try to browse certain sites on a corporate laptop and you get blocked. A warning message then pops up stating certain sites are not permitted on the laptop. These messages help to deter people from trying to browse certain sites on company laptops.

Advertise Monitoring (Administrative)   Many companies make it known that admin account activities are logged and reviewed, which helps deter people from using those accounts to do bad things.

Employee onboarding (administrative): During onboarding, you can highlight the penalties for misconduct in the workplace, which helps deter employees from engaging in bad behaviors.

Recovery Controls   These controls try to get your systems back to a normal state following a security incident. Some examples of recovery controls and their types are as follows:

Reissue Access Cards (Physical)   In the event of a lost or stolen access card, the card needs to be deactivated and a new access card issued.

Repair Physical Damage (Physical)   In the event of a damaged door, fence, or lock, you need to have a process in place for getting it repaired quickly.

Make System and Data Backups (Technical)   Your company should be performing regular backups of important information and have a process in place for quickly restoring a last-known good backup in the event of a security incident.

Implement Patching (Technical)   In the event of possible vulnerability that places your company at risk, you should have a process in place for quickly getting a patch pushed out in order to return your company to a "secure state."

Develop a Disaster Recovery Plan (Administrative)   This plan outlines how to get your company back to a normal state of operations following a natural or human-made disaster.

Develop an Incident Response Plan (Administrative)   An incident response plan outlines the steps you can take to return to normal business operations following a cybersecurity breach.

Configuring Azure's Threat Modeling Solution

Now that we have discussed threat modeling in general, let's focus on the Microsoft Threat Modeling tool. This tool is an important element of the Microsoft Security Development Lifecycle (SDL). It's designed to help software architects identify and mitigate potential security issues during software development as well as after its release. Developed with non-security experts in mind, it can be used by all developers and it's easily understood by any audience. The tool comes with many features and capabilities; here are some of the most important ones:

Automation of creating a model: It gives you guidance and feedback while creating the threat model.

Reporting: Reporting is the action of providing detailed reports for your security activities.

Designed for developers and center on software: Threat modeling can focus on different points of view, such as from the asset's or attackers' point of view. The Microsoft Threat Modeling Tool focuses on threat modeling that is centered on software and creates information that is easily digestible for software developers.

STRIDE Analysis per threat: This tool integrates a threat modeling framework called *STRIDE* that performs analysis for each potential threat. Created by Microsoft, STRIDE aims to help applications meet the security directives of the CIA triad (confidentiality, integrity, and availability) as well as authentication, authorization, and nonrepudiation. STRIDE stands for Spoofing, Tampering, Repudiation, Information Disclosure, Denial of service (DoS), and Elevation of privilege, which are broken down as follows:

Spoofing: Spoofing is impersonating another person or computer (e.g., IP address) without their knowledge. It violates the principle of proper authentication.

Tampering: Tampering involves making unauthorized modifications to memory, disk, network, etc., and violates the principle of integrity.

Repudiation: Repudiation is the act of claiming that you didn't do something when you actually did. If repudiation is possible, people cannot be held accountable for their actions. It's important that nonrepudiation be upheld so that an action can be linked back to the person who did it.

Information disclosure: Information should only be disclosed to an authorized user; improper information disclosure occurs whenever information is made available to a user who isn't authorized to see it.

Denial of service: This is an attack that exhausts the resources necessary for a business to continue to offer services. For example, a DoS attack includes sending a huge amount of data packets to google.com web servers to prevent users from being able to access that website. Such an attack compromises a company's availability to meet the needs of its customers or employees.

Elevation of privilege: This occurs when a user is able to escalate their level of access beyond what they need for normal use. For example, say an error in a website allows a normal user to become an administrator; it would allow someone to perform actions on the website that they are not authorized to do.

Configuring the Threat Modeling Tool

The first step in using the Microsoft Threat Modeling Tool is to download it. Go to the Download Center (`https://docs.microsoft.com/en-us/azure/security/develop/threat-modeling-tool`).

Once you've downloaded the tool, open the tool. You'll be presented with the preview shown in Figure 4.4.

FIGURE 4.4   Threat modeling tool preview

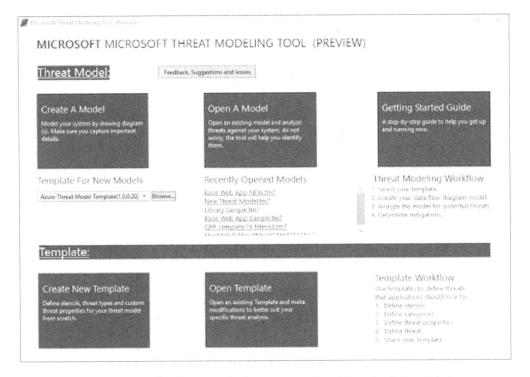

Table 4.1 contains is a breakdown of what you can do with each of these sections (`https://docs.microsoft.com/en-us/azure/security/develop/threat-modeling-tool-getting-started`).

TABLE 4.1   Threat modeling tools

Component	Details
Feedback, Suggestions, and Issues	Clicking this button will take you to the MSDN Forum for all things related to the Software Development Lifecycle (SDL). It gives you an opportunity to read through what other users are doing and the issues they are facing, along with workarounds and recommendations. You can also email tmtextsupport@microsoft.com to get in touch with the Microsoft Support team.
Create a Model	This opens up a blank canvas for you to draw your threat modeling diagram. Be sure to select the correct template you'd like to use for your model.

Component	Details
Template for New Models	You need to select a template to use before creating a model. Microsoft's main template is the Azure Threat Model Template. This contains Azure-specific stencils, threats, and mitigations. If this doesn't meet your needs, Microsoft provides generic models that you can access by selecting the SDL TM Knowledge Base from the drop-down menu. If you want to create your own custom template or submit a new one for all users, then you should check out Microsoft's Template Repository GitHub page (`https://github.com/microsoft/repo-templates`) to learn more about that option.
Open a Model	This will open previously saved threat models. The Recently Opened Models feature is a good option if you need to open your most recent files. When you hover over this selection, you'll see two ways to open models: **Open from this Computer:** This is the classic way of opening a file from your local storage. **Open from OneDrive:** This allows teams to use folders in OneDrive to save and share all their threat models from a single location.
Getting Started Guide	This will open the Microsoft Threat Modeling Tool's main page.

Azure Monitor

The Azure Monitor tool provides you with a means of collecting, analyzing, and acting on the information from your cloud and on-premises environments. It provides a lot of information on how your applications are performing, and it can proactively identify potential issues with the applications themselves and the resources on which they depend. All the data collected by Azure Monitor fits into one of two types:

Metrics   Metrics are numerical values that describe an aspect of a system at a certain point in time. Metrics are capable of supporting near-real-time scenarios. For example, a CPU metric would be something such as percentage of CPU usage.

Logs   Logs contain different data types that have been organized into records, with different sets of properties for each type. Information like events and traces are stored as logs, in addition to performance data. These can be combined for more effective analysis. Log data that has been collected by Azure Monitor can be analyzed with queries to quickly retrieve, consolidate, or analyze the data.

Here are some examples of the categories of data that Azure Monitor collects:

Application monitoring data: Data about an application's performance and functionality

Guest operating system (OS) monitoring data: Data that notes whether your OS is running on Azure, another cloud platform, or on-premises

Azure resource monitoring data: Data about the operation of a specific Azure resource

Azure subscription monitoring data: Data about the operation and management of an Azure subscription and the health and operation of the Azure subscription itself

Azure tenant-monitoring data: Data about the operation of tenant-level Azure services (e.g., Azure Active Directory)

Another important aspect of Azure Monitor is the alert function. The alert function helps proactively notify users of critical conditions in the environment, and in some cases, automates corrective action. Alert rules can be based on metrics or log data. Alert rules based on metrics can provide near-real-time alerts but are based on simpler information. Rules based on logs will be further from real time, but they can be configured to allow for complex logic across data from multiple sources.

Visualizations in Azure Monitor

The Azure dashboard allows you to combine multiple types of data into a single display that you can see via the Azure portal (see Figure 4.5). It's completely customizable, allowing you to add the output of any log query or metrics chart directly to the dashboard.

FIGURE 4.5 Data visualization

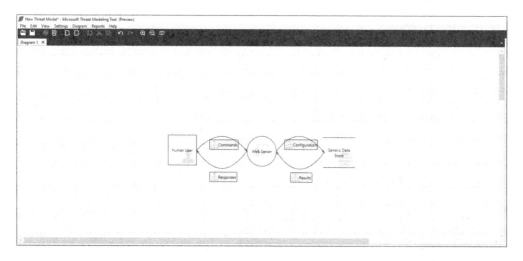

Configuring and Managing Security Monitoring Solutions

An important aspect of cloud security is being able to monitor your environment for any malicious activities. In this section, we discuss how to configure and manage security monitoring solutions for your Azure environment.

Creating and Customizing Alert Rules by Using Azure Monitor

Within Azure Monitor, there are three types of alerts that you must be able to create and customize, including metric alerts, log alerts, and activity log alerts. Let's begin by looking at metric alerts.

Creating Metric Alerts

A *metric alert* in Azure Monitor is a process setup where you're notified when one of your environment's metrics crosses a threshold that you set. For example, if you want to make sure that only 50 endpoints can connect to a specific server, you set it as the threshold. Once the 51st endpoint connects to that server, it triggers a metric alert and sends out an alert that you have exceeded the 50-endpoint threshold.

You define a metric alert rule by first specifying the target resource that you want to be monitored, then selecting a metric name, a condition type (i.e., static or dynamic), and the conditions (i.e., an operator, a metric threshold, and an action group to be triggered when the alert rule activates). Your condition types will affect the way thresholds are determined.

Follow these steps:

1. In the Azure portal, in the Favorites section, click Monitor.

2. Click Alerts, then click Create and select Alert Rule.

3. On the Scope tab, click Select Scope. In the next pane, select the target resources for which you want to create an alert. You can use the drop-down options of Filter By Subscription, Filter By Resource Type, or Filter By Location, or use the search bar to find the resource(s) you want to monitor.

4. Not all resources have metrics that you can create alerts on. If the resource you have selected has metrics that you can create alert rules on, the available signal types listed on the bottom right will include metrics from which you can choose.

5. Once you have selected the resource you want, click Done.

6. Next, select the Condition tab. In the Select A Signal pane you will see a list of signals supported for the selected resource. Choose the metric on which you want to create an alert.

7. Next, you will see a chart showing the metric's behavior for the last six hours; you can use the Chart Period drop-down to view more of that metric's history. If you already know what threshold you want, this information may be irrelevant to you, but it can be useful if you don't know what threshold you want. You can use this information to establish a baseline for what is normal, and then determine what a good threshold would be based on that.

8. If the metric you choose has dimensions, you will see a Dimensions table. You can then select one or more values per dimension. For example, if you create a metric rule and you want to monitor two specific instances, you can add a dimension for this rule that includes two instances.

   Let's look at an example where you have an App Service plan for your company's website. In this situation, you want to monitor CPU usage on multiple instances running your website or app. Here's how you can do that using a metric alert rule:

   - Target Resource: myAppServicePlan
   - Metric: Percentage CPU
   - Condition Type: Static
   - Dimensions: Instance = InstanceName1, InstanceName2
   - Aggregation Type: Average
   - Period: Over the last 3 mins
   - Frequency: 2 mins
   - Operator: GreaterThan
   - Threshold: 30

   If you want to create a rule that monitors all instances as they are created without specifying any particular instances, you can use a rule like this:

   - Target Resource: myAppServicePlan
   - Metric: Percentage CPU
   - Condition Type: Static
   - Dimensions: Instance = *
   - Aggregation Type: Average
   - Period: Over the last 3 mins
   - Frequency: 2 mins
   - Operator: GreaterThan
   - Threshold: 30

9. Next, you need to select three things: your threshold type, operator, and aggregation type. These will determine the logic that the metric alert rule will use to evaluate whether or not something complies:

Threshold type: You can choose between having a *static threshold* or a *dynamic threshold*. A static threshold is a number that you set, whether it's an absolute number or a percentage. A dynamic threshold leverages Microsoft's Machine Learning algorithm to learn the metric's historical behavior and comes up with an appropriate threshold based on the sensitivity that you choose. This number will not be fixed and will change over time. In terms of sensitivity, you can choose High, Medium, or Low. If you choose High sensitivity, then even a small deviation will trigger an alert, whereas if you choose Low sensitivity, then the alert rule will only trigger on large deviations.

Operator: This selection determines how the threshold will be used to trigger the alert. You have four options for when the alert will be triggered:

- Greater than the upper threshold (default)
- Greater than or equal to the upper threshold
- Less than or equal to the lower threshold
- Less than the lower threshold

Aggregation Type: This selection is how you will combine the information to use for your calculations. For example, if you create an alert rule for multiple instances and select Average, an alert will be triggered when the Average number value across all instances exceeds the threshold. You can also select Maximum or Minimum, but typically it's best to choose Average.

10. You can choose to set Aggregation Granularity and Frequency Of Evaluation. Aggregation Granularity is the time period used to aggregate the values together. Frequency Of Evaluation is how often you want the system to check for any violations that would trigger an alert.

11. Now, click Done.

    Optional: If you need the alert to monitor something else, you can add another criterion here.

12. Now that you have created the alert, you'll need to define what will happen when the alert rule is triggered. You will be taken to the Actions tab, which is where you'll define what happens when the alert is triggered. If you have an *action group* created, you can select it or create a new action group. (An action group is a collection of notification preferences defined by the owner of an Azure subscription, such as Azure Monitor.) Each action is a combination of three elements (`https://docs.microsoft.com/en-us/azure/azure-monitor/alerts/action-groups`):

    - Type: This element determines the notification or action that will be performed. Common examples include sending SMS messages, sending a recorded voice call, or sending an email.
    - Name: This element determines the unique identifier within the action group.
    - Details: This element provides additional information that varies by type.

13. Next, proceed to the Details tab. Under Project Details, you can select the subscription and resource group in which the alert rule resource will be saved. Then, under Alert Rule Details, you'll specify the Severity and Alert Rule Name. You can also provide an Alert Rule Description, select Enable Upon Creation to enable to alert rules, and select Automatically Resolve Alerts if needed.

14. Next, on the Tags tab, select the tags that you want on the alert rule you're creating.

15. Lastly, proceed to the Review + Create tab. This is your chance to review your selection before creating the alert rule. The system will perform a quick automatic validation to see if you are missing any information or anything that needs to be corrected. Once you are satisfied with your selections, click Create.

Creating Log Alerts

The second type of alert we are going to be looking at is a *log alert*. A log alert is a type of alert that allows users to create a Log Analytics query that will evaluate resource logs on a specified frequency and generate alerts based on the results. Just like a metric log, these rules can trigger multiple actions using action groups.

Prerequisites

Unlike metric logs, there are a few prerequisites that you need to meet to enable log alerts. Log alerts use queries on Log Analytics data. In order for them to work, you must start by collecting log data in a Log Analytics Workspace. Once you have log data to query, you can begin querying that data and configuring log alerts. You will also need a role that gives you the access you'll need. Azure Monitoring Contributor is a common rule used for creating, modifying, and updating log alerts.

Creating a Log Alert

Similar to a metric alert, the log alert is defined by three components:

Target: The specific Azure resource that you want to monitor

Criteria: The logic that needs to be evaluated for the alert to fire

Action: The response that the alert will trigger; it will typically be notifications or an automated response

Here's how to create the alert:

1. In the Azure portal, select the resource you want to monitor.

2. From the Resource menu, under Monitoring, select Alerts.

3. In the top command bar, click Create (see Figure 4.6), and then click Alert Rule.

4. The Create Alert Rule Wizard will open to the Select A Signal page of the Condition tab. The scope should already be defined based on the resource you've selected.

FIGURE 4.6   Creating alert rules

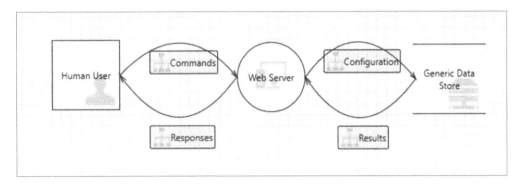

5. Click the Custom Log Search signal.

6. Write a query to identify the conditions for triggering alerts.

7. Once you have created your query, click Run to confirm that the query correctly identifies the data that you want on your alert.

8. Once you are satisfied that the query works how you like, click Continue Editing Alert.

9. The Condition tab will then open, populated with your log query.

10. Next, in the Measurement section, select values for the Measure, Aggregation Type, and Aggregation Granularity fields.

11. Choose the option Split By Dimensions if you want.

12. In the Alert Logic section, specify the following: Operator, Threshold Value, and Frequency.

13. Optionally, in the Advanced Options section, you may set the number of violations required to trigger the alert.

14. You will then be taken to the Preview chart, where you can view the query evaluation results over time. Here, you can adjust the time period to see how your query would be evaluated over different periods, which can help you tune your query.

15. From this step forward, you have everything you need to create the alert and can select Review + Create at any time. However, there are a few more things you may want to add to have an effective alert.

16. On the Actions tab, select or create the action groups you want to use for the alert.

17. Next, on the Details tab, define Project Details and Alert Rule Details.

18. Optionally, in the Advanced Options section, you can choose several features, including Enable Upon Creation and the option to mute actions for a period after an alert rule fires (Figure 4.7).

FIGURE 4.7 Choosing advanced options

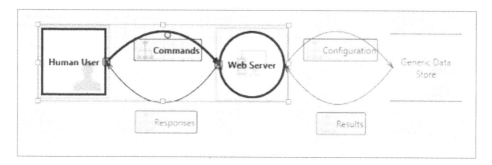

19. On the Tags tab, set any required tags on the Alert Rule resource.

20. Now that you've created all of the optional configurations, it's time to select the Review + Create tab. This will run a validation and inform you of any issues, as well as give you a chance to review your selections.

21. Once you pass the validation and review your settings, click Create to create the alert rule.

Activity Log Alerts

Activity log alerts are alerts that activate when a new activity log event occurs. This alert type varies from a regular log alert in that a regular log alert focuses on resource logs, whereas an activity log alert is looking for a certain set of events and flagging the activity logs that correspond to those events. For example, you may use a regular log alert for monitoring CPU usage and use an activity log to monitor user logins. Typically, you create activity log alerts to receive notifications for two categories of events:

Specific Operations You can configure log alerts for specific operations that occur on resources in Azure. These alerts are often scoped to particular resource groups or resources. For example, you may want to be notified any time a VM is deleted in a particular resource group.

Service Health Event These are events that affect the health of your resources. These events typically include the notification of incidents and maintenance events that apply to those resources.

Activity log alerts have a few main options:

Category This option includes Administrative, Service Health, Auto Scale, Security, Policy, and Recommendations.

Scope   This option centers on the individual resource or set of resources for which the alert is being defined. The scope for an activity log alert may be defined at different levels:

> **Resource Level**   This option is when it's set for an individual resource, such as a specific VM.
>
> **Resource Group Level**   This option is when you set the alert for a group of resources, such as all the VMs in a specific resource group.
>
> **Subscription Level**   This option is when you create the alert for all resources or a subset of resources within a subscription, such as all VMs in a subscription or all resources in a subscription.

Resource Group   By default, the alert rule will be saved in the same resource group as the target defined in Scope. You may also define a resource group where the alert rule will be stored.

Resource Type   The Resource Manager will define a namespace for the target of the alert.

Operation Name   This option is the Azure resource provider operation name used for Azure RBAC. If an operation is not registered with the Resource Manager, then it cannot be used in an activity log alert rule.

Level   This option is the severity level of the event and includes the following options: Informational, Warning, Error, or Critical.

Status   This option details the status of the event: typically, Started, Failed, or Succeeded.

Event Initiated By (the Caller)   This option is the email address or Azure Active Directory identifier of the user who performed the operation.

The last thing to know about activity log alerts is that for each associated severity level they will have one of the values discussed in Table 4.2.

TABLE 4.2   Activity log alert severity levels

Severity	Description
Critical	Describes serious events that require the immediate attention of an administrator. It can also indicate that an application or system has stopped working or stopped responding.
Error	Indicates a problem but isn't serious enough to require immediate attention.
Warning	Indicates a warning of potential problems, but they *do not* indicate an actual error. May indicate that your resource is not in the ideal state, and it may degrade later into showing errors or critical events.
Informational	More or less an FYI to pass noncritical information to your network administrator.

Creating Activity Log Alerts

Here's how you create activity log alerts:

1. In the Azure portal, select Monitor.

2. Select Alerts ➢ Create ➢ Alert Rule.

3. On the Scope tab, click Select Scope. Next, in the Context pane, select the target resource(s) on which you want to place the alert. As shown in Figure 4.8, you can use the Filter By Subscription, Filter By Resource Type, and Filter By Location options to find the resource you want to monitor. You can also use the search bar.

   If the resource that you selected has activity log operations that you can create alert rules on, it will appear in the Resources section.

FIGURE 4.8   Selecting a resource

4. Once you have selected the target resource, click Done.

5. Next, go to the Condition tab. Within the loaded Context pane, you will see a list of signals supported for each resource. Select the activity log signal or operation for which you need to create an alert rule. To only find activity log–related signals, sort by signal type.

6. You will find a chart for the activity log operation for the past six hours. You can use the Chart Period drop-down menu to choose the period of time you want to see.

7. Under Alert Logic, you have the option to define more criteria for filtering. Examples include:

   Event Level: This option refers to the severity level that we covered earlier: Informational, Warning, Error, or Critical.

   Status: The status of the event can be Started, Failed, or Succeeded.

   Event Initiated By: This option is the email address or Azure Active Directory identifier of the user who performed the operation that triggered the alert.

8. On the Actions tab, define which actions and notifications are triggered when the alert rule fires by either selecting an existing action group or creating a new action group.

9. Select the Details tab. Under Project Details, select the resource group in which the alert rule resource will be saved. Under Alert Rule Details, specify the alert rule name and provide a rule description.

10. Proceed to the Tags tab and set any tags that you want your alert rule to have.

11. Proceed to the Review + Create tab and review your selections before creating the alert rule. An automatic validation will be performed and will notify you of any missing information or fields that need correction. Once you're finished, click Create.

Configuring Diagnostic Logging and Retention Using Azure Monitor

Before you enable diagnostic logging, we first need to discuss the concept of platform logs. *Platform logs* are logs that provide detailed diagnostic and auditing information for Azure resources and the platform on which they depend. They are automatically generated, but you will need to configure them to be forwarded to one or more destinations to be retained. Table 4.3 lists the different types of platform logs.

TABLE 4.3 Various platform log types and descriptions

Log	Layer	Description
Resource Logs	Azure Resources	Previously referred to as diagnostic logs, these provide you with insights into the operations that were performed in a specific Azure resource. For example, you can use this to monitor Azure Key Vault to see when someone accesses a secret or when a request is made to a database. The content you will find in the resource log varies, depending on the Azure service and resource type.
Activity Log	Azure Subscription	This log type provides you with insights into the operations of every Azure resource in a subscription, as well as updates on the service's health events.
		You can use activity logs to identify what, who, and when for any write operations on the resources in your subscription.
Azure Active Directory Logs	Azure Tenant	This log type contains a history of all sign-in activity and changes made in the Azure AD for that Azure tenant.

As previously mentioned, to enable diagnostic logging, you will be sending these logs to different destinations based on your monitoring requirements. You do this by creating a diagnostic setting. But first, take note of the different destinations to which we can send these logs (see Table 4.4).

TABLE 4.4   Various log destinations and descriptions

Destination	Description
Log Analytics Workspace	Log Analytics Workspace allows you to analyze the logs that are aggregated from all your Azure resources. It also allows you to take advantage of all the features in Azure Monitor Logs, such as log queries and log alerts. Then, you can pin the results of those queries to an Azure dashboard or include them as part of a workbook in an interactive report.
Event Hub	Using an event hub is a good option if you want to send platform log data outside of Azure. One case where you'd want to do that is when you send the log data to a third-party SIEM or custom telemetry platform.
Azure Storage	This is an archive where you can store logs for audit or backup.

Creating Platform Metrics and Logs in the Azure Portal

There are two elements to gathering diagnostic information in the Azure environment: platform metrics and platform logs. Platform metrics are automatically sent to Azure Monitor metrics by default without configuration and require no work on your end.

Platform logs that include an Azure activity log and resource logs provide diagnostic and auditing information for Azure resources and the Azure platform on which they depend. The activity log exists on its own but can be sent to other destinations, whereas resource logs are not collected unless they are being routed to a destination.

Though a single diagnostic setting supports selecting multiple destination types, you can only select one destination within each of those types. Each resource in Azure can have up to five diagnostic settings. To create a diagnostic setting, take the following steps:

1.   First, you must configure the diagnostic setting. Where in the Azure portal you configure this setting depends on the resource:

   - For an individual resource, go to the resource's menu and click Diagnostic Settings under Monitor.

   - For multiple resources, select Diagnostic Settings under Settings in the Azure Monitor menu, and then click the resources you want.

   - For the activity log, choose Activity Log from the Azure Monitor menu, then Diagnostic Settings. Be sure to disable any legacy configurations.

2.   If no diagnostic settings exist on the resource you selected, you will receive a prompt to create a setting. Click Add Diagnostic Setting. If there are existing settings, you can select Edit Setting to edit an existing one.

3. Give the setting a name if it doesn't have one already.

4. Select the logs and metrics you want to route. For your logs, either choose a category group or check the individual boxes for each category of data you want to send to the destinations that you will specify later. The list of categories you have to choose from varies for each Azure service. Select allMetrics if you want to store metrics in Azure Monitor Logs as well.

5. Select Destination Details. Here, you will check the box for each destination to which the logs should be sent. When you check each box, options will appear that allow you to add the following additional information (see Figure 4.9):

   a. **Log Analytics:** Here, enter the log's subscription and workspace. If you don't have a workspace, you will need to create one before you can continue.

   b. **Event Hubs:** Here, you need to specify the following:

      i. First, specify the subscription of which the event hub is part.

      ii. Second, you will need an event hub namespace. If you don't have one yet, you need to create one:

         (1) Optional: You can create an event hub name to send all of your data to. If you choose not to create a name, an event hub will be created for each log category.

         (2) Optional: You can create an event hub policy that defines the permissions that the streaming mechanism has.

   c. **Storage:** Here, you choose the subscription, storage account, and retention policy for your log.

   d. **Partner Integration:** You must install a partner integration in your subscription; the options will vary depending on the partner.

6. Click Save.

Monitoring Security Logs Using Azure Monitor

Azure Monitor has two features for monitoring security logs:

- Azure Monitor Logs
- Azure Monitor Metrics

First, let's look at Azure Monitor Logs—a feature that collects, aggregates, and organizes log and performance data from monitored Azure resources. It allows you to consolidate data from multiple resources into a single workspace. These sources can include:

- Platform logs from Azure services
- Log and performance data from VM agents
- Usage and performance data from applications

FIGURE 4.9 Destination Details

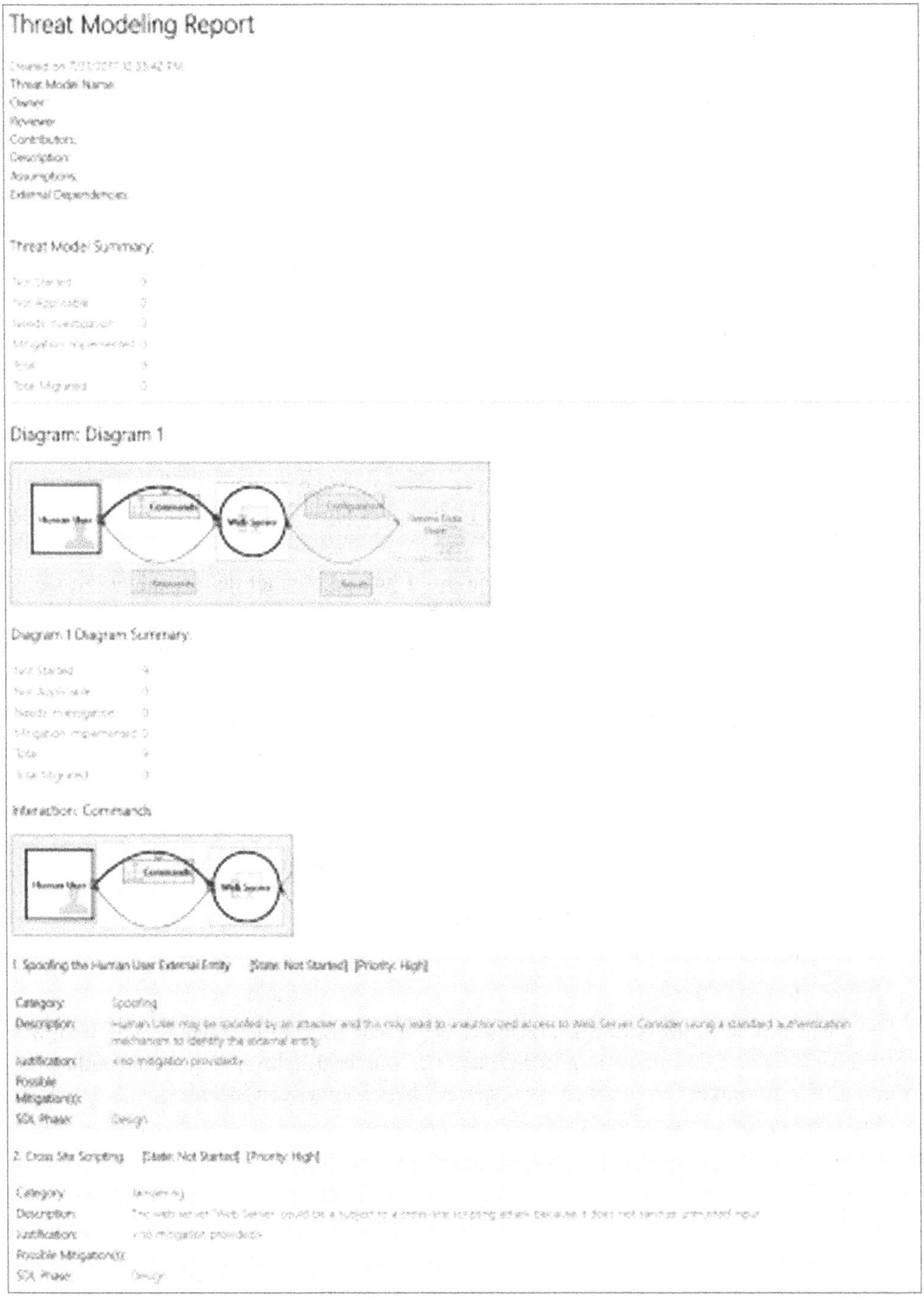

In addition to consolidation, Azure Monitor Logs allow you to perform quick analysis. The feature supports a query language that is capable of analyzing millions of records at a time. The results of these queries can then be used in alert rules or visualized in a workbook or dashboard.

Features of Azure Monitor Logs (`https://docs.microsoft.com/en-us/azure/azure-monitor/logs/data-platform-logs`) can be found in Table 4.5.

TABLE 4.5   Features of Azure Monitor Logs

Feature	Description
Analyze	You can use Log Analytics via the Azure portal to write log queries that allow you to interactively analyze log data using Microsoft's Analysis Engine.
Alert	You can configure a log alert rule that will send a notification or take automated action when the results of a query match a specified result.
Visualize	You can pin query results in the form of tables or charts to an Azure dashboard.
	You can also create a workbook to combine multiple sets of data into a single report.
	You can export the results of a query to Power BI (a data visualization tool) to create different visualizations and share the results with users outside Azure.
Get Insights	Azure Monitor Logs supports Insights that provide you with a customized monitoring experience for several applications and services.
Retrieve	You can access log query results multiple sources:
	Command line via the Azure CLI or Azure PowerShell cmdlets
	Custom app via the REST API or client library for .NET, Java, JavaScript, or Python
Export	You have the option to configure automated exporting of log data to an Azure storage account or Azure event hub.
	You can create a custom workflow to retrieve log data and copy it to an external location via Azure Logic Apps.

Configuring Azure Monitor Logs

The first step to using Azure Monitor Logs for diagnostic work is to configure a data collection. To do this, you must ensure that you have created a Log Analytics workspace, which is where you will be sending the data. A workspace defines the following:

- The geographic location of the information
- Access rights that decide which users can access data
- Configuration settings, including the pricing tier and data retention rules

Here are the steps to create a Log Analytics workspace:

1. Go to the Azure portal and click All Services. In the list of resources, type **Log Analytics** and select Log Analytics Workspaces from the search results.

2. Next, select Create and then fill in the following information as appropriate:

   ▪ Select a subscription from the drop-down menu.

   ▪ For resource groups, you can choose to use an existing resource group or create a new one.

   ▪ Create a name for the new Log Analytics workspace. This name must be unique per each resource group.

   ▪ Select an available region. (Note that not all regions have Log Analytics available.)

3. Select Review + Create to review the settings, and then select Create The Workspace. This will select the default pricing tier of pay-as-you-go, meaning that you will not incur any charges until you start collecting a sufficient amount of data.

Now that you have your Log Analytics workspace set up, you need to configure the resources you want to send data to that workspace. How you do this will vary, depending on the type of data source:

▪ For Azure resources, you have to create diagnostic settings to send resource logs to the workspace.

▪ For VMs, you need to enable VM Insights to collect data from VMs.

▪ To collect events and performance data, you must configure data sources on the workspace itself.

Using Log Queries to Retrieve Data

You retrieve data from a Log Analytics workspace through a *log query,* which is a read-only request to process data and return results. All log queries are written in Kusto Query Language (KQL). You can write log queries in Log Analytics to analyze the data that have been collected, to use them in alert rules, or to include their results in workbooks or dashboards for reporting purposes. You have the option to create custom queries, but Insights include prebuilt queries that you can use to analyze your data without having to write any code from scratch. If you would like to learn more about log queries, how to use them, and how to create them, Microsoft has a documentation page dedicated to them: `https://docs` `.microsoft.com/en-us/azure/azure-monitor/logs/log-query-overview`.

Azure Monitor Metrics

Azure Monitor Metrics is a feature of Azure Monitor that collects numeric data from monitored Azure resources into a time series database. Metrics in Azure Monitor can detect data in near real time, which is great for the alerting and detection of issues. Once data is collected, it can be analyzed using a tool called Metrics Explorer.

Table 4.6 illustrates what you can do with Azure Monitor Metrics (`https://docs` `.microsoft.com/en-us/azure/sentinel/quickstart-onboard`).

TABLE 4.6   Azure Monitor Metrics features and descriptions

Feature	Description
Analyze	Using Metrics Explorer allows you to analyze collected metrics on a chart and compare metrics across multiple resources.
Alert	This feature allows you to configure a metric alert rule that will send a notification or take an automated action when the metric value crosses a threshold.
Visualize	You can pin a chart from Metrics Explorer to the Azure dashboard for easy viewing. You can also create a workbook to combine multiple sets of data in an interactive report.
Automate	You can use the auto scale feature to increase or decrease resources based on a metric value threshold.
Retrieve	You can access metric values from a number of sources: Command line via the Azure CLI or Azure PowerShell cmdlets Custom app via the REST API or client library for .NET, Java, JavaScript, or Python
Export	You can route metrics to logs to analyze data in Azure Monitor Metrics alongside data in Azure Monitor Logs. Then you can store these metric values for up to 93 days. If you want to route metrics to an external system, then you need to stream the metrics to an event hub.
Archive	This feature allows you to archive the performance or health history of your resources for compliance, auditing, or offline reporting.

Data Collection

Azure Monitor collects metrics from the following four types of sources. Once these metrics are collected and added to the metric database, they can be evaluated together (see Figure 4.10):

Azure Resources   These are platform metrics that are created by Azure resources. They give you visibility into a resource's health and performance. Each resource type creates a unique set of metrics without any need for configuration. Platform metrics can be collected from all available Azure resources at a frequency of one-minute intervals, unless otherwise specified.

Applications   Applications Insights is an Azure tool that creates metrics for all your monitored applications to help you detect performance issues and track trends for how your applications are being used. For example, you can get information about server response time and browser exceptions by using Applications Insights.

Virtual Machine (VM) Agents   Metrics will be collected from the guest OS of a virtual machine in your environment. You may enable guest OS metrics for Windows VMs via the Windows diagnostic extension. To enable metrics for Linux VMs, use the InfluxData Telegraf agent.

Custom Metrics   You have the option to define custom metrics, in addition to the standard metrics that are available by default. You can create custom metrics in any monitored application with Application Insights or for any Azure service by using the custom metrics API.

FIGURE 4.10   Custom metrics

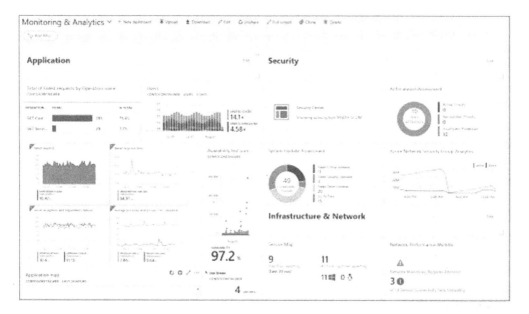

Using Metrics Explorer

Metrics Explorer allows you to interactively analyze the data collected in your metric database. In addition, it allows you to create data visualizations to chart the values of multiple metrics over time. You can see an example in Figure 4.11.

Creating a Metric Chart

To use Metric Explorer to create a metric chart, follow these steps:

1. From your resource, resource group, subscription, or Azure Monitor's View, open the Metrics tab.

2. Click Select A Scope to open the Resource Scope Picker, which allows you to select the resources for which you want to see metrics.

3. Depending on the resource chosen, you may need to pick a namespace, which is just a label that allows you to organize metrics so that you can easily find them.

4. Select a metric from the list of available metrics.

5. Optional: You can change the metric aggregation. For example, you can have a chart showing minimum, maximum, or average values of the selected metric.

FIGURE 4.11   Metric database data chart

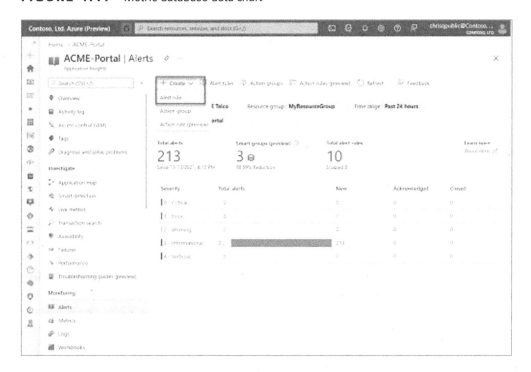

Selecting a Time Range

The charts you create by default will show the last 24 hours' worth of metrics data. You can use the Time Picker in the top right of the display to change the time range for your chart (see Figure 4.12).

Applying Dimension Filters and Splitting

Two important features to understand for your analysis are filtering and splitting. They allow you to show various metric segments that impact the overall value of the metric you are investigating and help in identifying potential outliers:

FIGURE 4.12   Changing the time range

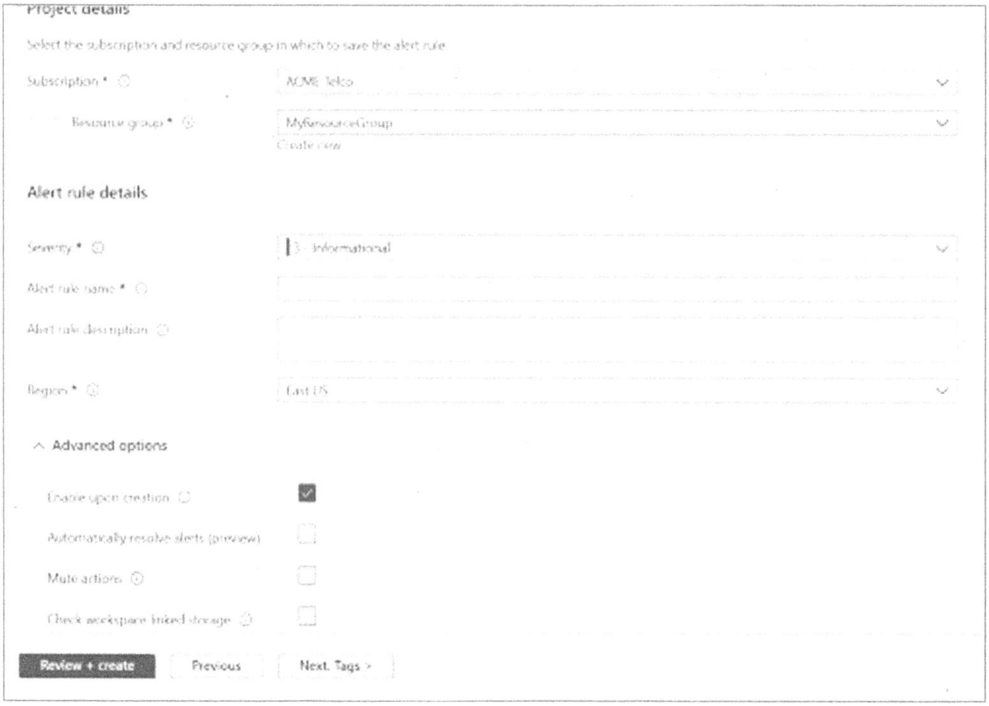

Filtering: This feature allows you to choose which dimension values are included in the chart. A common example is if you are looking at requests to a server and you want to filter the successful requests from the unsuccessful requests. This is where you would need to use filtering. To add a filter to your chart, select Add Filter above the chart you are working on.

Splitting: This feature controls whether the chart displays separate lines for each value of a dimension or if it aggregates the values into a single line. Say you are looking at the average response time across all servers in your environment. You can choose to have a single line showing the average time of all servers or you can have a separate line for each server. To do a split in your chart, select Apply Splitting above the chart.

In addition, you can use other chart settings to change chart style, title, and other mostly cosmetic features. Once you are done with your customization, pin your chart to a dashboard to save your work so that you will always be able to access it.

Microsoft Sentinel

Microsoft Sentinel is the cloud-native security information and event management (SIEM) and security orchestration, automation, and response (SOAR). First, let's look at the SIEM aspect of it. A SIEM is responsible for collecting and analyzing security data, which is collected from the different systems within a network to find abnormal behavior and potential cyberattacks. A SOAR helps coordinate, execute, and automate tasks between different people and tools within a single platform. Some common technologies that feed data into a SIEM for analysis are firewalls, antivirus software, applications, and network infrastructure devices. SIEMs provide their analysis in two main ways:

- They create reports on incidents and events that can be used to determine what is occurring on your network.
- They can be set up to send alerts when a certain set of events takes place, using predetermined rules. For example, you can set up a rule that if an admin account has more than five failed logins in a row, an alert is sent out because it may indicate an attempted unauthorized login.

How Does a SIEM Work?

A SIEM works in the following ways:

It collects data from different sources: First, you must configure your SIEM to get data from all the data sources of interest to you. These sources include network devices, endpoints, domain controllers, and any other device or service that you want to monitor and do analysis on.

It aggregates the data: Once all the devices and services you care about are connected to the SIEM, the SIEM must aggregate and normalize the data coming from all those different sources so that it can be analyzed. *Aggregation* is the process of moving data from different sources into a common repository; think of it as collecting data from all devices in one place. *Normalization* means taking different events from several different places and putting them into common categories so that analysis can begin. For example, if you have devices in different time zones, the SIEM can convert them all to one time zone so that a consistent timeline can be created. Last, the SIEM can perform *data enrichment* by adding supplemental information such as geolocations, transaction numbers, or application data that will allow for better analysis and reporting.

It creates policies and rules: SIEMs allow you to define profiles, which specify how a system should behave under normal conditions. Some SIEMs use machine learning to automatically detect anomalies based on this normal behavior. However, you can also manually create rules and thresholds that determine which anomalies are considered a security incident. Then when the SIEM is analyzing the data that comes in, it compares it to your normal profile and the rules you created to determine if something is wrong with your systems that requires investigation.

It analyzes the data: The SIEM will look at the data to determine what has happened among the different data sources, and then it will identify trends and discover any threats based on the data. Also, if you create rules for a certain threshold, such as five failed login attempts in a row, then the SIEM can raise alerts when those rules are violated.

It assists in the investigation: Once an investigation has begun, you can query the data stored in the SIEM to pinpoint certain events of interest. This allows you to trace back events to find the root cause of an incident and provide evidence to support your conclusions.

The next aspect to Microsoft Sentinel is security orchestration, automation, and response (SOAR). SOAR is a combination of software that enables your organization to collect data about security threats and to respond to security events without the need for human intervention.

Security Orchestration

This aspect focuses on connecting and integrating different security tools/systems with one another to form one cohesive security operation. Some of the common systems that may be integrated are vulnerability scanners, endpoint security solutions, end-user behaviors, firewalls, and IDS/IPS. It can also connect external tools like an external threat intelligence feed. By collecting and analyzing all of this information together, you can gain insights that may not have been found if you'd analyzed all that information separately. However, as the datasets become larger, more and more alerts will be issued—and ultimately a lot more false positives and noise that must be sorted to get to the useful information.

Security Automation

The data and alerts collected from the security orchestration is then used to create automated processes that replace manual work. Traditional tasks, which would need to be performed by analysts—tasks such as vulnerability scanning, log analysis, and ticket checking—can be standardized and performed solely by a SOAR system. These automated processes are defined in *playbooks*, which contain the information required for the automated processes. The SOAR system can also be configured to escalate a security event to humans if needed. As you can imagine, this system can save your company a lot of money and time on human capital. Also, machines tend to be more reliable and consistent than humans, which leads to fewer mistakes in your security processes.

Security Response

As the name suggests, this aspect is all about providing an efficient way for analysts to respond to a security event. It's where a SOAR creates a single view for analysts to provide planning, managing, monitoring, and reporting of actions once a threat is detected. See Figure 4.13.

FIGURE 4.13   SOAR and SIEM elements in Azure

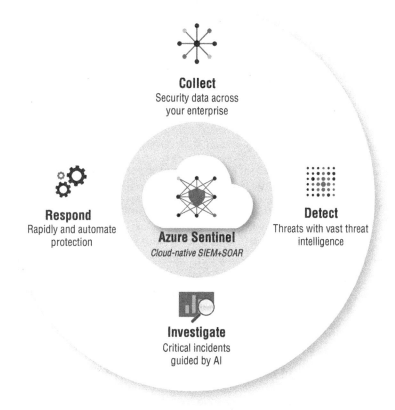

Threat Hunting

Microsoft Sentinel offers one more very useful feature for a security engineer: threat-hunting capabilities. Sentinel's threat-hunting search and query tools are based on the MITRE framework, and they enable you to proactively hunt for threats across your Azure environment. You can use Azure's prebuilt hunting queries, or you can create your own custom detection rules.

Creating and Customizing Alert Rules in Microsoft Sentinel

Now that you have been introduced to Microsoft Sentinel and its main features, let's talk about how to use it in a practical sense. The first step based on the exam objectives is to create and customize alert rules. In order to do this, you first need to ensure that you have connected all the data sources that you want to Sentinel. To do so, make sure that you satisfy some prerequisites:

Global Prerequisites

An Active Azure Subscription: If you don't have one, create a free account.

Log Analytics workspace: You need to create a Log Analytics workspace.

By default, you have a 90 days retention in the Log Analytics workspace to be used for Microsoft Sentinel.

Permissions

To enable Microsoft Sentinel: You need contributor permissions to the subscription in which the Microsoft Sentinel workspace resides.

To use Microsoft Sentinel: You need either contributor or reader permissions on the resource group to which the workspace belongs.

Additional permissions may be needed to connect specific data sources. Microsoft Sentinel is a paid service, so you must have an active subscription to use it.

Once you have satisfied all of these prerequisites, enable Microsoft Sentinel by following these steps:

1. Go to the Azure portal within the subscription where Microsoft Sentinel has been created.
2. Search for and select Microsoft Sentinel.
3. Click Add.
4. Choose the workspace you want to use or create a new one. You can run Microsoft Sentinel across more than one workspace, but the data will be isolated to a single workspace.
5. Click Add Microsoft Sentinel.

Configuring Connectors in Microsoft Sentinel

Microsoft Sentinel ingests data from services and applications by connecting to the service and forwarding the events and logs of interest to itself. To get data from physical and virtual machines, you can install a log analytics agent to collect the logs and forward them to

Microsoft Sentinel. For firewalls and proxies, you need to install the log analytics agent on a Linux syslog server, and from there, the agent will collect the log files and forward them to Microsoft Sentinel. Here's how to configure this:

1. From the main menu of Sentinel, select Data Connectors (which should be on the bottom left) to open the Data Connectors Gallery.

2. This gallery contains a list of all the data sources you can connect to Sentinel. Select a data source, and then click the Open Connector Page button.

3. The Connector page will show instructions for configuring the connector and any additional instructions that are necessary for that particular resource. Follow these instructions to finish the configuration.

4. The Next Steps tab on the Connector page will show built-in workbooks, sample queries, and analytics rule templates that go along with the data connectors. You can use them to immediately start receiving insights from the data you are collecting.

With this last step, all your data sources are connecting and streaming data to Microsoft Sentinel. You can start using queries to investigate the data in Log Analytics.

Using Built-in Detection Templates

Now that you have connected all the data sources you want to Microsoft Sentinel, we can begin discussing how to use this information to detect suspicious behavior. In order to assist people with this process, Microsoft Sentinel comes with prebuilt detection templates that you can use to create threat detection rules in your environment. These templates were designed by Microsoft's in-house security experts and analysts based on known threats, common attack vectors, and known patterns of suspicious activity. Much research occurred before these templates were built, so you may want to consider using them in your own environment. If you prefer not to use them, you have the option of customizing them to your liking or creating your own. Now let's look at how you can access these built-in templates:

1. To view the built-in detection templates, navigate to Microsoft Sentinel and then select Analytics ➤ Rule Templates. A tab will open containing all the built-in Microsoft Sentinel rules shown in Table 4.7.

TABLE 4.7   The built-in Microsoft Sentinel rules and their descriptions

Rule type	Description
Microsoft Security	These templates automatically create Microsoft Sentinel incidents in real time from the alerts created in other Microsoft Security products.
Fusion	Sentinel leverages the Fusion correlation engine with scalable machine-learning algorithms to allow for advanced detection of multistage attacks. It detects by correlating alerts and events across multiple products into actionable incidents. It's important to note that the logic of Fusion is hidden and therefore cannot be customized. Fusion is enabled by default.

TABLE 4.7   The built-in Microsoft Sentinel rules and their descriptions *(continued)*

Rule type	Description
Machine-learning (ML) Behavioral Analytics	ML Behavioral Analytics templates use Microsoft's machine-learning algorithms to detect attacks and malicious behavior. These are proprietary, and so like Fusion you cannot see the internal logic, and therefore, cannot customize it.
Anomaly	The Anomaly Rule templates utilize machine learning to detect specific types of suspicious behavior. Each rule in the template has its own unique parameters, thresholds, and sets of behavior that are being analyzed. The configurations of the templates can't be changed, but you can get around that by duplicating a rule and then changing the duplicate. This allows you to achieve the same effect as editing the rule itself.
Scheduled	These are scheduled analytics rules that are based on built-in queries created by Microsoft security experts. You are able to see the query logic and make changes as you see fit, enabling you to create new rules.
Near-real-time (NRT)	NRT rules are a limited set of scheduled rules, designed to run once every minute, to supply you with information as up-to-the-minute as possible. They function mostly like scheduled rules and are configured similarly, with some limitations.

Using the Built-In Analytics Rules

In this section we are going to explain how to use Azure's built-in analytics rules for monitoring.

1. In Microsoft Sentinel, select Analytics and then the Rule Templates page. Here, you select the template name that you want to use, and then click Create Rule in the Details pane.

> Each template has its own set of required data sources. Once you open a template, the system will automatically check all data sources for availability. If there is an availability issue with any of the data sources, the Create Rule button may be disabled or you might see a warning mentioning the issue.

2. Once you click Create Rule, the Rule Creation Wizard opens, based on the selected template. All of the details will be automatically filled in based on the template; however, you can customize the logic and rule settings as you like. You can repeat this process to create as many rules as you like, based on the built-in templates. Once you are satisfied with the rule, follow the prompts to finish creating the rule. The new rule(s) will then appear on the Active Rules tab.

Creating Custom Analytics Rules

Here are the steps for customizing analytics rules:

1. From the Microsoft Sentinel navigation menu, select Analytics.

2. In the action bar at the top, select Create and click Scheduled Query Rule, which opens the Analytics Rule Wizard. In this window, you will need to provide information about the rule you want to create:

   a. First, provide a unique name and a description for the rule.

   b. In the Tactics field, you must choose from among different categories of attacks to classify the rule. The options are based on the MITRE ATT&CK framework. For example, if you want a rule that will help you detect when a hacker is moving laterally through your network, you can choose Lateral Movement for the tactic. If you want a rule for detecting privilege escalation, then select that from the drop-down menu.

   c. Set the appropriate alert severity.

   d. Once you create the rule, its status will be enabled by default, so it will run immediately after you finish creating it. If you don't want to run it right away, select Disabled. When disabled, the rule won't run, but you can always go to your Active Rules tab and enable it if you need it.

Defining the Query Logic

On the Set Rule Logic tab, you can write a query directly into the Rule Query field, which will define the query's logic (functionality). Alternatively, you can create a query in Log Analytics and then copy and paste it. These queries are written in KQL.

Performing Alert Enrichment

Alert enrichment is all about making your alerts more useful through customization. This enrichment reduces the time needed to investigate alerts by providing you with more useful information within the alerts themselves. There are three ways you can do this in Azure:

Entity Mapping   Use entity mapping in the configuration section to map parameters from your query results to specific entities. Entities in Azure include the following:

- User account
- Host
- IP address
- Malware
- File
- Process
- Cloud application

- Domain name
- Azure resource
- File hash
- Registry key
- Registry value
- Security group
- URL
- Internet of Things (IoT) device
- Mailbox
- Mail cluster
- Mail message
- Submission mail

Once you have these configured, when alerts are either sent or generated by Microsoft Sentinel and Sentinel understands what kind of entity a data item represents, it can perform a deeper analysis. It will be able to compare insights about that item across all data sources and can track it more effectively across the environment, providing you—the end user—with better analytics, investigation, remediation, threat hunting, and so on.

Custom Details   As the name suggests, this allows you to extract event data from your query and have it surface in the alerts produced by the rule. You'll get immediate event content visibility in your alerts, rather than having to manually obtain that information.

Alert Details   This allows you to change the alert's presentation details to match its content. You then can have incidents in your queue named to match the alert itself, which can instantly clarify your actual threat landscape.

Query Scheduling and Alert Threshold

In the Query Scheduling section, set the following parameters:

1. Set Run Query to Every to control how often the query is run. The most frequently you can run a query is every 5 minutes and the most infrequently is every 14 days.

2. Set Lookup Data From The Last to specify the time period of the data covered by the query. The furthest back you can look up data is 14 days.

3. In the Alert Threshold section, you can define the sensitivity level for the rule that will determine how many query results you need to generate an alert. For example, you may want to generate an alert when the number of matching events is greater than 100. If you want to register an alert for every event, then enter 0.

Results Simulation

In the Results Simulation section, you can select Test With Current Data to generate a graph of the results that a query would have generated over the last 50 times it would have run, based on the schedule you have selected. This way, you can see if your query would generate too many or too few alerts for your liking, and you can fine-tune your alert threshold accordingly. You'll want to ensure that you aren't producing so much noise to the point that the alerts are no longer helpful in detecting real issues.

Evaluating Alerts and Incidents in Microsoft Sentinel

In this section, we discuss how to evaluate alerts and incidents in Sentinel. You'll learn how to quickly evaluate the seriousness of a potential security issue.

Incident Creation Settings

To understand the importance of creating incidents, you must know the difference between an alert and an incident in Azure. *Alerts* are notifications that proactively notify you when issues are found in your infrastructure or application using the data provided to Sentinel. An *incident,* on the other hand, is a group of related alerts that together create an actionable potential threat that requires an investigation and resolution. Sentinel uses analytics to correlate alerts into incidents. Now that you understand the difference, let's look at how you can create incidents.

On the Incident Settings tab, you can select whether and how Sentinel will turn alerts into actionable incidents. By default, Sentinel will create a single, separate incident for each alert. You may choose not to create any incidents or to group several alerts together into a single incident using this tab's settings (see Figure 4.14).

FIGURE 4.14   Creating incident alerts

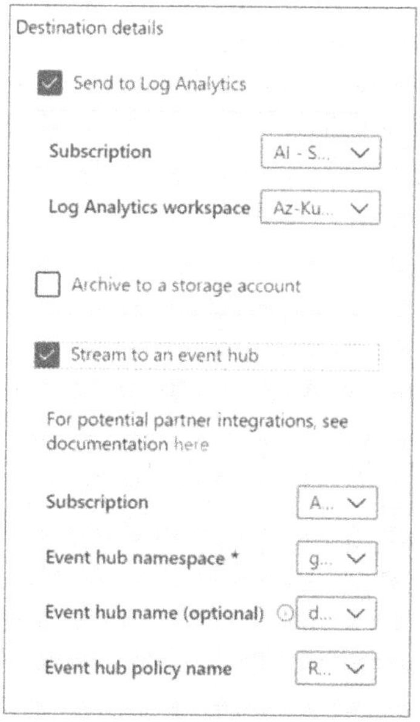

Setting Automated Responses

Automated responses in Microsoft Sentinel are facilitated by automation rules. Automation rules allow you to triage incidents. You can use them to do things like assign incidents to the right people, close noisy incidents/false positives, and change an incident's severity or add tags to incidents without having to perform these tasks manually. Automation rules also allow you to run playbooks in response to incidents.

A *playbook* is a set of procedures that can be executed by Sentinel as an automated response to an alert or an incident. Playbooks are used to automate and orchestrate your response and can be configured to run automatically in response to specific alerts or incidents. This automated run is configured by attaching the playbook to an analytics rule or an automation rule. Playbooks can also be triggered manually, if need be.

To set an automated response, follow these steps:

1. Select the Automated Responses tab. Here, you can set the automated response based on the alert (or alerts) generated by the rule you created or by the incidents created by the alerts:

   Alert-based automation: From the Alert Automation drop-down list, select any playbook you want to run automatically once an alert is generated.

   Incident-based automation: This allows you to select or create an automation rule under Incident Automation (Preview).

2. Once you've made your alert choices, click Review + Create to review all the settings for your new rule. Once you do, click Create to create the new alert rule.

Viewing Your Rule and Its Output

To find your custom rules, go to the main Analytics screen on the Active Rules tab. From here, you can enable, disable, or delete any rule.

If you would like to view the results of the alert rules you created, navigate to the Incidents page. Here, in addition to seeing your results, you can triage, investigate your incidents, and remediate potential threats.

Summary

This chapter focuses on managing security operations. Security operations include the people, processes, and technology responsible for preventing, detecting, assessing, monitoring, and responding to cybersecurity threats. The technology we discussed in this chapter will allow you to monitor your environment for any signs of malicious activity or malfunctioning. Through custom policies, you can mandate what is and isn't allowed in your environment, which should limit the actions that lead to potential security issues. You learned how to deploy Microsoft Defender for Cloud and Microsoft's native threat modeling tool to secure your infrastructure from potential threats. Finally, you learned how to use Azure's monitoring solutions to help you identify any issues that might occur despite the actions you took previously. Overall, this implementation will allow you to respond quickly to any issues found on your network.

Exam Essentials

Understand the role and function of Azure Policy. Azure Policy allows you to define a set of properties that your cloud resources should have, and then it will compare that defined list of properties to the actual properties of your resources to find those that are not compliant.

Be able to explain what a policy definition is and how it affects Azure resources. A policy definition expresses what you want your policy to evaluate and what actions it should take based on each resource to which it is assigned.

Know how policy effects work in regard to a policy definition. Each policy definition that you create in Azure Policy has an effect, which determines what will happen when a policy rule is evaluated to match. This effect can be applied whether it's the creation of a new resource, an updated resource, or an existing resource.

Know the order of evaluation for policy effects. The policy order of evaluation is (1) Disabled, (2) Append and Modify, (3) Deny, and (4) Audit.

Be able to explain what Microsoft Defender is and what its main features are. Microsoft Defender for Cloud is one of the primary tools that you use for cloud workload protection. Its three main features are endpoint detection and response, advanced protection capabilities, and vulnerability management.

Be able to explain what threat modeling is and how it is used in threat mitigation. Threat modeling is the process of identifying risks and threats that are likely to affect your organization. It's important for you to appropriately plan (i.e., model) your countermeasures and security controls to mitigate these threats.

Understand what Azure Monitor is and what the tool is used for. This tool provides you with a means of collecting, analyzing, and acting on the information from your cloud and on-premises environments.

Be able to explain what the Azure Monitor Logs feature is used for and what its data sources are. This feature collects and organizes log and performance data from monitored resources. It allows you to consolidate data from multiple sources into a single workspace. These sources include platform logs from various Azure services, log and performance data from VM agents, and usage and performance data collected from applications.

Understand what Azure Monitor Metrics does and how it adds security to your Azure environment. This feature of Azure Monitor gathers numeric data from monitored Azure resources into a time series database. Metrics are numerical values collected at regular intervals that are used to describe some aspect of a system at a particular point in time. Metrics in Azure Monitor can detect data in near-real-time, which is great for alerting and fast issue detection. Once data is collected, it can be analyzed using a tool called Metrics Explorer.

Be able to explain what the Metrics Explorer tool does.   This tool allows you to interactively analyze the data collected in your metric database. It also allows you to create data visualizations to chart the values of multiple metrics over time.

Understand how metric alerts are used for notification purposes in Azure.   In Azure Monitor, a metric alert is a way to be notified when a metric in your environment crosses a set threshold. For example, if you want to ensure that only 50 endpoints can connect to a specific server, you set a metric alert that triggers once the 51st endpoint connects to that server. You are then notified that you have exceeded the 50-endpoint threshold.

Be able to explain what a log alert is.   A log alert is a type of alert that allows users to create a Log Analytics query to evaluate resource logs on a set frequency and to create an alert based on the results.

Be able to explain what an activity log alert is.   These alerts activate when a new activity log event occurs. A regular log alert focuses on resource logs, whereas an activity log is looking for a certain set of events and flagging the activity logs that correspond to those events. For example, you may use a regular log alert for monitoring CPU usage and use an activity log to monitor user logins.

Understand what Microsoft Sentinel is and its purpose.   Sentinel is the cloud-native security information and event management (SIEM) and security orchestration, automation, and response (SOAR) tool.

Be able to explain what a data connector is and how it integrates with Sentinel.   Data connectors are all of the data sources you can connect to Sentinel.

Be able to explain what a prebuilt detection rule is in Sentinel.   Sentinel comes with prebuilt detection templates you can use to create threat detection rules in your environment.

Understand the uses for automation rules in Azure.   Automation rules allow you to triage incidents in Sentinel. You can use them to assign incidents to the right people, close noisy incidents/false positives, change an incident's severity, or add tags to incidents without having to perform these tasks manually. They also allow you to run playbooks in response to incidents.

Be able to define a playbook.   A playbook is a set of procedures that can be run from Sentinel as an automated response to an alert or an incident. Playbooks are used to automate and orchestrate your responses. They can be configured to run automatically when specific alerts or incidents are created by attaching them to an analytics rule or an automation rule. Playbooks can also be triggered manually, if need be.

Review Questions

1. What does security operations include?

   A. Performing all security-related activities

   B. Preventing, detecting, assessing, monitoring, and responding to cybersecurity threats

   C. Securing IT infrastructure

   D. Resolving security alerts and incidents

2. What is threat modeling?

   A. Creating visualizations of potential threats

   B. Identifying risks and threats that are likely to affect your organization

   C. Simulating the activity of threats to your company

   D. A type of security assessment

3. What does Azure Policy do?

   A. Defines the properties of your cloud resource and scans for compliance

   B. Allows you to create policy documentation

   C. Creates rules for IT administrators to follow

   D. Provides information on Azure best security practices

4. What is a policy definition?

   A. A template for creating policies

   B. The rules for creating your policies

   C. The details of a prebuilt policy in Azure Policy

   D. A definition that describes what you want your policy to evaluate and what actions it should take on each resource to which it is assigned

5. What's the difference between an alert and an incident in Microsoft Sentinel?

   A. Alerts are actionable, whereas incidents are not.

   B. Alerts can be created automatically, whereas incidents must be created manually.

   C. Alerts are notifications, whereas incidents are actionable potential threats.

   D. There is no significant difference.

6. Which of the following is not an entity in Microsoft Sentinel?

   A. IP addresses

   B. File

   C. Encryption key

   D. User account

7. Which of the following is not a feature of Microsoft Defender for Cloud?

  A. Automated compliance assessments

  B. Endpoint detection and response

  C. Advanced protection capabilities

  D. Vulnerability management

8. What is an effect in Azure Policy?

  A. The aftereffect of enabling a policy

  B. The effect determines what will happen when a policy rule is evaluated to match

  C. A change in configuration caused by implementing a policy

  D. A type of a policy

9. Which of the following is not an example of an effect in Azure Policy?

  A. Append

  B. Audit

  C. Deny

  D. Remediate

10. What is the correct order of evaluation for a policy definition?

  A. Append and modify, deny and audit, disabled

  B. Disabled, append and modify, deny and audit

  C. Deny and audit, disabled, and append and modify

  D. Disabled, deny and audit, append and modify

  E. This is the order in which a policy definition will execute effects for out-of-compliance resources.

11. What commercial software does Azure's vulnerability scanner integrate?

  A. QualysGuard

  B. Metasploit

  C. OpenVas

  D. Nmap

12. Which of the following is not an element of the STRIDE threat modeling framework?

  A. Spoofing

  B. Denial of service

  C. Tampering

  D. Enumeration

13. What is the purpose of Azure Monitor?

   A. To scan your environment for potential threats

   B. To monitor network resources for errors

   C. To provide you with a means for collecting, analyzing, and acting on the information from your cloud and on-premises environments

   D. To monitor the internal network as part of threat-hunting activities

14. What is not a severity level for a log alert?

   A. Urgent

   B. Critical

   C. Error

   D. Warning

15. What is not a feature of Azure Monitor Logs?

   A. Analyze

   B. Alert

   C. Remediate

   D. Visualize

16. What is *not* a feature of Azure Monitor Metrics?

   A. Analyze

   B. Alert

   C. Visualize

   D. Importing

17. What best describes filtering in Log Analytics?

   A. Allows you to choose which dimension values will be included in the chart

   B. Excludes unnecessary information

   C. Enriches query results

   D. Refines the information shown in data visualizations

18. What best describes splitting in Log Analytics?

   A. Configuring data connectors to send information to different places

   B. Separating data items within an alert

   C. Separating alerts into different incidents

   D. Controlling whether the chart displays separate lines for each value of a dimension or aggregates the values into a single line

19. What is Microsoft Sentinel?

    A. An endpoint protection solution

    B. A cloud-native SIEM and SOAR system

    C. A network monitoring solution

    D. A tool for incident detection and remediation

20. In what language are queries written for Microsoft Sentinel?

    A. Kusto Query Language (KQL)

    B. Perl

    C. Python

    D. C++

Chapter

5

Securing Data and Applications

THE MCA MICROSOFT CERTIFIED ASSOCIATE AZURE SECURITY ENGINEER ASSESSMENT TEST TOPICS COVERED IN THIS CHAPTER INCLUDE:

✓ **Configure security for storage**

- Configure access control for storage accounts

- Configure storage account access keys

- Configure Azure AD authentication for Azure Storage and Azure Files

- Configure delegated access

✓ **Configure security for data**

- Enable database authentication by using Azure AD

- Enable database auditing

- Configure dynamic masking on SQL workloads

- Implement database encryption for Azure SQL Database

- Implement network isolation for data solutions, including Azure Synapse Analytics and Azure Cosmo Database

✓ **Configure and manage Azure Key Vault**

- Create and configure Key Vault

- Configure access to Key Vault

- Manage certificates, secrets, and keys

- Configure key rotation

- Configure backup and recovery of certificates, secrets, and keys

This chapter focuses on how to secure data and applications on the Azure platform, including secure data storage, creating data backups seamlessly, database security, and leveraging Azure tools like Microsoft Defender and Key Vault. It will also cover how to protect the application's backend databases by implementing encryption, authentication, and auditing.

Configuring Security for Storage in Azure

In Azure, data storage is facilitated through an Azure Storage account, which contains all of the Azure Storage data objects: blobs, file shares, queues, tables, and disks. Storage accounts give you a unique namespace that allows you to access all of your data over HTTP or HTTPS. Also, all data in your storage account is automatically encrypted on the service side. You can have several different types of storage accounts and each supports different feature types in Azure (see Table 5.1).

TABLE 5.1   Various storage accounts and their usage

Type of storage account	Supported storage services	Usage
Standard general-purpose v2	Blob (including Data Lake Storage*), Queue, Table storage, and Azure Files	This is the standard storage account for blobs, file shares, queues, and tables. You will want to use this for the majority of scenarios in Azure Storage.
Premium block blobs^	Blob storage (including Data Lake Storage*)	This is the premium storage account for blobs and appended blobs. It should be used in scenarios where there are high transactions rates, where smaller objects are being used, or in situations that require consistently low storage latency.
Premium file shares^	Azure Files	This is a premium storage account for file shares. It should be used for enterprise or high-performance applications. It is a storage account that can support both SMB and NFS file shares.
Premium page blobs^	Page blobs only	This is a premium storage account for page blobs only.

*https://docs.microsoft.com/en-us/azure/storage/files/
storage-files-identity-auth-active-directory-domain-service-enable?tabs=azure-portal

^https://docs.microsoft.com/en-us/azure/storage/files/storage-files-identity-ad-ds-configure-permissions

One of the common use cases people have for a storage account is migration. Migration can be complicated, and there are several different options depending on what you are looking to do, as outlined in Table 5.2.

TABLE 5.2 Migration scenario breakdown

Migration scenario	Details
Move a storage account to a different subscription.	Azure Resource Manager provides options for moving a resource to a different subscription.
Move a storage account to a different resource group.	Azure Resource Manager provides options for moving a resource to a different resource group.
Move a storage account to a different region.	To move a storage account, create a copy of your storage account in another region. Then, move your data to that account by using AzCopy or another tool of your choice.
Upgrade to a general-purpose v2 storage account.	You can upgrade a general-purpose v1 storage account or blob storage account to a general-purpose v2 account. Note that this action cannot be undone.
Migrate a classic storage account to Azure Resource Manager.	The Azure Resource Manager deployment model is superior to the classic deployment model in terms of functionality, scalability, and security.

Storage Account Access Keys

For your storage account, your access keys are similar to a root password and can be used to authorize access to data in that storage account via shared key authorization. Whenever you create a storage account, Azure generates two 512-bit storage account access keys. It's best to use Azure Key Vault to manage your access keys and regularly rotate and regenerate your keys. Common security best practices for access keys include not giving access keys to other users and not hard-coding them or saving them anywhere in plaintext.

Configuring Access Control for Storage Accounts

Whenever you want to access data in a storage account, the client application will make a request over HTTP/HTTPS to Azure Storage. By default, every resource in Azure Storage is secured, meaning that the request must be authorized. This authorization ensures that the client application making the request has the proper permission to access data in the storage account.

You can use the following options to authorize access to data in storage accounts:

Azure Active Directory Integration   Microsoft recommends this method for authorizing data access requests. They recommend it because it has great overall security and is relatively easy to use compared to other options on this list. You can use Azure's role-based access control (RBAC) to control your security principal's permissions to access blobs, queues, and table resources in your storage accounts. You can also use Azure's attribute-based access control (ABAC) to put extra conditions on your Azure's role assignments for blob resources. However there are situations where this can't be done, such as accessing Azure files over REST.

Azure Active Directory Domain Services Authentication   This can only be used for accessing Azure files. Azure files allow for identity-based authorization over Server Message Block (SMB) via Azure AD DS. You can still use RBAC for fine-grained access control to Azure files. To achieve this Azure AD DS works along with Azure AD.

On-premises Active Directory Domain Services Authentication   This option utilizes your on-premises AD synced with Azure AD to access Azure files. SMB access to Azure files is provided via AD DS, and you can use RBAC to manage share-level access while using New Technology File System (NTFS) discretionary access control lists (DACLs) for directory- and file-level permissions.

To enable access to Azure files over SMB using Azure AD, you first need to ensure that you meet the following prerequisites:

1. You must select or create an Azure AD tenant.

2. Enable Azure AD Domain Services on the Azure AD tenant.

3. Domain-join an Azure VM with Azure AD DS.

4. Create and select a file share.

5. Lastly, you need to verify that Azure Files has connectivity. You do this by mounting your Azure file shares using your storage account key.

If all of these prerequisites are fulfilled, then follow these steps to grant access to the Azure file resources with Azure AD credentials:

1. First, you must enable Azure AD DS authentication via SMB for your storage account in order to register the storage account with the associated Azure AD DS deployment.

2. Next, you need to assign access permissions for the file share to an Azure AD identity.

3. Configure NTFS permissions over SMB for directories and files

4. Lastly, mount the Azure file share from a VM within the domain.

This process is summarized in Figure 5.1.

FIGURE 5.1 Granting access to Azure file resources with Azure AD credentials

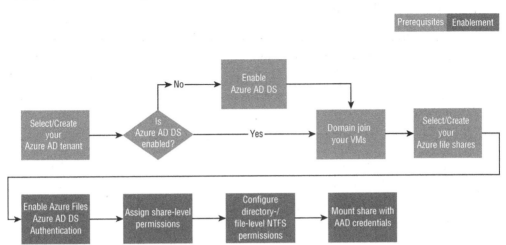

Shared Key Authorization This option can be used for accessing blobs, files, queues, and tables. It requires every client who needs access to have a storage account access key. Then the client will pass a header with each request that has been signed using the storage account access key to gain access.

Whenever you create a storage account, Azure will automatically generate two 512-bit storage account access keys for the account. You can use these keys to authorize access to data via shared key authorization. To view your access keys, follow these steps:

1. Go to the Azure portal and select your desired storage account.

2. Under Security + Networking, select Access Keys. This will display your account access keys as well as the entire connection string for every key.

3. Select Show Keys to view your access keys and their connection strings and to enable buttons to copy the values.

4. Under key1, you can find the key's value and copy the account key.

Alternatively, you can copy the entire connection string.

Note that while you can use either of the keys to access Azure Storage, it's advised that you use the first key and save the second key for when you need to rotate the keys.

To view the account's access keys, the user must have the Service Administrator role or be assigned an Azure role that has the Microsoft.Storage/storageAccounts/listkeys/action permission. Several built-in roles have this action, including the Owner, Contributor, and Storage Account Key Operator Service Roles.

Shared Access Signature (SAS) These signatures provide limited delegated access to resources on a storage account, namely blobs, files, queues, and tables. You also have the option to add time constraints on the time that the signature will be valid or on the permission that it grants, which gives you more flexibility in access control. There are three types of shared access signatures:

User Delegation SAS   This is secured using Azure Active Directory credentials and with SAS-specified permissions. This type of SAS is applied to Blob storage only.

Service SAS   This type of SAS is secured using the storage account key and delegates access to an Azure resource in any one of the following Azure Storage services: blob, queue, table, or Azure Files.

Account SAS   An account is secured using a storage account key and also delegates access to resources in one or more of the storage services. You can also delegate access to service-level operations and read, write, and delete operations that aren't permitted with a service SAS.

A SAS can be in one of two forms:

Ad Hoc SAS   If you choose to create an ad hoc SAS, you will be able to specify the start time, expiry time, and permission in the SAS unique resource identifier (URI).

Service SAS with Stored Access Policy   A stored access policy is applied to a resource container and is used to create constraints for one or more service SAS. Once you associate a service SAS with a stored access policy, the SAS will then inherit the constraints defined in that stored access policy.

How a SAS Works

A SAS is a signed unique resource identifier (URI) that is associated with one or more storage resources. This URI includes a token that has a special set of query parameters, and it will indicate how the resource will be accessed by the client. One of the most important query parameters (i.e., the signature) is constructed via the SAS parameters and signed using the key that was used to create the SAS. The signature is then used by Azure Storage to grant access to the storage resource.

SAS Token

The SAS token is a string that you generate on the client side. The SAS tokens you create are not tracked by Azure Storage, and you can create an unlimited number of tokens. Once you create these SAS tokens, you distribute them to any client application that requires access to resources in your storage account.

Whenever a client application makes a data request, they will provide the SAS URI to Azure Storage. The service will check the SAS parameters and its signature to verify its validity, and then the request will be authorized. Otherwise, the request will be declined with an error code 403.

To generate a SAS token in the Azure portal, follow these steps:

1. In the Azure portal, go to the storage account that you want to access under the Settings section and then select Shared Access Signature.

2. Select the desired permission for the SAS tokens as well as their start/end times.

3. Once you are done, click Generate SAS And Connection String to create the token.

4. Once this is done, you will see the SAS token populate and you can then copy and paste it wherever you like.

Anonymous Public Read Access

This method is for containers and blobs. Once anonymous access is configured, clients will be able to read blob data without authorization. You can disallow this access at any time and all further requests will require authorization. Two settings will affect public access:

- **Allowing public access for the storage account:** By default a storage account will allow users with the appropriate permission to make the container publicly accessible. However, the blob data will not be available for public access until the user explicitly configures the container's public access setting.

- **Configure public access settings:** By default this will be disabled, meaning that every request to the container or its data requires authorization. However, with the right permission, you can modify the container's public access setting to allow for anonymous access, but only after anonymous access has been allowed for the storage account.

To allow/disallow public access for a storage account from the Azure portal, follow these instructions:

1. Go to the storage account in the Azure portal.

2. Go to the Configuration setting under Settings.

3. Lastly, set Blob public access to Enabled/Disabled as desired.

If you want to update the public access level for one or more containers from the Azure portal, follow these steps:

1. Go to the storage account in the Azure portal.

2. Under Data Storage, choose Containers from the menu.

3. Select the container(s) for which you want to set the public access level.

4. Click the Change Access Level button to open the public access settings.

5. Select the public access level you want from the drop-down menu and then click OK to apply the changes.

Configuring Storage Account Access Keys

As mentioned previously, whenever you create a storage account Azure will create two storage account access keys for that account that can be used to authorize access to data in your storage account. We've already discussed how to find your access keys, but in this section, we will discuss how to configure, protect, and use these keys securely in Azure.

Protecting Your Access Keys

Access keys function similarly to a root password for your storage account; they provide users with access to the account and should be properly protected at all times. Microsoft recommends that you use Azure Key Vault for the management of your access keys, which includes managing, rotating, and regenerating keys if they are lost. To properly protect your access keys, you want to avoid sharing them with other users, avoid hard-coding them into any code you create, and avoid saving them anywhere in plaintext that may be accessible to others. If you believe that a key may have been compromised, you should rotate the key immediately.

Creating a Key Expiration Policy

A key expiration policy allows you to set a rotation reminder for the account access keys. The reminder will display only if the time interval that you have selected has passed and the keys have not been rotated. This is a great way to ensure that you meet your internal standards. To create a key expiration policy, follow these steps:

1. Go to the Azure portal and then go to your storage account.

2. Under Security + Networking, choose Access Keys. Your account's access keys will appear along with the connection string for each key.

3. Click the Set Rotation Reminder link.

4. Select the Enable Key Rotation Reminders checkbox and then set the frequency of the reminder.

5. Click Save.

Preventing Expired Keys

You can monitor your storage accounts with Azure Policy to ensure that the account access keys have been rotated within the time period that you have set. Azure Storage even has a built-in policy for ensuring that the storage account access keys do not expire. This policy is called Storage Account Keys Should Not Be Expired. If you would like to assign this built-in policy for a resource scope, follow these steps:

1. Go to the Azure portal, and then search for Policy to display the Azure Policy dashboard.

2. In the Authoring section, choose Assignments.

3. Click Assign Policy.

4. On the Basics tab of the Assign Policy page, in the Scope section, specify the scope for the policy assignment. Click the More button to choose the subscription and optional resource group.

5. In the Policy Definition field, click the More button and enter storage account keys in the Search field. Then select the policy definition named Storage Account Keys Should Not Be Expired.

6. Click Review + Create to assign the policy definition to the specified scope.

Monitoring Compliance with the Key Expiration Policy

In this section, we are going to discuss how to monitor compliance for your key expiration policy:

1. Navigate to the Azure Policy dashboard and locate the built-in policy definition for the scope that you specified in the policy assignment. To find it, you can search for **Storage Account Keys Should Not Be Expired** in the search box to filter for that built-in policy.

2. Select the policy name with the desired scope.

3. On the Policy Assignment page for the built-in policy, click View Compliance. Any storage accounts within the specified subscription and resource group that do not meet the policy requirements will appear in the compliance report.

Configuring Azure AD Authentication for Azure Storage and Azure Files

In this section, we will look at configuring secure authentication for Azure Storage using Azure AD Authentication.

Step 1: Enabling AD DS Authentication for Your Azure File Shares

The recommended means of enabling Azure AD authentication for Azure Storage is through the `AzFilesHybrid` PowerShell module. The first thing you want to do is download the `AzFilesHybrid` module using the following steps.

As a prerequisite, you will need to install .NET Framework 4.7.2. It is required for the module to be imported successfully. In addition, you can follow these steps to install it if needed:

1. Download and unzip the `AzFilesHybrid` module (i.e., GA module: `v0.2.0+`).

2. Install and execute the module on a device that is domain-joined to the on-premises AD DS. It must have credentials with the permissions to create a service logon account or a computer account in the desired AD.

3. Run the script using an on-premises AD DS credential that is synced with your Azure AD. This on-premises AD DS credential must be assigned either the Owner or the Contributor role on the storage account.

Once you have the module installed, you want to run the `Join-AzStorageAccount` cmdlet; this will create an account in your AD domain. The AD DS account created by the cmdlet will represent the storage account. If the account is created under an organization unit that enforces password expiration, be sure to update the password *before* the maximum password age or it will result in authentication failures. Lastly, you need to replace the placeholder values with your desired parameters before executing:

```
# Change the execution policy to unblock importing AzFilesHybrid.psm1 module
Set-ExecutionPolicy -ExecutionPolicy Unrestricted -Scope CurrentUser
```

```
# Navigate to where AzFilesHybrid is unzipped and stored and run to copy the
files into your path
.\CopyToPSPath.ps1


# Import AzFilesHybrid module
Import-Module -Name AzFilesHybrid


# Login with an Azure AD credential that has either storage account owner or
contributer Azure role assignment
# If you are logging into an Azure environment other than Public (ex.
AzureUSGovernment) you will need to specify that.
# See https://docs.microsoft.com/azure/azure-government/documentation-
government-get-started-connect-with-ps
# for more information.
Connect-AzAccount


# Define parameters, $StorageAccountName currently has a maximum limit of 15
characters
$SubscriptionId = "<your-subscription-id-here>"
$ResourceGroupName = "<resource-group-name-here>"
$StorageAccountName = "<storage-account-name-here>"
$DomainAccountType = "<ComputerAccount|ServiceLogonAccount>" # Default is set
as ComputerAccount
# If you don't provide the OU name as an input parameter, the AD identity that
represents the storage account is created under the root directory.
$OuDistinguishedName = "<ou-distinguishedname-here>"
# Specify the encryption algorithm used for Kerberos authentication. Default
is configured as "'RC4','AES256'" which supports both 'RC4' and 'AES256'
encryption.
$EncryptionType = "<AES256|RC4|AES256,RC4>"


# Select the target subscription for the current session
Select-AzSubscription -SubscriptionId $SubscriptionId


# Register the target storage account with your active directory environment
under the target OU (for example: specify the OU with Name as "UserAccounts" or
DistinguishedName as "OU=UserAccounts,DC=CONTOSO,DC=COM").
# You can use to this PowerShell cmdlet: Get-ADOrganizationalUnit to find the
Name and DistinguishedName of your target OU. If you are using the OU Name,
specify it with -OrganizationalUnitName as shown below. If you are using the OU
```

DistinguishedName, you can set it with -OrganizationalUnitDistinguished Name. You

can choose to provide one of the two names to specify the target OU.

```
# You can choose to create the identity that represents the storage account as
either a Service Logon Account or Computer Account (default parameter value),
depends on the AD permission you have and preference.
# Run Get-Help Join-AzStorageAccountForAuth for more details on this cmdlet.


Join-AzStorageAccount `
        -ResourceGroupName $ResourceGroupName `
        -StorageAccountName $StorageAccountName `
        -DomainAccountType $DomainAccountType `
        -OrganizationalUnitDistinguishedName $OuDistinguishedName `
        -EncryptionType $EncryptionType


#Run the command below if you want to enable AES 256 authentication. If you
plan to use RC4, you can skip this step.
Update-AzStorageAccountAuthForAES256 -ResourceGroupName $ResourceGroupName -
StorageAccountName $StorageAccountName


#You can run the Debug-AzStorageAccountAuth cmdlet to conduct a set of basic
checks on your AD configuration with the logged on AD user. This cmdlet is
supported on AzFilesHybrid v0.1.2+ version. For more details on the checks
performed in this cmdlet, see Azure Files Windows troubleshooting guide.
Debug-AzStorageAccountAuth -StorageAccountName $StorageAccountName
-ResourceGroupName $ResourceGroupName -Verbose
```

Once you have executed the `Join-AzStorageAccount` script, confirm that it worked by running the following script:

```
# Get the target storage account
$storageaccount = Get-AzStorageAccount `
        -ResourceGroupName "<your-resource-group-name-here>" `
        -Name "<your-storage-account-name-here>"
```

It's a command line argument so please keep as is List the directory service of the selected service account:

```
$storageAccount.AzureFilesIdentityBasedAuth.DirectoryServiceOptions
```

It's a command line argument so please keep as is List the directory domain information if the storage account has enabled AD DS authentication for file shares:

```
$storageAccount.AzureFilesIdentityBasedAuth.ActiveDirectoryProperties
```

If the script was successful, the output should look like this:

```
DomainName:<yourDomainHere>
NetBiosDomainName:<yourNetBiosDomainNameHere>
ForestName:<yourForestNameHere>
DomainGuid:<yourGUIDHere>
DomainSid:<yourSIDHere>
AzureStorageID:<yourStorageSIDHere>
```

MANUAL CONFIGURATION

If, for whatever reason, you can't run this script, you can also configure it manually. For manual configuration, you need to check the state of your environment:

1. Ensure that Active Directory PowerShell is installed and that the shell is being executed with admin privileges.

2. Confirm that Az.Storage 2.0 module or a later version is installed.

3. Check your AD DS to see if there is a computer account or service logon account that has already been created with SPN/UPN as cifs/*your-storage-account-name-here*.file.core.windows.net. If you don't have this account already, you can create one using these steps:

    a. First create a new Kerberos key for your storage account, which will act as the password for your account using the PowerShell cmdlets below. (This will only be used during setup.)

    Create the Kerberos key on the storage account and get the Kerb1 key as the password for the AD identity to represent the storage account:

    ```
    $ResourceGroupName = "<resource-group-name-here>"

    $StorageAccountName = "<storage-account-name-here>"

    New-AzStorageAccountKey -ResourceGroupName $ResourceGroupName -Name
    $StorageAccountName -KeyName kerb1

    Get-AzStorageAccountKey -ResourceGroupName $ResourceGroupName -Name
    $StorageAccountName -ListKerbKey | where-object{$_.Keyname -contains
    "kerb1"}
    ```

    b. Once you have the key, create either a service or computer account under your organization unit (OU). Use the following specification while replacing the example text with your storage account name:

    ```
    SPN: "cifs/your-storage-account-name-here.file.core.windows.net" Password:
    Kerberos key for your storage account.
    ```

    c. If your OU enforces password expiration, then you must update the password before the maximum password age to prevent authentication failures.

    d. Keep the Security Identifier (SID) of the newly created identity for the next step.

ENABLE THE FEATURE ON YOUR STORAGE ACCOUNT

To manually enable the feature on your account, modify the following command to include the configuration details for the domain properties and run it to enable the feature. The storage account SID will be the SID of the identity you created in the previous step:

Set the feature flag on the target storage account and provide the required AD domain information:

```
Set-AzStorageAccount `
        -ResourceGroupName "<your-resource-group-name-here>" `
        -Name "<your-storage-account-name-here>" `
        -EnableActiveDirectoryDomainServicesForFile $true `
        -ActiveDirectoryDomainName "<your-domain-dns-root-here>" `
        -ActiveDirectoryNetBiosDomainName "<your-domain-dns-root-here>" `
        -ActiveDirectoryForestName "<your-forest-name-here>" `
        -ActiveDirectoryDomainGuid "<your-guid-here>" `
        -ActiveDirectoryDomainsid "<your-domain-sid-here>" `
        -ActiveDirectoryAzureStorageSid "<your-storage-account-sid>"
```

HOW TO MANUALLY PERFORM DEBUGGING

If you would like, you can run the `Debug-AzStorageAccountAuth` cmdlet to run a set of basic checks on your AD configuration with the logged-on AD user:

```
Debug-AzStorageAccountAuth -StorageAccountName $StorageAccountName -
ResourceGroupName $ResourceGroupName -Verbose
```

HOW TO CONFIRM THAT THE FEATURE WAS ENABLED

If you want to run an overall check that the feature has been enabled on the storage account, use this script:

Get the target storage account:

```
$storageaccount = Get-AzStorageAccount `
        -ResourceGroupName "<your-resource-group-name-here>" `
        -Name "<your-storage-account-name-here>"
```

List the directory service of the selected service account:

```
$storageAccount.AzureFilesIdentityBasedAuth.DirectoryServiceOptions
```

List the directory domain information if the storage account has enabled AD DS authentication for file shares:

```
$storageAccount.AzureFilesIdentityBasedAuth.ActiveDirectoryProperties
```

Step 2: Assigning Share-Level Permissions to an Identity

Now that you have enabled AD DS authentication on your storage account, the next step is to configure share-level permissions to gain access to your file shares. You can do this in two ways. First, you can assign the permissions to specific AD users/user groups. Second, you can assign the permissions to all the authenticated identities as a default share-level permission.

CHOOSING THE CONFIGURATION METHOD

Microsoft suggests that most users assign share-level permissions to specific Azure AD users or groups, rather than making it a default permission. Then they should use Windows ACLs for granular access control at the directory and file levels, as this is considered the most secure configuration option.

Microsoft has identified two scenarios where they recommend using the second approach of default share-level permissions assigned to all authenticated identities (https://docs.microsoft.com/en-us/azure/storage/files/ storage-files-identity-ad-ds-configure-permissions):

1. If you are having issues syncing your on-premises AD DS to Azure AD, this is a good time to use a default share-level permission. By assigning a default share-level permission, you will be able to work around the sync requirement as you don't need to specify the permission to identities in Azure AD. To ensure you still have good security, you can then use Windows ACLs for granular permission control of your files and directories.

2. If you have a situation where the on-premises AD DS that you're using is synced to a different Azure AD than the Azure AD where the file share is deployed, then you should opt for using default permissions.

Option 2 is a common situation when you are managing multitenant environments. By using the default share-level permission, you can bypass the requirement for an Azure AD hybrid identity. Then you can use Windows ACLs on your files and directories to control permissions for individuals and groups. See a list of built-in roles below Table 5.3:

TABLE 5.3   Built-in share-level permissions (https://docs.microsoft.com/en-us/ azure/storage/files/storage-files-identity-ad-ds-configure-permissions)

Supported built-in roles	Description
Storage File Data SMB Share Reader	This allows for read-level access to files and directories in Azure file shares. It is similar to a file share ACL for read access on a Windows File server.
Storage File Data SMB Share Contributor	This allows the user to have read, write, and delete access for files and directories in Azure file shares.
Storage File Data SMB Share Elevated Contributor	This allows the user to have read, write, delete, and modify ACLs for files and directories in Azure file shares.

OPTION 1: SHARE-LEVEL PERMISSIONS FOR SPECIFIC AZURE AD USERS OR GROUPS

To use this method, the identity must be a hybrid identity that exists on both on-premises AD DS and Azure AD. Then you simply assign the share-level permission to that user account. The same concept applies to groups or service principals in Azure. Therefore, you must sync the users and groups from your on-premises AD DS to Azure AD, using Azure AD Connect Sync.

Share-level permissions must be assigned to the Azure AD identity that represents that same user or group in AD DS to support AD DS authentication to your Azure file share. Authentication and authorization for identities that exist only in Azure AD are not supported with AD DS authentication. Here's how to assign built-in roles to the Azure AD identity for a user via the Azure portal for granting share-level permissions:

1. In the Azure portal, navigate to the desired file share or create a file share.

2. Click Access Control (IAM).

3. Click Add A Role Assignment.

4. In the Add Role Assignment section, select the built-in role you want from the provided role list.

5. Leave Assign Access To Set to the default setting of Azure AD User, Group, or Service Principal. Then select the target Azure AD identity by name or email address. As mentioned previously, the selected Azure AD identity must be a hybrid identity and cannot be a cloud-only identity.

6. Click Save to complete the assignment.

OPTION 2: SHARE-LEVEL PERMISSIONS FOR ALL AUTHENTICATED IDENTITIES

With this option, you will be adding a default share-level permission that will be added to your storage account that will give all authenticated users and groups the same set of permissions. Authenticated users or groups will be identified as their given identity, which can then be authenticated against the on-premises AD DS with which the storage account is associated. This cannot be done using the Azure portal, so let's look at how to do this in the Azure PowerShell.

Use the following script to configure default share-level permissions on your storage account. You can only enable default share-level permission on storage accounts that have been associated with a directory service for Files authentication:

```
$defaultPermission = "None|StorageFileDataSmbShareContributor|StorageFileDataS
mbShareReader|StorageFi
leDataSmbShareElevatedContributor" # Set the default permission of your choice
$account = Set-AzStorageAccount -ResourceGroupName "<resource-group-name-here>"
-AccountName "<storage-account-name-here>" -DefaultSharePermission
$defaultPermission
$account.AzureFilesIdentityBasedAuth
```

WHAT HAPPENS IF YOU USE BOTH CONFIGURATIONS ON A STORAGE ACCOUNT?

You can use a combination of both of these options if you prefer. With this configuration, a specific user or group will have whatever the higher-level permission is between the default share-level permission and the RBAC assignment.

Once you have assigned the share-level permission, the next step is to configure the directory- and file-level permissions.

Step 3: Configuring Directory- and File-Level Permissions over SMB

Now that you have assigned share-level permissions, you need to configure Windows ACLs at the root, directory, and file levels to have granular access control. The share-level permissions determine whether a user can access the share as a whole, but now you want to create ACLs that will control what resources within that share that a user can access. It's important to note that both share-level and file-/directory-level permissions are enforced when a user attempts to access a file/directory, so if there are any conflicts between the two, the most restrictive one will be applied. Azure File supports the full set of basic and advanced Windows ACLs. The following permissions are included on the root directory of a file share (`https://docs.microsoft.com/en-us/azure/storage/files/storage-files-identity-ad-ds-configure-permissions`). See Table 5.4 for details:

- BUILTIN\Administrators:(OI)(CI)(F)
- BUILTIN\Users:(RX)
- BUILTIN\Users:(OI)(CI)(IO)(GR,GE)
- NT AUTHORITY\Authenticated Users:(OI)(CI)(M)
- NT AUTHORITY\SYSTEM:(OI)(CI)(F)
- NT AUTHORITY\SYSTEM:(F)
- CREATOR OWNER:(OI)(CI)(IO)(F)

TABLE 5.4   Users and their definitions

Users	Definition
BUILTIN\ Administrators	These are all users who are domain admins of the on-premises AD DS environment.
BUILTIN\Users	This is a built-in security group within AD that includes authenticated users by default.
NT AUTHORITY\ SYSTEM	This is the OS service account for the file server.
NT AUTHORITY\ Authenticated Users	These are all the users in AD who can receive a valid Kerberos token.
CREATOR OWNER	Every object that is created, whether it's a directory or file, will have an owner. You can create ACLs and assign them to this role to control their permissions as defined by the ACL.

Azure files supports the full suite of basic and advanced Windows ACLs. To view and configure your Windows ACLs for directories and files in an Azure file share, you must mount the share and then use Windows File Explorer. To enforce these permissions, you must mount the share by using your storage account key from your domain-joined virtual machine (VM). Follow these instructions to mount an Azure file share using the command prompt to configure your Windows ACLs.

To mount a file share from the command prompt, you use net use. Use the following command and replace the placeholder values with your own values:

```
$connectTestResult = Test-NetConnection -ComputerName <storage-account-
name>.file.core.windows.net -Port 445
if ($connectTestResult.TcpTestSucceeded)
{
  net use <desired-drive-letter>: \\<storage-account-
name>.file.core.windows.net\<share-name> /user:Azure\<storage-account-name>
<storage-account-key>
}
else
{
  Write-Error -Message "Unable to reach the Azure storage account via
port 445.
Check to make sure your organization or ISP is not blocking port 445, or use
Azure P2S VPN,  Azure S2S VPN, or Express Route to tunnel SMB traffic over a
different port."
}
```

CONFIGURING YOUR WINDOWS ACLS

Once the file share has been mounted using your storage account key, you can configure your windows ACLs (i.e., NTFS permissions). The two options to do this are Windows File Explorer and icacls.

CONFIGURING WINDOWS ACLS WITH WINDOWS FILE EXPLORER

You can use Windows File Explorer to grant full permission to any directories and files under the file share, even the root directory. Here's how you do it:

1. Open Windows File Explorer and right-click the file or directory you want to configure access for and then click Properties.

2. Click the Security tab.

3. Click Edit to change your permissions.

4. You can modify the permissions of existing users or click Add to grant permissions for a new user.

5. If you are granting permissions to a new user, a prompt window will appear. Enter the username of the user that you want to grant permissions to in the "Enter the object names to select" box, and click Check Names to find the full name of the chosen user.

6. Click OK.

7. On the Security tab, select all the permissions you want to grant the user.

8. Click Apply.

If you are unable to load the AD domain information in Windows File Explorer, it's normally due to the trust configurations in your on-premises AD environment. The client machine was unable to reach the AD domain controller registered for Azure Files authentication. If this occurs, then you can use icacls for configurating Windows ACLs. (icacls is a command-line tool for modifying the NTFS file system permissions in Windows.)

CONFIGURING WINDOWS ACLS WITH *ICACLS*

The configuration of Windows ACLs with icacls is much simpler than using Windows File Explorer. You can use the following Windows command to grant a user full permission to all directories and files under a file share. Be sure to replace the placeholder values:

```
icacls <mounted-drive-letter>: /grant <user-upn>:(f)
```

Step 4: Mount a File Share from a Domain-Joined VM

The process that we are going to complete here will verify that your file share and access permissions are set up correctly and that you can access an Azure file share from a domain-joined VM. Here are the prerequisites that you need to satisfy before you can mount a file share (https://docs.microsoft.com/en-us/azure/active-directory/fundamentals/active-directory-how-subscriptions-associated-directory#associate-a-subscription-to-a-directory):

1. If you are mounting the file share from a client that has previously mounted the file share using your storage account key, then you need to make sure that you have disconnected the share, you have removed the persistent credentials of the storage account key, and you are currently using AD DS credentials for authentication.

2. Your client must have access to your AD DS. If your machine/VM is outside the network managed by your AD DS, you will need to enable VPN to reach AD DS for authentication.

Once these prerequisites are met, the first thing you must do is sign into the client machine using the credentials to which you gave permissions. Then, in the Azure PowerShell, use the following command to mount the Azure file share, making sure that you replace the placeholder values with your own. You always need to mount using the path shown:

Be sure to always mount your share using .file.core.windows.net, even if you choose to set up a private endpoint for your share.

```
$connectTestResult = Test-NetConnection -ComputerName <storage-account-
name>.file.core.windows.net -Port 445
if ($connectTestResult.TcpTestSucceeded)
{
  net use <desired-drive letter>: \\<storage-account-name>.file.core.windows.
net\<fileshare-name>
}
else
{
  Write-Error -Message "Unable to reach the Azure storage account via
port 445.
Check to make sure your organization or ISP is not blocking port 445, or use
Azure P2S VPN, Azure S2S VPN, or Express Route to tunnel SMB traffic over a
different port."
}
```

If the command is successful, then you have officially succeeded in enabling and configuring on-premises AD DS authentication for your Azure file shares. Next, we will look at what you need to do if your storage account is in a domain or OU that enforces password rotation.

UPDATING THE PASSWORD OF YOUR STORAGE ACCOUNT IDENTITY IN AD DS

After you register the AD DS identity/account that represents your storage account in an OU or domain using password expiration time, you must change the password before the maximum password age. The worst-case scenario if you don't change your password in time is that your account may be deleted, and you may lose access to your Azure file shares.

To facilitate a password rotation, you can run the `Update-AzStorageAccountADObjec tPassword` command from the `AzFilesHybrid` module in PowerShell.

In order for this to work, the command must be run in an on-premises AD DS–joined environment using a hybrid user with owner permissions to the storage account and AD DS permissions to change the password of the identity representing the storage account. Once you run the command, it will obtain the second Kerberos key of the storage account and use it to update the password of the registered account in AD DS. Then it will regenerate the target Kerberos key of the storage account and update the password of the registered account in AD DS. You can use the following script to do this:

```
# Update the password of the AD DS account registered for the storage account
# You may use either kerb1 or kerb2

Update-AzStorageAccountADObjectPassword `
      -RotateToKerbKey kerb2 `
```

```
-ResourceGroupName "<your-resource-group-name-here>" `
-StorageAccountName "<your-storage-account-name-here>"
```

If you would like to avoid having to use password rotations, then during the onboarding of the Azure storage account in the domain, place the Azure storage account into a separate organizational unit in AD DS. Next, disable the Group Policy inheritance on that organizational unit to prevent default domain policies or specific password policies from being applied.

Configuring Delegated Access for Storage Accounts

A shared access signature (SAS) provides secure delegated access to resources in your storage accounts. SAS allows for granular (i.e., detailed) control over how someone can assess this data. Some examples are:

- What resources can be assessed

- What permissions they have when assessing those resources

- How long the SAS will be valid

In this section, we will cover how to configure user-delegated access with SAS.

A SAS secured with Azure AD credentials is called a user delegation SAS, and it's recommended by Microsoft that you use Azure AD credentials whenever possible as a security best practice. Whenever your application design requires shared access signatures, employ user delegation SAS for the best possible security. But keep in mind that this is only possible for blobs.

To create a user delegation SAS, follow these steps:

1. Use RBAC to grant the desired permissions to the security principal who will be requesting the user delegation key.

   Every SAS is signed with a key and, therefore, your first step in creating a user delegation SAS is to request a user delegation key. To do so, you need a security principal that has been assigned the `Microsoft.Storage/storageAccounts/blobServices/generateUserDelegationKey` action. An Azure security principal can be a user, group, service principal, or managed identity; the important thing is that it has the required permission to request a delegation key. You can explicitly assign the security principal the permissions it needs or you can use one of the following built-in roles:

   - Contributor

   - Storage Account Contributor

   - Storage Blob Data Contributor

   - Storage Blob Data Owner

   - Storage Blob Data Reader

   - Storage Blob Delegator

One important thing to remember is that the Get User Delegation Key operation acts at the level of the storage account; therefore, the `Microsoft.Storage/storageAc counts/blobServices/generateUserDelegationKey` must be scoped at the level of the storage account, the resource group, or the subscription for it to work. This is important to keep in mind when creating custom roles, as all of the built-in roles listed previously have this enabled at default.

Alternatively, if you have a situation where the security principal is assigned a role that permits data access but that is scoped at the level of a container, you can assign the Storage Blob Delegator role to that security principal at the level of the storage account, resource group, or subscription. This role grants the security principal permissions to request the user delegation key.

2. Acquire an OAuth 2.0 token from Azure AD.

    To get a user delegation key, you should first request an OAuth 2.0 token from Azure AD, which will be used with the bearer scheme to authorize the call to the Get User Delegation Key operation. OAuth2.0 makes use of what are called *bearer tokens*—security tokens that grant the "bearer" access to a protected resource. These tokens are acquired from the application that you want access to and include:

    - Web apps
    - Mobile apps
    - Desktop apps
    - Web APIs

    Once you acquire the OAuth 2.0 token from the resource you want access to, you can use it to request the user delegation key.

3. Use the token to request the user delegation key by calling the Get User Delegation Key operation.

    You can use the Get User Delegation Key operation to obtain a key that can be used to sign a user delegation SAS. This request (which requires HTTPS) can be made by calling the operation in Table 5.5.

TABLE 5.5 Calling the Get User Delegation Key operation

POST method request URI	HTTP version
`https://myaccount.blob.core.windows.net/?restype=service &comp=userdelegationkey`	HTTP/1.1

If you need to make a request against the local storage service, you must specify the local hostname and blob service port as 127.0.0.1:10000. This will be followed by the local storage account name (see Table 5.6).

TABLE 5.6   Specifying the local hostname and blob service port

POST method request URI	HTTP version
http://127.0.0.1:10000/devstoreaccount1/?restype=service &comp=userdelegationkey	HTTP/1.1

You have option of adding the optional timeout parameter in the request URI to obtain a parameter for timeouts expressed in seconds. Table 5.7 describes the request headers. Request headers typically provide information about the request.

TABLE 5.7   Request headers

Request header	Description
Authorization	This header is required, and it specifies the authorization scheme.
x-ms-version	This header is required for all authorized requests.
x-ms-client-request-id	This is an optional header that provides a client-generated opaque value that will be recorded in the analytics logs when enabled. Microsoft recommends this header for correlating client-side activities with requests received by the server.

The format for the request body is:

```
<?xml version="1.0" encoding="utf-8"?>
<KeyInfo>
    <Start>String, formatted ISO Date</Start>
    <Expiry>String, formatted ISO Date </Expiry>
</KeyInfo>
```

4. The element <start> sets the start time for the user delegation SAS. It must be a valid date and time within seven days of the current time.

5. The <expiry> elements mark the expiry time of user delegation SAS. They must be a valid date and time within seven days of the current time.

Once you have the user delegation key, you can use it to construct an unlimited number of user delegation SASs over the lifetime of the key. The user delegation key will be independent of the OAuth 2.0 token used to acquire it, and therefore, the token will not need to be renewed as long as the key is valid. You can configure the key to be valid for up to seven days.

6. Use the user delegation key to construct the SAS token with the appropriate fields.

Table 5.8 shows all the supported fields that can be used when creating a user delegation SAS token:

TABLE 5.8   Supported fields when creating a user delegation SAS token (https://docs.microsoft.com/en-us/azure/active-directory/fundamentals/active-directory-how-subscriptions-associated-directory#associate-a-subscription-to-a-directory)

SAS field name	SAS token parameter	Required or optional	Version support	Description
signedVersion	Sv	Required	11-09-2018 or later	Indicates the version of the service used to construct the signature field, and specifies the service version that handles a request made with this shared access signature.
signedResource	Sr	Required	All	Specifies which blob resources are accessible via the shared access signature.
signedStart	St	Optional	All	The time at which the shared access signature becomes valid, expressed in one of the accepted ISO 8601 UTC formats. If omitted, the current UTC time is used as the start time.
signedExpiry	Se	Required	All	The time at which the shared access signature becomes invalid, expressed in one of the accepted ISO 8601 UTC formats.

TABLE 5.8 Supported fields when creating a user delegation SAS token *(continued)*

SAS field name	SAS token parameter	Required or optional	Version support	Description
signedPermissions	Sp	Required	All	Indicates which operations a client who possesses the SAS may perform on the resource. Permissions may be combined.
signedIp	sip	Optional	2015-04-05 or later	Specifies an IP address or an inclusive range of IP addresses from which to accept requests.
signedProtocol	spr	Optional	2015-04-05 or later	Specifies the protocol permitted for a request made with the SAS. Includes this field to require that requests made with the SAS token use HTTPS.
signedObjectId	skoid	Required	2018-11-09 or later	Identifies an Azure AD security principal.
signedTenantId	skitid	Required	2018-11-09 or later	Specifies the Azure AD tenant in which a security principal is defined.
signedKeyStartTime	skt	Optional	2018-11-09 or later	Value is returned by the Get User Delegation Key operation. Indicates the start of the lifetime of the user delegation key, expressed in one of the accepted ISO 8601 UTC formats. If omitted, the current time is assumed.

SAS field name	SAS token parameter	Required or optional	Version support	Description
signedKeyExpiryTime	ske	Required	2018-11-09 or later	Value is returned by the Get User Delegation Key operation. Indicates the end of the lifetime of the user delegation key, expressed in one of the accepted ISO 8601 UTC formats.
signedKeyService	sks	Required	2018-11-09 or later	Indicates the service for which the user delegation key is valid. Currently only the Blob service is supported.
signedAuthorizedObjectId	saoid	Optional	2020-02-10 or later	Specifies the object ID for an Azure AD security principal that is authorized by the owner of the user delegation key to perform the action granted by the SAS token. No additional permission check on POSIX ACLs is performed.
signedUnauthorizedObjectId	suoid	Optional	2020-02-10 or later	Specifies the object ID for an Azure AD security principal when a hierarchical namespace is enabled. Azure Storage performs a POSIX ACL check against the object ID before authorizing the operation.
signedCorrelationId	scid	Optional	2020-02-10 or later	Correlates the storage audit logs with the audit logs used by the principal generating and distributing SAS.

TABLE 5.8 Supported fields when creating a user delegation SAS token *(continued)*

SAS field name	SAS token parameter	Required or optional	Version support	Description
signedDirectoryDepth	sdd	Required when sr=d	2020-02-10 or later	Indicates the number of directories beneath the root folder of the directory specified in the canonicalized Resource field of the string-to-sign.
signedEncryptionScope	ses	Optional	2020-12-06 or later	Indicates the encryption scope to use to encrypt the request contents.
Signature	sig	Required	All	The signature is an HMAC computed over the string-to-sign and key using the SHA256 algorithm, and then encoded using Base64 encoding.
Cache-Control response header	rscc	Optional	2013-08-15 or later	Azure Storage sets the Cache-Control response header to the value specified on the SAS token.
Content-Disposition response header	rscd	Optional	2013-08-15 or later	Azure Storage sets the Content-Disposition response header to the value specified on the SAS token.
Content-Encoding response header	rsce	Optional	2013-08-15 or later	Azure Storage sets the Content-Encoding response header to the value specified on the SAS token.

SAS field name	SAS token parameter	Required or optional	Version support	Description
Content-Language response header	rscl	Optional	2013-08-15 or later	Azure Storage sets the Content-Language response header to the value specified on the SAS token.
Content-Type response header	rsct	Optional	2013-08-15 or later	Azure Storage sets the Content-Type response header to the value specified on the SAS token.

To create the SAS token, you can use PowerShell, Azure CLI, or .NET.

PowerShell

The first thing you need to do is ensure that you have PowerShell version 1.10.0 or later of the Az-Storage module installed. Follow these steps to install the latest version of the module:

1. You need to uninstall any previous installations of Azure PowerShell. You can do this in one of two ways:

    - Use the Apps & Features setting located under Settings.

    - Remove all Azure modules from %Program Files%\WindowsPowerShell\ Modules.

2. Open the Windows PowerShell window and run this command to install the latest version of PowerShellGet:

    ```
    Install-Module PowerShellGet -Repository PSGallery -Force
    ```

3. Close and reopen the PowerShell window after running the previous command.

4. Install the latest version of Azure PowerShell:

    ```
    Install-Module Az -Repository PSGallery -AllowClobber
    ```

5. Once you have PowerShell version 3.2.0 or later installed, run the following command to install the latest version of the Azure Storage PowerShell module:

    ```
    Install-Module -Name Az.Storage -Repository PSGallery -Force
    ```

6. Close and reopen the PowerShell window.

    You can check the version of the Az.Storage module installed by using this command:

```
Get-Module -ListAvailable -Name Az.Storage -Refresh
```

Signing into Azure PowerShell with Azure AD

It's important to note that when you create a user delegation SAS with PowerShell, the user delegation key will be implicitly created for you and the start time and expiry time that you use for the SAS will be used for the user delegation key. The maximum time you can set is seven days.

Now, to create a user delegation SAS for a container or blob, you first need to create a new Azure Storage context object—it uses the -UseConnectedAccount parameter. This parameter will create the context object under the Azure AD account with which you signed in. You can use the following command:

```
$ctx = New-AzStorageContext -StorageAccountName <storage-account>
-UseConnectedAccount
```

Creating a User Delegation SAS for Containers

To create a user delegation SAS for containers, you want to call NewAzStorageContainer SASToken and pass in the Azure Storage context object that you created previously. You can use this command to generate the token for a given container (replacing the placeholders with the appropriate values):

```
New-AzStorageContainerSASToken -Context $ctx `
    -Name <container> `
    -Permission racwdl `
    -ExpiryTime <date-time>
```

Creating a SAS Token for a Blob

Similar to the previous function used to create a SAS token for a blob, you use the New-AzStorageBlobSASToken command and pass it the Azure Storage context object that you created previously. Use the following command to generate the token (replacing the place-holders with the appropriate values):

```
New-AzStorageBlobSASToken -Context $ctx `
    -Container <container> `
    -Blob <blob> `
    -Permission racwd `
    -ExpiryTime <date-time>
    -FullUri
```

This example uses the -FullUri parameter, which means that it will return the blob URI with the SAS token appended to it. The output will look like the following:

```
https://storagesamples.blob.core.windows.net/sample-container/blob1.txt?sv=
2018-
11-09&sr=b&sig=<sig>&skoid=<skoid>&sktid=<sktid>&skt=2019-08-
06T21%3A16%3A54Z&ske=2019-08-07T07%3A00%3A00Z&sks=b&skv=2018-11-09&se=2019-08-
07T07%3A00%3A00Z&sp=racwd
```

Revoking a User Delegation SAS in PowerShell

If you ever need to revoke a user delegation SAS in PowerShell, use the `Revoke-AzStora` `geAccountUserDelegationKeys` command. This command revokes all the user delegation keys associated with the storage accounts, thus invalidating all the SASs associated with those keys. You can use the following command (replacing the placeholders with the appropriate values):

```
Revoke-AzStorageAccountUserDelegationKeys -ResourceGroupName
<resource-group> `
    -StorageAccountName <storage-account>
```

Creating a User Delegation SAS for a Container or Blob with Azure CLI

The first step in this process is to make sure that you have Azure CLI installed on your machine. The exact instructions vary depending on what type of machine you are using, but they can easily be found in the Azure documentation under "How to install the Azure CLI."

You need to log into the Azure CLI using your preferred method, through either the web browser or the Azure command line using the following command:

```
az login -u <username> -p <password>
```

Using Azure AD Credentials to Secure the SAS with Azure CLI

Similar to PowerShell, when creating the delegation SAS with Azure CLI, the user delegation key used to sign the SAS is created for you implicitly. The start and expiry time you specify will also be the start and expiry time for the user delegation key.

When creating the SAS, you must include the `--auth-mode login` and the `--as-user` parameters. You need to specify the `--auth-mode login` parameter so that the requests made to Azure Storage are authorized with your Azure AD credentials. Next, you must specify the `--as-user` parameter to indicate that the SAS should be returned as a user delegation SAS.

Creating a User Delegation SAS for a Blob

To create a user delegation SAS for a blob, you use the `az storage blob generate-SAS` command. The supported permissions for a user delegation SAS on a blob includes Add, Create, Delete, Read, and Write. You can use the following command to return a user delegation SAS for a blob. Please note that this example uses the `--full-uri` that you used earlier so that it will return the blob URI with the SAS token appended at the end:

```
az storage blob generate-sas \
    --account-name <storage-account> \
    --container-name <container> \
    --name <blob> \
    --permissions acdrw \
```

```
--expiry <date-time> \
--auth-mode login \
--as-user \
--full-uri
```

Revoking a User Delegation SAS Using the Azure CLI

To revoke a user delegation SAS using the Azure CLI, you call the `az storage account revoke-delegation-keys` command. This command revokes all the user delegation keys associated with the specified storage account, and thus invalidates all of the SASs associated with those keys:

```
az storage account revoke-delegation-keys \
    --name <storage-account> \
    --resource-group <resource-group>
```

Creating a User Delegation SAS with .NET

.NET is a free, cross-platform open-source developer platform. Within Azure, .NET allows you to host web applications with ASP.net—a set of tools and libraries for building web apps and services. In this instance, we are just using it to execute C# code. The first step for using .NET is to obtain a token credential that your code can use to authorize requests to Azure Storage. To do this, you will create an instance of the `DefaultAzureCredential` class. The following example shows this process for creating a service client for blob storage:

```
// Construct the blob endpoint from the account name.
string blobEndpoint = string.Format("https://{0}.blob.core.windows.net",
accountName);


// Create a new Blob service client with Azure AD credentials.
BlobServiceClient blobClient = new BlobServiceClient(new Uri(blobEndpoint),
                                                     new
DefaultAzureCredential());
```

Next, you need to obtain the user delegation key that will be used to sign the user delegation SAS. You can use one of the following two methods to request the user delegation key:

- `GetUserDelegationKey`
- `GetUserDelegationKeyAsync`

In the following example, we use the second option:

```
// Get a user delegation key for the Blob service that's valid for seven days.
// You can use the key to generate any number of shared access signatures over
the lifetime of the key.
UserDelegationKey key = await
blobClient.GetUserDelegationKeyAsync(DateTimeOffset.UtcNow,
DateTimeOffset.UtcNow.AddDays(7));
```

```
// Read the key's properties.
Console.WriteLine("User delegation key properties:");
Console.WriteLine("Key signed start: {0}", key.SignedStartsOn);
Console.WriteLine("Key signed expiry: {0}", key.SignedExpiresOn);
Console.WriteLine("Key signed object ID: {0}", key.SignedObjectId);
Console.WriteLine("Key signed tenant ID: {0}", key.SignedTenantId);
Console.WriteLine("Key signed service: {0}", key.SignedService);
Console.WriteLine("Key signed version: {0}", key.SignedVersion);
```

Creating a User Delegation SAS Using the *GetUserDelegationSasContainer* Command

This example uses the GetUserDelegationSasContainer command:

```
async static Task<Uri> GetUserDelegationSasContainer(BlobContainerClient
blobContainerClient)
{
    BlobServiceClient blobServiceClient = blobContainerClient.
GetParentBlobServiceClient();

    // Get a user delegation key for the Blob service that's valid for
seven days.
    // You can use the key to generate any number of shared access signatures
    // over the lifetime of the key.
    Azure.Storage.Blobs.Models.UserDelegationKey userDelegationKey =
        await
    blobServiceClient.GetUserDelegationKeyAsync(DateTimeOffset.UtcNow,
    DateTimeOffset.UtcNow.AddDays(7));

    // Create a SAS token that's also valid for seven days.
    BlobSasBuilder sasBuilder = new BlobSasBuilder()
    {
        BlobContainerName = blobContainerClient.Name,
        Resource = "c",
        StartsOn = DateTimeOffset.UtcNow,
        ExpiresOn = DateTimeOffset.UtcNow.AddDays(7)
    };

    // Specify racwl permissions for the SAS.
    sasBuilder.SetPermissions(
        BlobContainerSasPermissions.Read |
```

```
        BlobContainerSasPermissions.Add |
        BlobContainerSasPermissions.Create |
        BlobContainerSasPermissions.Write |
        BlobContainerSasPermissions.List
        );


    // Add the SAS token to the container URI.
    BlobUriBuilder blobUriBuilder = new BlobUriBuilder(blobContainer
Client.Uri)
    {
        // Specify the user delegation key.
        Sas = sasBuilder.ToSasQueryParameters(userDelegationKey,
                                        blobServiceClient.AccountName)
    };


    Console.WriteLine("Container user delegation SAS URI: {0}",
blobUriBuilder);
    Console.WriteLine();
    return blobUriBuilder.ToUri();
}
```

The following code block is a test that you can run to see if the SAS is valid. If the SAS is not valid, it should return an error code 403 (i.e., forbidden).

```
private static async Task ListBlobsWithSasAsync(Uri sasUri)
{
    // Try performing a listing operation using the container SAS provided.

    // Create a container client object for blob operations.
    BlobContainerClient blobContainerClient = new BlobContainerClient(sasUri,
null);

    // List blobs in the container.
    try
    {
        // Call the listing operation and return pages of the specified size.
        var resultSegment = blobContainerClient.GetBlobsAsync().AsPages();

        // Enumerate the blobs returned for each page.
        await foreach (Azure.Page<BlobItem> blobPage in resultSegment)
        {
            foreach (BlobItem blobItem in blobPage.Values)
            {
```

```
                    Console.WriteLine("Blob name: {0}", blobItem.Name);
                }
                Console.WriteLine();
            }


        Console.WriteLine();
        Console.WriteLine("Blob listing operation succeeded for SAS {0}",
sasUri);
        }
    catch (RequestFailedException e)
    {
        // Check for a 403 (Forbidden) error. If the SAS is invalid,
        // Azure Storage returns this error.
        if (e.Status == 403)
        {
            Console.WriteLine("Blob listing operation failed for SAS {0}",
sasUri);
            Console.WriteLine("Additional error information: " + e.Message);
            Console.WriteLine();
        }
        else
        {
            Console.WriteLine(e.Message);
            Console.ReadLine();
            throw;
        }
    }
    }
}
```

Creating a User Delegation SAS for a Directory

This section discusses how you can create a user delegation SAS for a directory rather than an individual file or resource. Following is an example of the code you can use to create a user delegation SAS:

```
async static Task<Uri> GetUserDelegationSasDirectory(DataLakeDirectoryClient
directoryClient)
{
    try
    {
        // Get service endpoint from the directory URI.
        DataLakeUriBuilder dataLakeServiceUri = new DataLakeUriBuilder(directory
Client.Uri)
```

```
        {
            FileSystemName = null,
            DirectoryOrFilePath = null
        };

        // Get service client.
        DataLakeServiceClient dataLakeServiceClient =
            new DataLakeServiceClient(dataLakeServiceUri.ToUri(),
                                    new DefaultAzureCredential());

        // Get a user delegation key that's valid for seven days.
        // You can use the key to generate any number of shared access
signatures
        // over the lifetime of the key.
        Azure.Storage.Files.DataLake.Models.UserDelegationKey
userDelegationKey =
            await
dataLakeServiceClient.GetUserDelegationKeyAsync(DateTimeOffset.UtcNow,

DateTimeOffset.UtcNow.AddDays(7));

        // Create a SAS token that's valid for seven days.
        DataLakeSasBuilder sasBuilder = new DataLakeSasBuilder()
        {
            // Specify the file system name and path, and indicate that
            // the client object points to a directory.
            FileSystemName = directoryClient.FileSystemName,
            Resource = "d",
            IsDirectory = true,
            Path = directoryClient.Path,
            ExpiresOn = DateTimeOffset.UtcNow.AddDays(7)
        };

        // Specify racwl permissions for the SAS.
        sasBuilder.SetPermissions(
            DataLakeSasPermissions.Read |
            DataLakeSasPermissions.Add |
            DataLakeSasPermissions.Create |
            DataLakeSasPermissions.Write |
            DataLakeSasPermissions.List
            );
```

```
        // Construct the full URI, including the SAS token.
        DataLakeUriBuilder fullUri = new
DataLakeUriBuilder(directoryClient.Uri)
        {
            Sas = sasBuilder.ToSasQueryParameters(userDelegationKey,
dataLakeServiceClient.AccountName)
        };

        Console.WriteLine("Directory user delegation SAS URI: {0}", fullUri);
        Console.WriteLine();
        return fullUri.ToUri();
    }
    catch (Exception e)
    {
        Console.WriteLine(e.Message);
        throw;
    }
}
```

The following code is a test that you can run to confirm that the user delegation SAS was created and running successfully.

```
private static async Task ListFilesPathsWithDirectorySasAsync(Uri sasUri)
{
    // Try performing an operation using the directory SAS provided.

    // Create a directory client object for listing operations.
    DataLakeDirectoryClient dataLakeDirectoryClient = new
DataLakeDirectoryClient(sasUri);

    // List file paths in the directory.
    try
    {
        // Call the listing operation and return pages of the specified size.
        var resultSegment = dataLakeDirectoryClient.GetPathsAsync(false,
false).AsPages();

        // Enumerate the file paths returned with each page.
        await foreach (Page<PathItem> pathPage in resultSegment)
        {
            foreach (PathItem pathItem in pathPage.Values)
            {
```

```
            Console.WriteLine("File name: {0}", pathItem.Name);
        }
        Console.WriteLine();
    }


    Console.WriteLine();
    Console.WriteLine("Directory listing operation succeeded for SAS {0}",
sasUri);
    }
    catch (RequestFailedException e)
    {
        // Check for a 403 (Forbidden) error. If the SAS is invalid,
        // Azure Storage returns this error.
        if (e.Status == 403)
        {
            Console.WriteLine("Directory listing operation failed for SAS
{0}", sasUri);
            Console.WriteLine("Additional error information: " + e.Message);
            Console.WriteLine();
        }
        else
        {
            Console.WriteLine(e.Message);
            Console.ReadLine();
            throw;
        }
    }
}
}
```

Best Practices for SAS

Microsoft has identified two primary risks when using SAS in your applications:

- If a SAS is leaked, it may be used by anyone who has it, which would constitute a compromise of your storage account.

- If a SAS provided to a client application expires before it can be replaced, then the application will be unable to function, which can lead to major business disruptions.

Here are the following recommendations for using SAS that aid in mitigating these potential risks:

Always use HTTPS.   Whenever you create or distribute a SAS, you should pass it over HTTPs. If a SAS is passed over HTTP, it can be intercepted and read by an attacker using a man-in-the-middle attack.

Use a user delegation SAS whenever possible.   User delegation SASs have better security compared to a service SAS or an account SAS. User delegation SAS is secured with Azure AD credentials, which means you don't need to store your account key with the code.

Have a plan for revoking all SASs.   In the event that a SAS is compromised, you need to be able to revoke it as soon as possible to prevent misuse of that access.

Define the stored access policy for your service SAS.   This definition gives you the option to revoke permission for a service SAS without having to regenerate the storage account keys. This way, you can then set the expiration date on storage account keys very far into the future and simply revoke permissions to any SAS you created as needed.

Use near-term expiration dates on ad hoc SASs.   Even if a SAS is compromised, it will only be for a short time period and there will be limited unauthorized access. It also limits the amount of data that can be written to a blob by limiting the time available to upload to it.

Configure your clients to automatically renew the SAS as necessary.   You should review the SAS well before expiration to allow time for retries if the service providing the SAS is unavailable. This way, you are more likely to always have a valid SAS to use for accessing applications.

Set your SAS start time to 15 minutes in the past.   If you set the start time for a SAS to the current time, you may have failures for the first few minutes. This is because different machines have different current times, and therefore, it may not be active yet. As a general rule, try to set your SAS start time at least 15 minutes in the past so that it will be valid on all machines. Or, you can also choose not to specify a start time just be safe.

Be mindful of the SAS date-time format.   Make sure you understand the date-time format that your SAS is using so that you can set it for exactly the right time. Otherwise, you may give more or less access than you intended over the wrong time period.

Be specific with the resource to be accessed.   This goes back to the practice of least privilege. You want to ensure that you are granting access to the least number of resources possible and sharing the SAS with the least number of people required for the job to get done. In the event that the SAS is compromised, it will have less impact because the SAS has less access to company resources.

Know that your account will be billed for any usage, including through SAS.   If a user uses your SAS to upload or download, then you will be charged for that usage. If you share to multiple users (maybe a few hundred or thousand), then these costs can add up quickly, so keep that in mind when assigning access and sharing it with users.

Validate data written using SAS.   When a client application writes data to a storage account, there can be problems with the data that could cause errors if it was later used by an application. Microsoft suggests that you perform data validation *after* the data is written and *before* it is used by any of your applications. This helps protect you against corrupt or malicious data being written to your account by a user who has access to the SAS.

Understand when not to use a SAS.   Often, the risk associated with an operation against your storage account may outweigh the benefits of using a SAS. In these situations, Microsoft suggests that you create a middle-tier service that writes to your storage account after performing a business rule validation, authentication, and auditing. It can also be much simpler to manage access in other ways, such as making the container for a blob public rather than providing a SAS to every client that needs access.

Use Azure Monitor and Azure Storage logs to monitor your applications.   Authorization can fail due to an outage of your SAS provider's service or an accidental removal of a stored access policy. You may leverage Azure Monitor and Azure Storage Analytics logging to monitor for any spike in authorization failures. This way, you can be alerted and take action to resolve the issue.

Configuring Security for Databases

In this section, we will discuss how to secure your Azure SQL databases.

Enabling Database Authentication by Using Azure AD

First, let's discuss Azure's database service, Azure SQL Database. This tool is a platform as a service (PaaS) database engine that handles the majority of database management functions in Azure. Most of these functions can be done without user involvement, including upgrading, patching, backups, and monitoring.

Azure SQL database allows you to create data storage for applications and solutions in Azure while also providing high availability and good performance. It allows applications to process both relational data and nonrelational structures, such as graphs, JSON, spatial, and XML.

Azure SQL database can be deployed in one of two ways in the Azure environment:

- **Single Database:** A fully managed and isolated database that can be moved in and out of an elastic pool after its creation

- **Elastic Pool:** A collection of individual databases that use a shared set of resources, such as memory

Scalable Performance and Pools for Databases

Azure allows you to define the amount of resources allocated for your databases regardless of whether it's single or part of an elastic pool:

- **Single Databases:** For a single database, each will have its own amount of computer memory and storage resources. You can dynamically scale the resources up or down, depending on the needs of that database.

- **Elastic Pools:** In this case, you assign resources to a pool of machines that will be shared by all databases in the pool. To save money, you will need to move existing single databases into the resource pool to maximize the use of the resources.

There are two ways that databases can scale as resources are being used: via dynamic scalability and autoscaling. Dynamic scalability allows for manual scaling of resources with minimal downtime, while autoscaling is when a service automatically scales based on certain criteria. For better automation, it's better to use elastic pools because the resources will be shared based on individual database needs without the need for human intervention. For single databases, you can also use scripts to help automate scalability. Look up "Use Power-Shell to monitor and scale a single database" on Google and consult the Microsoft documentation if that is of interest to you.

Monitoring and Alerting Capabilities

Azure SQL Database comes with built-in monitoring and troubleshooting features to help you find out how your databases are performing and to help you monitor and troubleshoot database instances. Query Store is a built-in SQL server-monitoring feature that records the performance of your queries in real time. It helps you find potential performance issues in addition to the top resources for consumers. It uses a feature called *automatic tuning*, which is an intelligent performance service that continuously monitors queries executed on a database and uses the information it gathers to automatically improve their performance. Automatic tuning in SQL database allows you to choose two options: First, you can manually apply the tuning recommendations by running the scripts required to fix the issue, or you can let SQL Database apply the fix automatically. Second, SQL Database can test and verify that the fix is beneficial. Based on its evaluation, it will then retain or revert the change.

In addition to the performance monitoring and alerting tools, Azure SQL Database gives you performance ratings that allow you to monitor the status of thousands of databases as you scale up or down. This allows you to view the effect of making these changes based on your current and projected performance needs. You can also generate metrics and resource logs for further monitoring of your database environment.

Database Resiliency Capabilities

Azure SQL Database has several features that help you continue business operations during disruptions. In traditional SQL Server environments, you have at least two machines set up locally that have exact, synchronously maintained copies of data to prevent against a failure of one of the machines. While this provides good availability, it doesn't protect against a natural disaster that destroys both physical machines.

Azure SQL provides options for ensuring that you have your data stored in locations far enough away that no single catastrophic event can bring down all your services. This is primarily done by spreading replicas of your database in different availability zones. Azure availability zones are physically separated and stored in different locations within each Azure region, which allows them to be tolerant to local failures. Azure defines *failures* as occurrences that can cause outages, such as software and hardware failures, earthquakes, floods, and fires. Azure ensures that a minimum of three separate availability zones are present in all availability zone–enabled regions. These datacenter locations are selected using vulnerability risk assessment criteria created by Microsoft that identify all significant datacenter-related risks. It also considers risks that may be shared between availability zones. You can use availability zones to design and operate databases that will automatically transition between zones as needed without interrupting any of your services.

The Azure service level agreement (SLA) helps you maintain ongoing service 24/7 by mandating that Azure takes certain actions on behalf of its customers. The Azure platform completely manages every database, and it guarantees no data loss with a high percentage of data availability. Azure also guarantees that it will handle patching; backups; replication; failure detection; underlying potential hardware, software, and network failures; deploying bug fixes; failovers; database upgrades; and a few other maintenance tasks.

The last notable features for SQL databases encompass its built-in business continuity and global scalability features, which include:

Automatic Backups   SQL Database will automatically create full, differential, and transaction log backups of your databases that will allow you to restore your data up to any point in time. You may also configure SQL databases to store full database backups in Azure Storage for long-term retention.

Point-in-Time Restores   All SQL database deployment options allow for recovery to any point in time within the automatic backup retention period for a database.

Active Geo-replication   For both single and pooled databases, you can configure up to four readable secondary databases in the same or globally distributed datacenters. This helps to prevent an overload on the primary databases due to read requests and allows for the use of auto-failover groups in the event of an issue with the primary databases.

Auto-Failover Groups   These are a means for ensuring high availability and load balancing at scale. SQL Database handles all of the monitoring, routing, and failover orchestration to databases distributed globally.

Zone-Redundant Databases   SQL Database allows you to provision critical databases or elastic pool replicas across availability zones to give you the ability to recover automatically from a datacenter failure without data loss.

Enabling Database Authentication by Using Azure AD

Azure AD authentication is a method for connecting to Azure SQL Database, Azure SQL Managed Instance, and Synapse SQL in Azure Synapse Analytics using identities in Azure AD. The benefit of Azure AD authentication is that you can manage the identities of database users and Microsoft services in one central location. Here are some of the other benefits of using Azure AD for database authentication:

- It's an alternative to SQL server authentication.
- All password rotation occurs in a single place.
- It eliminates the need for storing passwords by enabling Integrated Windows Authentication and other types of authentication supported by Azure AD.

- It supports token-based authentication for applications that need to connect to SQL Database and SQL managed instances.

- It supports multifactor authentication, which adds an extra layer of strong authentication using easy verification options, such as phone calls, text message, and smartcards with PIN or mobile app notification.

The configuration steps for using Azure AD authentication are as follows:

1. Create and populate Azure AD.

2. Optional step: Associate or change the AD that is currently associated with your Azure subscription.

3. Create an Azure Active Directory Administrator.

4. Configure your client computers.

5. Create contained database users in your database mapped to Azure AD identities.

6. Connect to your database by using Azure AD identities.

Creating and Populating Azure AD

To use Azure AD, you need to have created Azure AD and populated it with the users that you want. It doesn't matter whether you sync your on-premises AD with Azure AD or if you created it from scratch, but it needs to have all the users that you plan to use set up.

Associating or Changing the AD Currently Associated with Your Azure Subscription

Every Azure subscription has a trust relationship with Azure AD to facilitate authentication of users, services, and devices. It's important to note that multiple subscriptions can trust the same Azure AD directory, but each subscription can only trust one directory.

It's important to know that when you associate a subscription with a different directory user that has roles assigned using Azure, RBAC will lose access. So, before you make the association, check the following.

1. Understand the following list of changes that will occur if you associate or add the subscription and how it could affect your environment:

    - Users that have been given roles using RBAC will lose their access, which can have a big impact on business operations.

    - Service administrators and co-administrators will lose their access.

    - If you have any key vaults, they'll become inaccessible and you'll have to fix them after the association.

    - For managed identities used by resources such as VMs or Logic Apps, you will need to re-enable or re-create them after the association.

    - If you have a registered Azure Stack, you'll need to re-register it after the association.

2. Make sure to sign in using an account that:

    ▪   Has an owner role assignment for the subscription

    ▪   Exists in both the current directory and new directory. The current directory should be associated with the subscription that you'll associate with the new directory.

    ▪   Make sure you are not using an Azure Cloud Service Provider (CSP) subscription (MS-AZR-0145P, MS-AZR-0146P, MS-AZR-159P), a Microsoft Internal Subscription (MS-AZR-0015P), or a Microsoft Azure for Students Starter subscription (MS-AZR-0144P).

3. To associate an existing subscription with your Azure AD directory (`https://docs.microsoft.com/en-us/azure/active-directory/fundamentals/active-directory-how-subscriptions-associated-directory#associate-a-subscription-to-a-directory`), follow these steps:

    a. First, sign in and select the subscription you want to use from the Subscriptions page in the Azure portal.

    b. Choose Change Directory.

    c. Review any warnings that appear and then select Change. After the directory has been changed for the subscription, you will receive a success message.

    d. Select Switch Directories on the Subscription page to go to your new directory.

It may take several hours for everything to show up correctly. Once you have made the change, use the directory switcher in the Azure portal to switch to the subscription associated with the domain.

Creating an Azure Active Directory Administrator

Each server in Azure that hosts an SQL Database starts with a single server admin account that will be the admin of the entire server. You want to use this account to create a second administrator account as an Azure AD account. This person will be a member of the db_owner role in every user database and enter each user database as the dbo user. To provision an Azure admin for your database, log in as Global Administrator and follow these steps:

1. In the Azure portal, go to the upper-right corner and select your connection from the drop-down list of possible Azure Active directories.

2. Choose the correct directory as the default Azure AD.

3. Navigate to the SQL database you want to use for the Azure AD integration.

4. Select the banner on top of the Active Directory Admin page and grant permission to the current user.

    After the operation is successful, you will receive a notification saying that it was successful.

5. Once the operation is completed, you can choose the Azure AD admin of your choice for your SQL Managed Instance. On the AD admin page, select the Set Admin command.

6. On the Azure Active Directory admin page, search and select the user or group for which you want to be an admin, and then choose Select. The Active Directory admin page should show all members and groups in your Active Directory. Users or groups who are grayed out can't be selected because they cannot be Azure AD admins.

7. At the top of the Active Directory admin page, select Save. It may take a few minutes for the change to take effect and for the new admin to appear in the Active Directory admin box.

Configuring Your Client Computers

On every client machine from which your applications or users connect to a SQL Database, you must install the following software:

- .NET Framework 4.6 or later
- Azure Active Directory Authentication Library for SQL Server (ADAL.DLL)

Creating Contained Database Users in Your Database Mapped to Azure AD Identities

SQL Managed Instance supports Azure AD server principals (logins) so that contained database users are not required to log in from Azure AD users, groups, or applications. However, using Azure AD authentication with SQL Database and Azure Synapse does require a contained database user based on an Azure AD identity. A contained database user does not have a login in the master database; instead, it maps to an identity in Azure AD that is associated with the database. This identity may be an individual user account or a group.

To create an Azure AD–based contained database user (with the exception of a server admin), connect to the database with an Azure AD identity as a user with at least the ALTER ANY USER permission. Then use the transact-SQL syntax here (replacing the placeholder with a legitimate name):

```
CREATE USER [<Azure_AD_principal_name>] FROM EXTERNAL PROVIDER;
```

To create a contained database user representing an application that will connect using an Azure AD token, use this syntax:

```
CREATE USER [appName] FROM EXTERNAL PROVIDER;
```

Once you create a database user, they will receive the CONNECT permission, which allows them to connect to that database as a member of the PUBLIC role. At first, the only permissions that the user will have within the database will be those granted to the PUBLIC role, or any permissions granted to any Azure AD groups of which the user is a member. Once you provision an Azure AD–based contained database user, you can grant the user additional permissions. You can still use RBAC by granting permissions to database roles and adding users to those roles.

Connecting to Your Database by Using Azure AD Identities

You can connect to a SQL database using an Azure AD identity and SQL Server Management Studio or SQL Server Database Tools.

AD Integrated Authentication

You can use this method as long as you are logged into Windows with your Azure AD credentials from a federated domain or a managed domain. These credentials must be configured for seamless SSO. Follow these steps to connect to the database using this method:

1. Start Management Studio or Data Tools. Enter the server name in the Server Name dialog box, and select Azure Active Directory–Integrated in the Authentication box.

2. Select the Options button. From the Connection Properties page, go to the Connect To Database box and type the name of the user database to which you want to connect.

AD Password Authentication

This method can be used to connect with an Azure AD principal name using the Azure AD managed domain. This method allows you to authenticate to the database in SQL Database or the SQL Managed Instance with Azure AD cloud-only identity users or those who use Azure AD hybrid identities. It is designed to support users who want to use their Windows credentials when their local machine is not joined with the domain (e.g., in remote access situations). In this type of authentication, a Windows user can indicate their domain account and password to authenticate to the database in SQL Database, the SQL Managed Instance, or Azure Synapse. Follow these steps to use this type of authentication:

1. Start Management Studio or Data Tools and navigate to the Authentication box. Then select Azure Active Directory Password.

2. Next, in the Username box, type your Azure AD username in the format ***myusername@ domain.com***. It must be a username from Azure AD or an account from a managed or federated domain with Azure AD.

3. In the Password box, type the user password for the account you have chosen.

4. Lastly, click the Options button and on the Connection properties page, go to the Connect To Database box and type the name of the user database to which you want to connect.

Using an Azure AD Identity to Connect from a Client Application

In order to use Integrated Windows Authentication, your domain's Active Directory must be federated with Azure AD or at least be a managed domain that is configured for seamless SSO for pass-through or password hash authentication.

The client application that wants to connect to the database must be running on a domain-joined machine under a user's domain credentials.

To successfully connect to a database using integrated authentication and an Azure AD identity, ensure that the `Authentication` keyword in the database connection string is set to `Active Directory Integrated`. You can use the following code to achieve this:

```
string ConnectionString = @"Data Source=n9lxnyuzhv.database.windows.net;
Authentication=Active Directory Integrated; Initial Catalog=testdb;";
SqlConnection conn = new SqlConnection(ConnectionString);
conn.Open();
```

Active Directory Password Authentication

To connect to a database using Azure AD cloud-only identity user account(s) who use Azure AD hybrid identities, you need to set the `Authentication` keyword to `Active Directory Password`. The connection string must contain the `User ID/UID` and `Pass word/PWD` keywords and their respective values. Here is a sample of this in C# code that uses ADO.Net:

```
string ConnectionString =
@"Data Source=n9lxnyuzhv.database.windows.net; Authentication=Active
Directory Password; Initial Catalog=testdb;  UID=bob@contoso.onmicrosoft.com;
PWD=MyPassWord!";
SqlConnection conn = new SqlConnection(ConnectionString);
conn.Open();
```

Azure AD Token

This authentication method allows Azure services to obtain JSON Web Tokens (JWTs) that can be used to connect to a database in SQL Database, SQL Managed Instance, or Azure Synapse via a token from Azure AD. This method allows Azure entities like service identities, service principals, and applications to authenticate using certificate-based authentication. There are four steps to using Azure AD token authentication:

1. Register your application with Azure AD, and then get the client ID from the application.
2. Create a database user representing the application.
3. Create a certificate on the client computer that runs the application.
4. Add the certificate as a key for your application.

Here is a sample of the connection string you would run to connect once you have fulfilled the previous requirements:

```
string ConnectionString = @"Data Source=n9lxnyuzhv.database.windows.net;
Initial Catalog=testdb;";
SqlConnection conn = new SqlConnection(ConnectionString);
conn.AccessToken = "Your JWT token";
conn.Open();
```

Enabling Database Auditing

In IT , an audit is an examination and evaluation of an organization's IT infrastructure, policies, and operations. The goal of the audit is to determine whether the IT controls are working correctly to protect corporate assets and ensure data integrity and availability, and to determine if they're properly aligned with the business's overall goals. This includes both the technical and physical security controls. Your primary objectives of an audit can be summarized as follows:

1. Evaluate the systems, controls, and processes that secure the company's data and systems.

2. Identify the risks to the company's information assets and the best methods to minimize those risks.

3. Ensure that your IT processes are in compliance with the appropriate laws, policies, and standards.

4. Identify any inefficiencies in IT systems and its associated management.

As mentioned previously, audits are aimed at ensuring that companies can adequately protect their information assets and this includes both prevention and detection. Databases are central repositories for company data and contain on average 43 percent (www .sqlshack.com/a-quick-overview-of-database-audit-in-sql) of all sensitive enterprise data held within the company. In a database audit, you are specifically inspecting the security controls that you have set in place to protect your databases from exploitation. During this inspection, you're primarily reviewing logging events that occurred on the server instance or in a database and were saved as audit files to be reviewed at a later date. Here are some components that you must focus on when auditing an SQL Database:

Access and Authentication As much as 48 percent (www.sqlshack.com/a-quick-overview-of-database-audit-in-sql) of data breaches result from the abuse of privileges. Therefore, you'll want to focus on measuring and understanding the controls on how your database authenticates its users, in addition to gathering details about who accessed which databases when and how.

Users and Administrator This component details the activities that were performed in the database by application users and administrators. It allows you to detect suspicious or potentially harmful behaviors.

Security Alerts This component includes identifying and flagging any suspicious activity and unusual or abnormal access to sensitive data.

Database Vulnerabilities and Threat Detection As part of the auditing process, you'll want to consistently scan your databases and the servers that they are running on for any vulnerabilities. Doing so will enable you to quickly take action to patch the vulnerabilities in those systems and to prevent hackers from being able to exploit them in order to gain access to company data.

Baseline Tracking You should understand what secure database configuration is for your environment. Part of your audit should include comparing your databases to that secure baseline and tracking any deviations from that baseline.

In Azure, SQL database auditing is summarized in three main areas:

Retain: This is an audit trail of chosen events, where you get to choose which categories of database actions you want to be audited.

Report: This allows you to use preconfigured reports to quickly visualize activities and events.

Analyze: This allows you to analyze reports and find suspicious events, unusual activity, and trends.

Server-Level vs. Database-Level Auditing Policy

Auditing in Azure is facilitated through the creation of an auditing policy, which can be defined for a specific database or as a default server policy in Azure (that will host SQL Database or Azure Synapse). A server policy will apply to all the existing and newly created databases on that server. If server auditing is enabled, it will always apply to the database regardless of the database auditing settings. Neither policy overrides the other. The database will therefore be audited twice in parallel—once by the server policy, then by the database policy.

Enabling Auditing for Your Server

To enable auditing on your server, follow these steps:

1. Navigate to the Azure portal.

2. Go to Auditing under the Security heading in the SQL database or under the SQL Server pane.

3. If you want to create a server auditing policy from scratch, then select the View Server Settings link on the Database Auditing page. You can view or modify the server auditing settings, and it will be applied to all existing and newly created databases on this server.

4. If you want to enable auditing on the database level, switch Auditing to On. Remember, you can enable server auditing and database auditing if you want them to exist side by side.

5. Once you have decided the type of auditing that you want to enable, you need to configure where the audit logs will be written, too. You can choose between storing them in an Azure Storage account, a Log Analytics workspace for integration with Azure Monitor logs, or an event hub for consumption. You can select any combination of these options, including all three.

6. Optional: Once you have selected where you will store your audit logs, you will be given the option Enable Auditing Of Microsoft Support Operations. This option allows you to track Microsoft Support Engineers (DevOps) operations on your server and writes them to an audit log in your Azure Storage account, Log Analytics workspace, or event hub.

7. Next, you must configure the audit logging to whatever storage destination you have selected:

- **Storage Account:** To configure writing audit logs for a storage account, select Storage in the Audit Log Destination section. Select the name of the Azure Storage account where the logs should be saved, select your desired retention period by opening Advanced Properties, and select Save. Any logs older than the retention period that you choose will be deleted. You have the option to keep the default value of 0 for a retention period, which that means that no logs will ever be deleted. Also, it's important to understand that changing the retention period only affects the logs that are written *after* the retention value is changed. All of the logs from before the change will be preserved.

- **Log Analytics Workspace:** To configure writing audit logs to a Log Analytics workspace, select Log Analytics in the Audit Log Destination section. From the Log Analytics drop-down list, select the Log Analytics workspace where the logs will be written and click OK.

- **Event Hub:** To configure writing audit logs to an event hub, select Event Hub in the Audit Log Destination section. Next, select the event hub where the logs will be written from the Event Hub Namespace drop-down list and click Save. For this to work, the event hub must be in the same region as your database and server.

We have finished enabling database audit logging. Next, we're going to look at how to analyze the audit logs and reports. Simply collecting the logs themselves isn't very useful if you don't know how to read and interpret the information contained within them.

Analyzing Audit Logs and Reports

Once you have the log files collected, you need be able to analyze these logs to find events of interest (EOIs). In this section, we will look at how to do this analysis and generate reports.

Log Analytics

If you choose to store your audit logs in Log Analytics, here are the steps you need to follow:

1. Navigate to the Azure portal and open the relevant database. At the top of the database's Auditing page, click View Audit Logs.

2. You have two options for viewing the logs.

   a. First, you can click Log Analytics at the top of the Audits Records page that just opened. Here you can change the time range and search queries. You can also select to view the dashboard at the top of the Audit Records page that will open a dashboard displaying the audit logs info (see Figure 5.2). Here you can navigate to Security Insights, access Sensitive Data (see Figure 5.3), and so on. It's designed to easily display Security Insights for your data based on your audit logs.

FIGURE 5.2 Audit log info

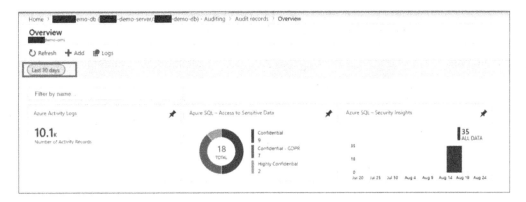

FIGURE 5.3 Security Insights

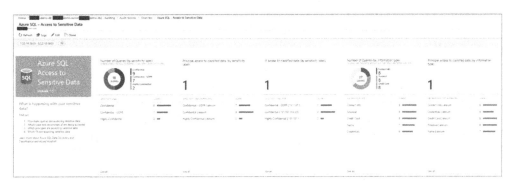

    b.   Your second option is to access the audit logs via the Log Analytics tab. To do so, open the Log Analytics workspace. In the General section, select Logs. Here you can perform queries to view audit logs. A simple example is running **search "SQLSe curityAuditEvents"**. In addition, you may also use Azure Monitor logs to run advanced searches on your audit logs.

Event Hub

If you choose to store your audit logs in Event Hub, you will need to set up a stream to consume events and write them to your target storage. When using Event Hub, audit logs are captured in the body of Apache Avro and later stored using JSON formatting and UTF-8 encoding. If you're not familiar with Apache Avro, it's a data serialization system in Azure. To read the audit logs, you will need to use Avro Tools (or something similar) to process the audit logs.

Azure Storage Accounts

There are multiple ways to view audit logs in an Azure Storage Account:

- You can explore audit logs via a tool like Azure Storage Explorer—a tool designed for uploading, downloading, and managing Azure Storage blobs, files, queues, and tables. In Azure Storage accounts, auditing logs are saved as a collection of blob files within a container called `sqldbauditlogs`.

- You can also explore audit logs via the Azure portal. Within the Azure Portal, open the database that you want to explore. At the top of the database's Auditing page, select View Audit Logs. This will open the Audit Records page and you'll be able to view the logs:
  - You can view specific dates by clicking Filter.
  - You can switch between the audit records created by using a Server Audit policy and your Database Audit policy by changing Audit Source.

- You can use the system function `sys.fn_get_audit_file` (T-SQL) to return the audit log data in a tabular format.

- Finally, you can use Merge Audit Files in SQL Server Management Studio (beginning with SSMS 17):
  - From the SSMS menu, select File ➤ Open ➤ Merge Audit Files.
  - The Add Audit Files dialog box will open. Select one of the Add options and choose to combine your audit files from a local disk or import them from Azure Storage. You will need to provide the Azure Storage details and account key.
  - After you have selected all the files you want to merge, click OK to complete the process.
  - The merged file will open in SSMS. Here you can view and analyze all of the log files as well as export them to an XEL or CSV file or into a table.

- You can use Power BI, which is a collection of software services, apps, and connectors that takes data from your Azure environment and turns it into interactive insights. You can view and analyze audit log data in Power BI.

- Lastly, you can download log files from your Azure Storage blob container via the portal or by using tools like Azure Storage Explorer.

Configuring Dynamic Data Masking on SQL Workloads

Dynamic data masking (DDM) is a technique for limiting sensitive data exposure by masking that data to nonprivileged users. DDM helps to improve an application's security by limiting the data that nonauthorized users can access. Refer back to Figure 5.3 for an example of what data masking would look like in a table of data.

When you use DDM, it allows customers to state how much sensitive data they want to reveal. DDM can be configured on specified database fields to hide sensitive data when returning results for a set of database queries. Using DDM doesn't change the data in the database; it simply changes what is displayed to users. This makes it very easy to use with existing applications because it doesn't need to change anything on the backend or even the actual queries themselves.

Defining a DDM Rule

You can define masking rules for a defined column in a table; this will allow you to obfuscate the data in that column (`https://docs.microsoft.com/en-us/azure/virtual-network/manage-network-security-group#before-you-begin`), as shown in Table 5.9:

TABLE 5.9   DDM rule descriptions

Function	Description
Default	This allows for full masking, depending on the data type in the designated field.
	For the string data type, you should use XXXX, depending on the number of characters that need to be masked.
	For the numeric data type, you would use a zero value instead of an X.
	For the date and time data type, you should use 01-01-1900 00:00:00.0000000.
	For the binary data type, you should use a single byte of ASCII value 0.
Email	This masking method will expose the first letter of the email address and the constant suffix of .com. It will take the form of an email address: sXX@XXX.com.
Random	This masking function can be used on any numeric type to mask the original value with a random value for a given range.
Custom String	This is a method that reveals the first and last letters of the string and adds a custom padding for the middle portion of the string.

DDM Permissions

The permissions required for creating a table with a DDM is the standard CREATE TABLE and ALTER on schema permissions. To add, replace, or remove the mask of a column, you need the ALTER ANY MASK permission and ALTER permission on that table. There's also an ALTER ANY MASK permission that you can assign to allow someone to alter any mask.

For users to view table data, they will need the SELECT permission on the table. Columns that are defined as masked will display only masked data. Grant a user the UNMASK permission to enable them to see unmasked data from the columns that have masking enabled.

The most powerful permission you can assign is the CONTROL permission. This includes both the ALTER ANY MASK and UNMASK permission.

Dynamic Masking Limitations

You cannot create a masking rule for the following column types (https://docs.microsoft.com/en-us/azure/virtual-network/manage-network-security-group#before-you-begin):

- Encrypted columns (Always Encrypted).

- FILESTREAM.

- COLUMN_SET or a column that is part of a column set.

- A mask cannot be configured on a computed column, but if the computed column depends on a column with a mask, then the computed column will return masked data.

- A column with data masking cannot be used as a key for a FULLTEXT index.

- A column in a PolyBase external table.

Adding a DDM cannot be implemented on a column with dependencies under normal conditions. To work around this, you would be required to remove the dependency, add the DDM, and then re-create the dependency.

If you have an expression referencing a column that has a data-masking function defined, then the expression will also be masked regardless of the type of function used to mask the column.

Cross-database queries that span two different Azure SQL databases, databases hosted on different SQL Server instances, and those that involve any kind of comparison or join operation using MASKED columns will not provide accurate results. This is because the data returned from the remote server will already be in MASKED form, and therefore will not reflect the true values of the data in the table.

Common Use Cases for DDM

The following are the common use cases for using DDM:

- Creating a mask on a column will not prevent updates to the column, meaning that while users may receive masked data when performing a query on that column, those same users may still have permissions to update the data if they have write permissions. Best practices for proper access control dictates that you should limit the update permissions for your databases, not just masking data (limiting view permission).

- Using SELECT INTO or INSERT INTO commands to copy data from a masked column into another table will result in masked data in the target table.

- When DDM is applied while running SQL Server Import and Export:

  - A database that has masked columns will result in an exported file with masked data (if the exporting user doesn't have UNMASK privileges).

  - An imported database will contain statically masked data.

Enabling Dynamic Data Masking

In this section we will look at how to enable DDM in Azure.

1. Navigate to the Azure portal, then to your database resource within the Azure portal.

2. Select the Dynamic Data Masking blade under Security, which opens the DDM Configuration page.

3. On the DDM Configuration page, you may see under Recommended Fields To Mask some database columns that Microsoft has recommended for masking. If you want to accept these recommendations, click Add Mask for the desired columns. Then click Save once you have made your selections.

4. To add a mask for any column in the database, select Add Mask to open the Add Masking Rule Configuration page.

5. On this page, under the Select What To Mask section, select Schema, Table, and Column to define the designated field for masking.

6. In the How To Mask section, choose the appropriate option from the list of masking options (see Figure 5.4).

FIGURE 5.4 Data masking

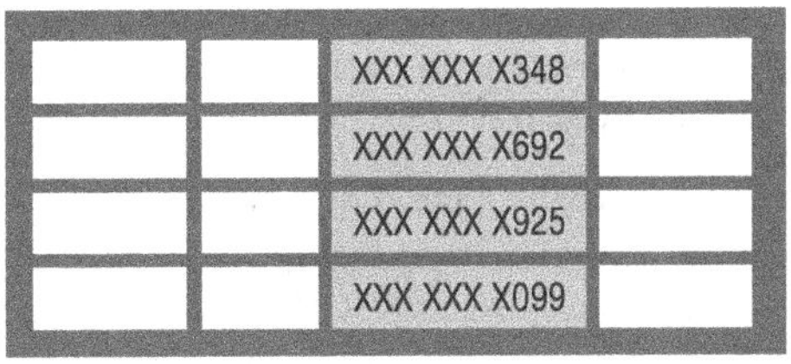

7. Select Add On The Data Masking Rule page to update the masking rules in the DDM policy.

8. If you want to exclude users from masking, go to the section titled SQL Users Excluded From Masking and type the SQL users or Azure AD identities that have access to unmasked sensitive data. These names should be separated by a semicolon. Users who have admin privileges always have access to unmasked data by default.

9. Finally, click Save on the Data Masking Configuration page to save the new or updated masking policy.

Implementing Database Encryption for Azure SQL Database

Transparent data encryption (TDE) encrypts SQL Servers, Azure SQL Database, and Azure Synapse Analytics data files. This type of encryption provides data encryption at rest. TDE provides real-time encryption and decryption of data and log files using a database encryption key (DEK) stored in the database boot record for availability during recovery. The DEK uses symmetric key encryption, meaning that it uses the same key for both encryption and decryption. This key is secured by a certificate that the server's master database stores or by an asymmetric key that an extensible key management (EKM) module protects. TDE can be used to protect data and log files, and it allows you to maintain compliance with the many laws/regulations and industry standards/guidelines established in different industries. TDE allows you to encrypt data using AES and 3DES encryption algorithms without altering your existing applications.

Encryption of database files using TDE is done at the page level. The way it works is that the pages in an encrypted database are encrypted *before* they're written to the disk, and they are decrypted when read into memory. By default, all newly deployed Azure SQL databases have TDE, but older databases must have it enabled. For a SQL-managed instance, the default setting is for TDE to be enabled at the instance level and for newly created databases. For Azure Synapse Analytics, TDE must be manually enabled.

Enabling TDE in the Azure Portal

To configure TDE through the Azure portal, you must be on an account that is an Azure Owner, Contributor, or SQL Security Manager. Here's how to enable TDE in the Azure portal:

1. For Azure SQL Database or Azure Synapse, you can manage TDE for the database from within the Azure portal. Simply navigate to the TDE settings under your user database, then toggle data encryption on or off.

2. Next, you are required to create the TDE master key (i.e., the TDE protector) at the server or the instance level. You also have the option of using bring your own key (BYOK) to encrypt data with a key from Key Vault. Simply open the TDE settings under your server and you will have the option to import your own key.

Implementing Network Isolation for Data Solutions, Including Azure Synapse

Network isolation is the practice of segmenting elements of your network from one another. It is commonly done in businesses so that anything that negatively affects one section of the network can't spread to other parts of the network. When it comes to data solutions in this instance, you want to isolate traffic belonging to one customer from others so that someone cannot gain unauthorized access to another customer's data.

In an Azure virtual network (VNet), you can logically separate your networks in many ways. For example, network security groups (NSGs) allow for network isolation by controlling which machines are allowed to communicate with one another. Another important example is Azure Private Link, which allows you to connect to Azure PaaS services over a private endpoint in the VNet. This allows you to ensure that traffic is traveling over the Microsoft network, rather than exposing it to the public Internet.

Implementing Network Isolation

Azure deployment features multiple layers of network isolation that are designed to ensure that Azure's network is isolated from the public Internet as well from other internal network elements. Figure 5.5 highlights all the various categories of controls available to implement network isolation.

FIGURE 5.5   Various category controls

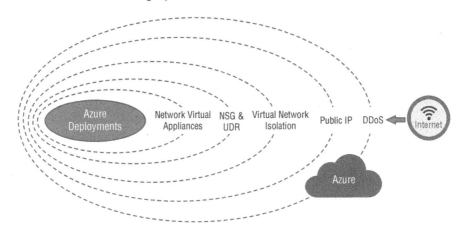

The first layer of isolation is Azure DDoS Protection (Basic), which doesn't require your configuration to implement, but it protects Azure from large-scale attacks (e.g., data requests) from the public Internet.

The next layer consists of the customer-defined public IP addresses. By giving customers the ability to define their public IP addresses, it allows you to determine which traffic can pass through the cloud service and to your virtual network, because only public IP addresses can be assessed from outside the network.

The third layer is the virtual network isolation, which is how you isolate machines within virtual networks in your environment. You have multiple options to choose from when it comes to implementing virtual network isolation:

Option 1—Subnets within a Single Virtual Network   Currently, Azure provides default routing across subnets within a single virtual network. However, you can prevent that by using Windows Firewall with Advanced Security. Figure 5.6 illustrates a simple example of Windows Firewall with Advanced Security.

Windows Firewall can be configured to block inbound connections based on your connection criteria. The inbound rules can be set up to determine the following:

- What local ports will accept connections
- What remote ports from which connections will be accepted

- What remote IP addresses from which connection requests will be accepted
- Which users will be authorized to make connections
- What computers are authorized to make connections

Option 2—Subnets in Different Virtual Networks   By separating virtual machines by subnet, you permit or deny network traffic using an access control list (ACL), which allows you to control traffic between subnets in different VNets (see Figure 5.7).

FIGURE 5.6   Azure Firewall

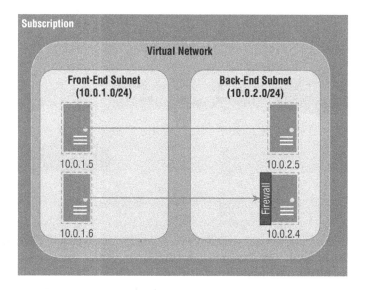

FIGURE 5.7   Network isolation through ACLs

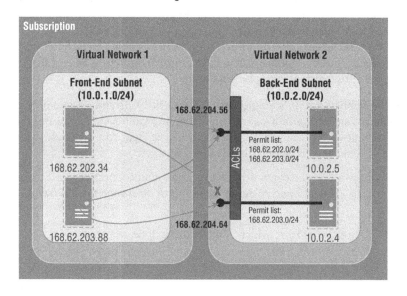

Next, you have network security groups (NSGs) and user-defined routing (UDR). NSGs contain security rules that allow or deny inbound/outbound network traffic for Azure resources. For each rule, you can specify its source and destination, in addition to port and protocols as filtering criteria for the network traffic. To create a network security group in Azure, follow these steps:

1. Navigate to the Azure portal menu or on the homepage and select Create A Resource.

2. Select Networking, and then select Network Security Group.

3. On the next page that opens, select the Basics tab and set the values for the following settings (`https://docs.microsoft.com/en-us/azure/virtual-network/man-age-network-security-group#before-you-begin`) shown in Table 5.10.

TABLE 5.10 Settings for creating a network security group in Azure

Setting	Action
Subscription	Select your desired subscription.
Resource Group	Either create a new group or select an existing resource group.
Name	Create a unique name within the resource group.
Region	Select your desired location.

4. Select Review + Create.

5. Azure will validate the NSG. Once you receive the Validation Passed message, click Create.

    User-defined routing (UDR) is when a user wants to define the way that traffic is routed (i.e., directed) on a network. Azure automatically routes traffic between Azure subnets, Vnets, and on-premises networks. However, if you want to change Azure's default routing, you can do so by creating a route table. To create a route table, follow these steps:

1. Go to the Azure portal and select Create A Resource.

2. Go to the search box and enter **route table**. Once Route Table appears in the results, select it.

3. On the Route Table page, click Create.

4. In the Create Route Table dialog box, do the following:

    a. Type a name for the route table.

    b. Select the appropriate subscription.

    c. Select a resource group—this can be an existing group or you can create a new one.

    d. Select a location.

    e. Select whether you want Virtual Network Gateway Route Propagation enabled or disabled.

5. Finally, click Create to create the new route table.

The next layer of network isolation is achieved through network virtual appliances, which can be used to create isolation boundaries between applications on the network. The most popular virtual appliance for achieving networking isolation is Azure Web Application Firewall. By using all of these different layers in conjunction, you can isolate machines and applications from one another within Azure.

Analytics and Azure Cosmo DB

Azure Cosmo DB is a solution for creating responsiveness in applications. Today's applications have a need to be highly responsive and always online for several reasons. First, one of the factors that search engines use for SEO is the response time of web pages. Second, users are extremely quick to leave applications and websites that have slow load times. So, for the sake of customer retention, it's important that your applications have low latency and high availability. To achieve both, instances of your applications need to be deployed in datacenters close to their end users. Additionally, applications need to respond in real time to large changes in usage to store growing volumes of data and to make this data easily and quickly accessible to users. Azure Cosmos DB was created to address all these issues.

    Azure Cosmos DB is a fully managed NoSQL database designed for modern app development. It allows for single-digit-millisecond response times, automatic and instant scalability, and guaranteed speed at scale. It provides business continuity through SLA-backed availability and a promise of enterprise-grade security. It supports faster app development thanks to turnkey multiregion data distribution to anywhere in the world, open-source APIs, and SDKs for commonly used programming languages. As a managed service, it also handles many of the common database administration tasks with automated managed updates and patching. Lastly, it can automate capacity management by providing serverless and automatic scaling options that can respond to the exact needs of the application and ensure that you meet the needs of your business. Table 5.11 summarizes the benefits of Azure Cosmos DB (`https://docs.microsoft.com/en-us/azure/cosmos-db/introduction`).

TABLE 5.11 Benefits of Cosmos DB

Benefit	Features
Guarantees speed at scale	It provides real-time access to applications and users with a guarantee of availability supported by SLAs.
	It allows for multiregional usage and allows you to distribute data to any Azure region easily.
	It allows for scaling of storage and throughput as needed across any Azure region, allowing you to handle unexpected traffic bursts with no business interruptions.

Benefit	Features
Simplified application development	It can be integrated with important Azure services for building applications, such as Azure Functions, IoT Hub, and App Service.
	You can choose from multiple database APIs to find the one that best suits your needs.
	Azure Change Feeds allow you to easily track and manage any changes made to database containers and creates triggered events via Azure Functions.
	Azure Cosmos DB's schema-less service will index all your data and allow you to quickly query data as needed.
Guaranteed business continuity and availability	Azure provides an SLA for Cosmos DB to ensure availability worldwide for customers.
	You can easily distribute data across any Azure region via automatic data replication, which helps ensure that you will have multiple backups and zero downtime.
	It comes with enterprise-grade encryption at rest.
	It allows you to use Azure RBAC to keep your data safe with fine-grained control.
Fully managed and cost-effective	Azure Cosmos DB is a fully managed service, meaning it comes with automatic maintenance, patching, and updates that saves developers time and money.
	You have multiple cost-effective options to choose from for handling unpredictable traffic.
	Azure Cosmos DB runs on a serverless model that allows for an automatic and responsive service to meet traffic demands.
	It comes with an auto-scale provisioned throughput that will automatically scale capacity to meet workloads instantly.
Azure Synapse Link for Azure Cosmos DB	It provides reduced analytics complexity with no ETL jobs to manage.
	It includes near real-time insights into operational data.
	It has no impact on operational workloads.
	It comes optimized for large-scale analytics workloads.
	It is cost-effective.
	It includes native integration with Azure Synapse Analytics.

Analytics with Azure Synapse

Azure Synapse Link for Azure Cosmos DB is a cloud-native hybrid transactional and analytical processing capability tool. It provides near-real-time analytics over operational data in Azure Cosmos DB. The Azure Synapse Link makes this possible by creating a seamless integration between Azure Cosmos DB and Azure Synapse Analytics. Azure Synapse Link utilizes the Azure Cosmos DB Analytical Store, which is a fully isolated column store that enables large-scale analytics against operational data in your Azure Cosmos DB without any impact on your workloads.

Figure 5.8 provides a visual representation of how it works.

FIGURE 5.8   Azure Synapse Link for Cosmos

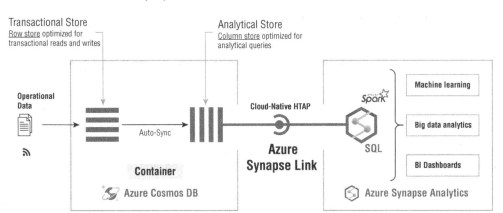

To allow for the analysis of large operational datasets, the operational data in Azure Cosmos DB was traditionally extracted and processed by extract-transform-load (ETL) pipelines. ETL is a data integration process that combines data from different sources into a single data store, which is then loaded into a data warehouse or another system where it can be used for analysis. As the name suggests, it features three main steps:

1. Extract data from legacy systems.

2. Cleanse data to improve data quality and establish consistency.

3. Load data into a target database.

When compared to the traditional ETL-based solutions, Azure Synapse link offers several advantages (`https://docs.microsoft.com/en-us/azure/cosmos-db/synapse-link`), as shown in Table 5.12.

TABLE 5.12   Benefits of Azure Synapse Link

Benefits	Description
Reduces complexity with no ETL jobs to manage	Azure Synapse Links allows you to access Cosmos DB using Azure Synapse Analytics, which allows you to run analytics against the store easily.
Near-real-time insights into your operational data	You can obtain insights into your operational data, which allows you to understand how your environment is running in real time by integrating with Azure Cosmos DB.
No impact on operational workloads	Azure Synapse Link allows you to run analytical queries against an Azure Cosmos DB analytical store. This provides a presentation of your data and allows you to run the analytics without consuming any of the provisioned throughput of your operational data.
Optimization for large-scale analytics	The Azure Cosmos DB analytical stores are designed to provide scalability, elasticity, and performance for analytical workloads. They have built-in support for Azure Synapse Analytics.
Cost-effectiveness	Azure Synapse Link eliminates the need for extra storage and compute layers required in traditional ETL pipelines when analyzing operational data. It also doesn't require you to provision any throughput that is needed for transactional workloads, making it an overall cost-effective solution.

Limitations of Azure Synapse Link

Azure Synapse Link does have the following limitations, however:

- Azure Synapse Link for Cosmos is only compatible with SQL API and Azure Cosmos DB API for MongoDB. Currently, it isn't supported for Gremlin API, Cassandra API, or Table API.

- Currently, you cannot access the Azure Cosmos DB Analytics store with the Azure Synapse Dedicated SQL Pool.

- The ability to enable Synapse Link on existing Cosmos DB containers is only supported for SQL API accounts. The Synapse Link can be enabled on new containers for both SQL API and MongoDB API accounts.

- Backup and restoration of data in analytical stores isn't currently supported.

- RBAC isn't supported when querying databases using Synapse SQL serverless pools.

Azure Synapse Security

Azure Synapse Links allows you to run near-real-time analytics for all types of company data in Azure Cosmos DB. This information can include personally identifiable information (PII), customer and financial information, and many other types of sensitive information that you want to protect from unauthorized viewers. It's important to ensure that your critical business data is stored securely when using analytical stores or transactional stores. Here are some of the security features that Azure Synapse Link for Azure Cosmos DB has to meet these security requirements:

Network Isolation Using Private Endpoints   As discussed earlier, *network isolation* is the process of segmenting your network into different parts. It can be done using private endpoints that can independently control network access to the data in both transactional and analytical stores. It's implemented using separate managed private endpoints for each store within the virtual networks in the Azure Synapse workspaces. To configure private endpoints for your analytical store, follow these two steps:

1. Set up an Azure Synapse Analytics workspace with a managed virtual network and data exfiltration. In your Azure Synapse Analytics workspace, you need to enable data exfiltration with data protection enabled, which ensures that malicious users cannot copy or transfer data from your Azure resources to locations outside your organization's scope. You can do this from the Networking tab in your Azure Synapse workspace.

2. Add a managed private endpoint for Azure Cosmos DB Analytical Store following these steps:

    a. Sign into the Azure portal.

    b. From the Azure portal, navigate to your Synapse Analytics workspace and open the Overview pane.

    c. Launch Synapse Studio by going to the Getting Started pane and selecting Open under Open Synapse Studio.

    d. In the Synapse Studio, open the Manage tab.

    e. Navigate to Managed Private Endpoints and select New.

    f. Select Azure Cosmos DB (SQL API) Account Type ➤ Continue.

    g. Complete the New Managed Private Endpoint form by filling in this information:

    Name: Provide a name for your new managed private endpoint. Keep in mind that this name cannot be updated once it's created.

    Description: Provide a description to identify this private endpoint, explain its function, and then provide any other information that you want.

    Azure Subscription: Select an Azure Cosmos DB account from a list of available accounts within your Azure Subscriptions.

Azure Cosmos DB Account Name: Select any existing Azure Cosmos DB account that is either SQL or MongoDB.

Target sub-resource: Select one of the following options: **Analytical,** if you want to create the private endpoint for an analytical store, or **SQL Or MongoDB,** if you want to add OLTP or a transactional account endpoint.

3. Once that is created, go to the Private Endpoint Name and select Manage Approvals in the Azure portal.

4. Go to your Azure Cosmos DB account, select the Private Endpoint, and then select Approve.

5. Navigate back to the Synapse Analytics workspace and click Refresh in the Managed Private Endpoints pane. Here, you need to verify that the private endpoint is in an Approved State.

Data Encryption with Customer-Managed Keys   Azure Synapse Link allows you to easily encrypt data across transactional and analytical stores using the same customer-managed keys in an automated and transparent manner.

Enabling an Azure Synapse Link for Azure Cosmos Accounts

Here we will look at how to enable Azure Synapse Link for Azure Cosmos.

1. Sign into the Azure portal.

2. Create a new Azure account or select an existing Cosmos DB account.

3. Navigate to your Azure Cosmos DB account and open the Features pane.

4. Choose Synapse Link from the Features list.

5. Next, you will be prompted to enable Synapse Link on your account. Select Enable.

After no more than 5 minutes, your account should be enabled to use Synapse Link.
It's important to note that turning on Synapse Link does not turn on the analytical store. Once you enable Synapse Link on a Cosmos DB account, the next step is to select Enable Analytical Store on containers to start using the Synapse Link for analytics.

Creating an Analytical Store–Enabled Container Using the Azure Portal

Here's how to create an analytical store–enabled container:

1. Sign into the Azure portal or Azure Cosmos DB Explorer.

2. Navigate to your desired Azure Cosmos DB account and open the Data Explorer tab.

3. On this tab, select New Container and create a name for your database, container, partition key, and throughput details. Then select the Analytical Store option. Once you do this, it will create a container with analytical TTL property set to the default value of –1, which means infinite retention. By default, this store will retain all the historical versions of records, but it can be changed later.

4. If you have not previously enabled Synapse Link on this account, you will be prompted to do so now because it's a prerequisite. (We discussed how to do this previously.) If you have already done so, you can skip this step.

5. Click OK to create an analytical store–enabled Azure Cosmos DB container.

6. Once the container is created, verify that the analytical store has been enabled by clicking Settings (which can be found below Documents in Data Explorer), and then check to ensure that the Analytical Store Time Live option is selected.

Configuring and Managing Azure Key Vault

Azure Key Vault is a cloud service for securely storing and accessing secrets. Microsoft defines a *secret* as anything for which you want to tightly control access. Some common examples of secrets are API keys, passwords, certificates, and cryptographic keys. The compromise of company secrets could provide an attacker with highly privileged access to your company's environment and cause major data breaches, which is why you want to ensure that they are properly protected. Azure's Key Vault Service supports two types of containers: vaults and managed hardware security module (HSM) pools. As of this writing, Azure Key Vault supports storing software and HSM-backed keys, secrets, and certificates. Here are some terms that you need to understand for our discussion about Azure Key Vault `https://docs.microsoft.com/en-us/azure/key-vault/general/basic-concepts`:

Vault Owner The vault owner is the user who can create a key vault and have full access and control over it. The vault owner also has the ability to set up auditing to log who is accessing the secrets and keys. Owners can also control the key life cycle, roll to a new version of the key, back up keys, and perform other key-related tasks.

Vault Consumer The vault consumer role allows you to perform actions on the secrets inside the vault key. The exact actions you can perform depend on the permission granted to the keys by the owner.

Managed HSM Administrators Users who are assigned this role have control over a managed HSM pool and have the ability to create role assignments to grant others delegated access.

Managed HSM Crypto Officer/User This role is typically assigned to users or service principals who will need to perform cryptographic operations using a key in managed HSM. They have the ability to create keys but cannot delete them.

Managed HSM Crypto Service Encryption User This built-in role is typically assigned to service accounts that need to encrypt data at rest with a customer-managed key.

Authentication in Azure Key Vault

Before you can perform any operations with Azure Key Vault, you first must authenticate (`https://docs.microsoft.com/en-us/azure/key-vault/general/basic-concepts`) to it. There are currently three ways to authenticate to Key Vault:

▪ **Managed identities for Azure resources:** These are identities that you assign to a VM or other Azure resource to give them access to Azure Key Vault. Whenever you need to deploy an app or a service, you must assign it an identity that will allow it to access Key

Vault. This is the recommended way of authenticating to Key Vault because the app or service doesn't manage the rotation of the secret.

- **Service principal and certificate:** The second option is to use a service principal and an associated certificate that allows for access to Azure Key Vault. This isn't a recommended approach because the application owner or developer must rotate the certificate, which means more overhead.

- **Service principal and secret:** Lastly, you can use a service principal and a secret to authenticate to Azure Key Vault. This isn't recommended by Microsoft, however, because it's hard to automate the rotation of the secret that's used to authenticate to Azure Key Vault.

Encrypting Data in Transit

Key Vault enforces Transport Layer Security (TLS) protocol to protect data when it's traveling between Azure Key Vault and any client. The successor of SSL, TLS is a cryptographic protocol designed to provide communications security over a computer network. TLS provides strong authentication, message privacy, and integrity, combined with the fact that it is easy to deploy and use.

Another aspect of encryption is Perfect Forward Secrecy (PFS), a specific key agreement protocol that helps prevent session keys from being compromised. PFS protects data on a network's Transport layer that uses TSL protocols. When PFS is used, encrypted communications and sessions that occurred in the past cannot be recovered or decrypted even if long-term secret keys or passwords are compromised in the future. This significantly reduces the risk associated with hackers compromising keys.

Key Vault Roles

Before we discuss how to create and configure Azure Key vault, let's examine some of the roles that it supports (Table 5.13). These roles will help you meet the needs of developers and security administrators (`https://docs.microsoft.com/en-us/azure/key-vault/general/basic-concepts`).

TABLE 5.13   Roles supported by Azure Key Vault

Role	Problem statement	Solved by Azure Key Vault
Developer for an Azure application	You want to write an application that uses keys for signing and encryption.	Your keys will be stored in Key Vault and accessed when needed using an URI.
	You need the keys to be external from your application so that it can be geographically distributed.	Keys are protected by Azure using strong algorithms, key lengths, and hardware security modules.
	You need the keys and secrets to be protected without having to write more code.	The keys will be processed in HSMs from the same Azure datacenters as your applications, which means better reliability and reduced latency when accessing them.
	You need the keys to be easy to use from your applications with proper performance.	

TABLE 5.13   Roles supported by Azure Key Vault *(continued)*

Role	Problem statement	Solved by Azure Key Vault
Developer for software as a service (SaaS)	You don't want to be liable for your customer's tenant keys and secrets. You want customers to own and manage their keys.	Customers can import their own keys in Key Vault and manage them. Whenever an application needs to perform cryptographic operations, Vault does this on behalf of the application. The application never sees the customers' keys.
Chief Security Officer (CSO)	You want to be compliant with FIPS 140-2 Level 2 or FIPS 140-2 Level 3 HSMs for key management. You want your organization in control of the key life cycle and monitoring key usage. You want to manage the keys from a single location in Azure.	You can select vaults for FIPS 140-2 Level 2 for compliance-validated HSMs. You can choose managed HSM pools for FIPS 140-2 Level 3 compliance validated HSMs. Key Vault is designed so that Microsoft does not see or extract your keys. Key usage is logged in near real time. The vault provides a single interface for managing all of your keys, regardless of how many vaults you have.

Creating a Vault in the Azure Portal

Follow these steps to create an Azure Key Vault:

1. From the Azure portal or from the homepage, select Create A Resource.

2. In the Search box, enter **Key Vault**.

3. From the Results list, select Key Vault.

4. In the Key Vault section, select Create.

5. In the Create Key Vault section, fill in the following information:

   Name: Enter a unique name.

   Subscription: Select a subscription.

   Resource Group: Either create a new resource group or enter a resource group name.

   Location: Select a location from the menu.

   You can leave the other options at their defaults.

6. Click Create. Once the vault is created, you will be provided with a vault URI that applications can use to connect via REST API.

Before we delve into configuring access to Azure Key Vault, here are some best practices for using Azure Key Vault provided by Microsoft:

Use Separate Key Vaults   Microsoft recommends that you use a separate vault per application, per environment, per region, because it ensures that you do not share secrets across environments and regions. Key vaults are used to define security boundaries for stored secrets. If you group secrets into the same vault, it increases the effective "blast radius" of a security event, because multiple secrets can be leaked in just that single security incident. To mitigate this, you should separate and store company secrets based on what the specific applications should have access to. For very large applications, Microsoft recommends that you use a more granular approach and consider separating secrets based on their related services within the application.

Control Access to Your Vault   While Azure Key Vault provides secure storage for your secrets, it's only as effective as your access control. It doesn't matter how secure the vault is, anyone with access can circumvent all its security features and view all the secrets stored in the vault. Therefore, you must be very careful with your access control procedures. You must secure access to your key vaults by allowing only authorized applications and users access. Microsoft suggest you do this in five ways:

- Restrict access to your subscription, resource group, and key vaults using RBAC.
- Create access policies for every vault you create.
- Implement the principle of least privilege access when granting access to your vault.
- Turn on a firewall and virtual network service endpoints to protect your vault.
- Regularly create backups. Backups should be performed whenever you update, delete, or create objects in your vault.

Configuring Access to Azure Key Vault

An Azure Key Vault access policy determines whether a given security principal can perform different operations on Key Vault secrets, keys, and certificates. Security principals, in this context, will primarily be a user, application, or user group. Currently, Key Vault supports up to 1,024 access policy entries. Each of these entries grants a distinct set of permissions to a particular security principal. Due to these restrictions, it's advised that you assign access policies to groups of users when possible, rather than assigning them to individuals, to preserve as many of these access policies as you can. Using groups also makes it much easier to manage permissions for multiple people in your organization because you don't have to manage everyone's permissions individually.

Here's how to assign an Azure Key Vault access policy:

1. In the Azure portal, navigate to the Key Vault resource for which you want to create the access policy.
2. Under Settings, select Access Policies, and then select Add Access Policy.
3. Select the permission you want to have under Certificate Permissions, Key Permissions, and Secret Permissions. You can do this manually, or you can select a template that contains commonly used permission combinations.

4. Under Select Principal, choose the None Selected link to open the Principal Selection pane. In that pane, enter the user's name, app, or service principal in the search field, and then click Select.

5. You will return to the Add Access Policy Page. There, click Add to save the new access policy.

6. You then will return to the Access Policies page. Here you must verify that your access policy is listed under Current Access Policies, and then click Save. Your access policies won't be applied until you save them.

Managing Certificates, Secrets, and Keys

Before we discuss managing these three elements with Azure Vault, we must define these three terms. *Certificates* are digital certificates used to authenticate a principal. For example, *server certificates* (SSL certificates) are used to authenticate the identity of a server. A *secret* is any piece of sensitive information that shouldn't be shared with unauthorized users. A common example of a secret is a user's password or access token. Lastly, we have *keys*, which are typically encryption keys that are used to encrypt and decrypt information. However, keys can also include access keys that allow you to access different types of resources. As the name suggests, keys simply provide you with access to some type of resource.

Using Azure RBAC Secret, Key, and Certificate Permissions with Key Vault

Using Azure RBAC secret, key, and certificate permissions with Key Vault is an alternative to using the vault access policy permissions approach we discussed previously. Here are the steps for using this method:

1. Ensure that you have an Azure Subscription.

2. To add the role assignments, you must have `Microsoft.Authorization/role Assignments/write` and `Microsoft.Authorization/roleAssignments/delete`.

To enable Azure RBAC permissions on Azure Key Vault, follow these steps:

1. To enable RBAC on a new key vault, navigate to the Access Policy tab, and under Permission Model, select Azure Role-Based Access Control (see Figure 5.9).

2. Repeat the same process for an existing vault.

Once you have performed these steps, you can assign roles to users that will allow them to access items in your Key Vault. Here's an example of assigning a role for viewing secrets:

1. Navigate to Azure Key Vault and open a previously created secret.

2. Click the Access Control (IAM) tab.

3. Click Add ≻ Add Role Assignment to open the Add Role Assignment page.

4. Assign the role of your choice.

FIGURE 5.9   RBAC in Azure Key Vault

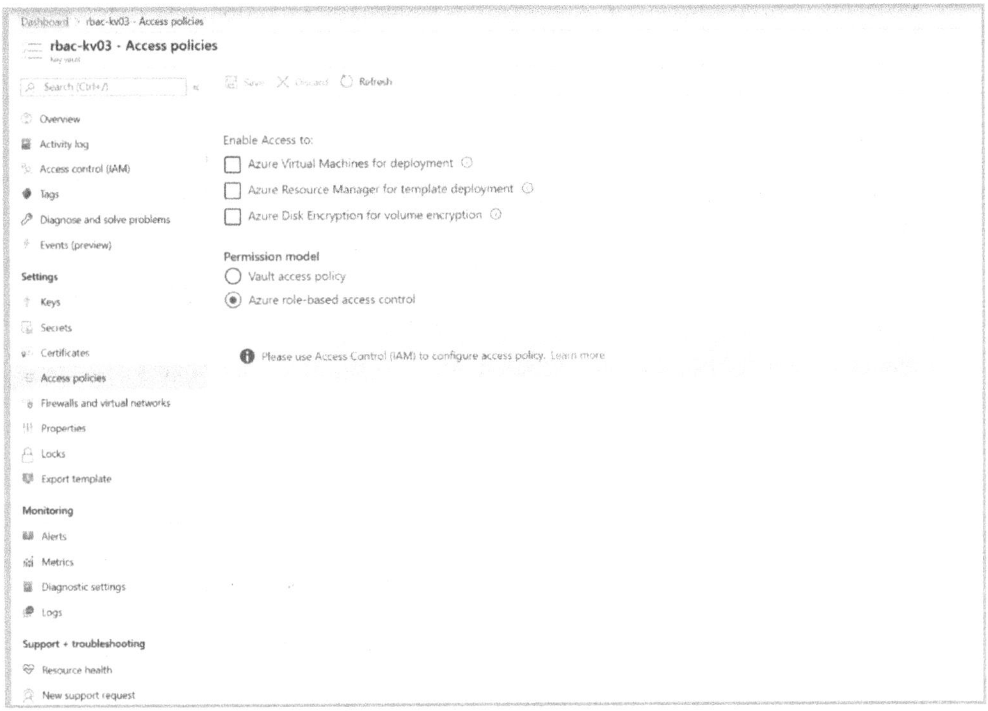

Configuring Key Rotation

Key rotation occurs when you retire an encryption key and replace the hold key with a newly generated cryptographic key. The act of rotating keys is important because it makes a potentially compromised key useless to an attacker. It also reduces the amount of content encrypted with a single key, which is good for protecting against authentication attacks. Regularly rotating keys is a necessary part of meeting industry standards and cryptographic best practices.

Key Vault makes key rotation easy by allowing users to configure Key Vault to automatically generate a new key version at a frequency they select. A rotation policy can be created in order to configure the rotation of each individual key. Microsoft recommends that encryption keys be rotated at least every two years as a best practice. This rotation allows users to enable end-to-end zero-touch rotation for encryption at rest for Azure services.

To enable Key Vault key rotation, you need key management permissions. To obtain such permissions, you must be assigned a Key Vault Administrator role to manage the rotation policy and on-demand rotation of encryption keys.

Configuring a Key Rotation Policy

You can configure the parameters of your key rotation via a key rotation policy. Here are the key rotation policy settings:

- **Expiry time:** This time is the key expiration interval and determines the expiration date of a newly rotated key. It has no effect on existing keys.

- **Enabled/disabled:** This setting is used to enable or disable the rotation of a key.

- **Rotation types:** There are two types of rotations from which you can choose. First, you can choose to automatically renew at a given time after creation (which is the default). Second, you can choose to automatically renew at a given time before expiry. This requires that you have an expiry time set on the rotation policy and an expiration date set on the key.

- **Rotation time:** This time is the key rotation interval—the minimum value is seven days from creation and seven days from expiration time.

- **Notification Time:** This time is for keys near expiry on which you want an event grid notification. It requires that you have expiry time set on the rotation policy and expiration date set on the key.

Creating a key rotation policy can be done when you create a key or for an existing key (see Figure 5.10). During the creation process, simply click the Not Configured link next to set key rotation policy.

To configure rotation policies on existing keys, you perform the same process—simply navigate to the key and click the Rotation Policy (see Figure 5.11).

In the rotation policy, you also have the option to select Rotate Now if you want to perform a manual rotation of your key at that point.

Configuring Backup and Recovery of Certificates, Secrets, and Keys

A backup in Key Vault is designed to provide you with an offline copy of all your secrets in the event that you lose access to your key vault. To facilitate this, Key Vault automatically provides features to help you maintain availability and prevent data loss. While creating backups is a good overall security control, it should only be done if you have a good business justification. Creating backups of your secrets in Key Vault can introduce operational challenges, such as having to maintain multiple sets of logs, permission, and so forth.

When creating backups in Key Vault, it's important to understand that there isn't a way to back up an entire vault in a single operation. Microsoft also warns that creating backups using the commands they provide to do an automated backup may result in errors and it won't be supported by Microsoft or the Azure Key Vault team. Here some common consequences that they warn of:

- Backing up secrets that have several versions can cause timeout errors.

- Backups create point-in-time snapshots. If a key is renewed during a backup, it can cause the mismatching of encryption keys.

- If you exceed the Key Vault service limits for requests per second, the backup will fail.

FIGURE 5.10   Creating a key rotation policy

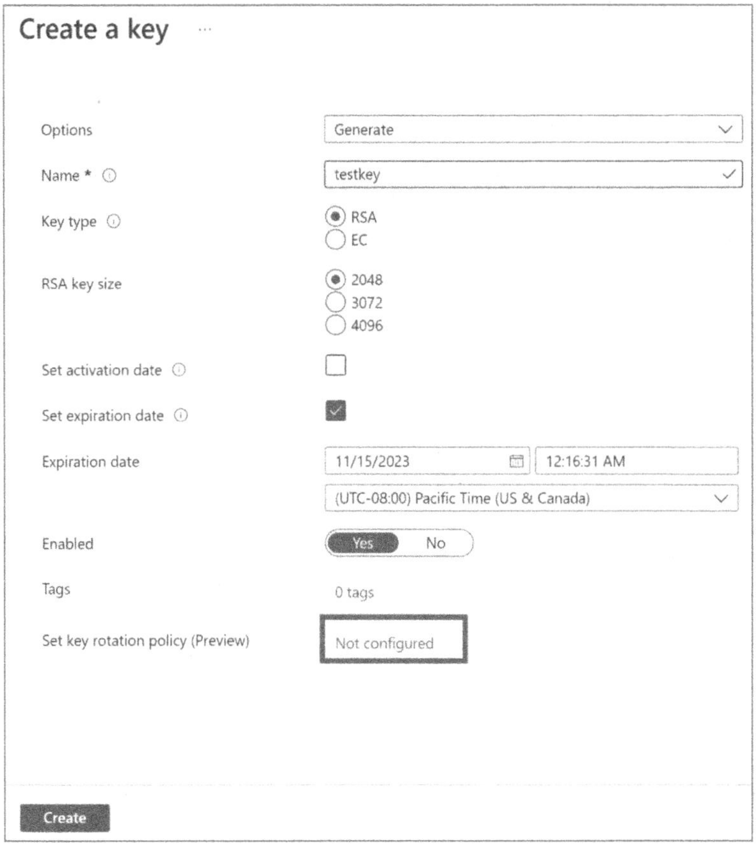

Create a key   ...

Options	Generate ⌄
Name * ⓘ	testkey ✓
Key type ⓘ	⦿ RSA ◯ EC
RSA key size	⦿ 2048 ◯ 3072 ◯ 4096
Set activation date ⓘ	☐
Set expiration date ⓘ	☑
Expiration date	11/15/2023 📅 12:16:31 AM (UTC-08:00) Pacific Time (US & Canada) ⌄
Enabled	(Yes No)
Tags	0 tags
Set key rotation policy (Preview)	Not configured

Create

FIGURE 5.11   Configuring a rotation policy

Home > Key vaults > jl-kv10 >

🔑 **testkey**   ...
Versions

＋ New Version   ◌ Refresh   🗑 Delete   ↓ Download Backup   ⚙ Rotation policy (Preview)

The last important consideration is that when you back up a Key Vault object, it will be downloaded as an encrypted blob that cannot be decrypted outside Azure. To get your data back using that encrypted blob, you must restore the blob into a Key Vault within the same Azure subscription and Azure geography.

Prerequisites

To back up a Key Vault object, you need to have the following:

- Contributor-level or higher permissions on an Azure subscription
- A primary Key Vault that contains the secrets you want to back up
- A secondary Key Vault where secrets will be restored

Configuring Backup and Restoration from the Azure Portal

To configure your backups from the Azure portal, follow these steps:

1. Go to the Azure portal.
2. Select your Key Vault.
3. Navigate to the object that you to back up and select it.
4. Select Download Backup.
5. Click Download.

To restore your backups from the Azure portal, follow these steps:

1. Go to the Azure portal.
2. Select the Key Vault of your choice.
3. Select the type of object you want to restore.
4. Select Restore Backup.
5. Go to the location where you saved the encrypted blob and click OK.

Summary

This chapter focuses on how to secure data and applications in Azure. Azure's infrastructure provides many options for collecting, securing, and analyzing data across your cloud network. In this chapter, we focused on three main aspects: First, we discussed how to securely store data on the Azure platform, which is done through proper database security and network segmentation. You want to ensure that you restrict access to those resources that are storing your data and encrypt the information at rest and in transit to and from those resources. Second, we covered securely storing data in databases, which includes utilizing database authentication using Azure AD, enabling database auditing to find potential security issues, enabling dynamic masking for SQL queries, implementing database encryption, and having proper network isolation. Finally, we discussed Azure Key Vault, which is a tool for securely storing secrets, certificates, and keys in Azure. We covered how to create a vault and access it using access control policies or RBAC, in addition to the importance of key rotation and how to back up the contents stored in Azure Key Vault.

Exam Essentials

Explain the function of the Azure storage account.   In Azure, data storage is facilitated through an Azure storage account, which contains all of your Azure Storage data objects: blobs, file shares, queues, tables, and disks. Storage accounts give you a unique namespace that will allow you to access all of your data over HTTP or HTTPS.

Know the purpose of a storage account access key.   For your storage account, your access keys are similar to a root password and can be used to authorize access to data in that storage account via shared key authorization. Whenever you create a storage account, Azure generates two 512-bit storage account access keys.

Explain the process of shared key authorization.   This option can be used for accessing blobs, files, queues, and tables. It requires every client that needs access to have a storage account access key. Then the client will pass a header with every request that is signed using the storage account access key in order to gain access.

Explain the function of a shared access signature (SAS).   These signatures provide limited delegated access to resources on a storage account, namely blobs, files, queues, and tables. You also have the option to add constraints on the time interval that the signature will be valid or on the permission that it grants, which gives you more flexibility in access control.

Be able to define a SAS token.   This is a string that you generate on the client side. The SAS token is not tracked by Azure Storage, and you can create an unlimited number of SAS tokens. Once you create a SAS token, you can distribute it to client applications that require access to those resources in your storage account.

Be able to define a key expiration policy.   A key expiration policy allows you to set a reminder for the rotation of the account access keys. The reminder will be displayed only if the time interval you have selected has passed and the keys have not been rotated. This is a great way to make sure you meet your internal standards.

Be able to describe the Azure SQL Database service.   This is a fully managed platform as a service (PaaS) database engine that handles the majority of database management functions in Azure. Most of these functions can be done without user involvement, including upgrading, patching, backups, and monitoring.

Explain how Azure Active Directory (Azure AD) authentication works.   Azure Active Directory (Azure AD) authentication is a method for connecting to Azure SQL Database, Azure SQL Managed Instance, and Synapse SQL in Azure Synapse Analytics using identities in Azure AD. The benefit of Azure AD authentication is that you can centrally manage the identities of database users and Microsoft services in one central location.

Be able to define an audit.   In IT, an audit is an examination and evaluation of an organization's information technology infrastructure, policies, and operations. The goal of the audit is to determine whether the IT controls are working correctly to protect corporate assets, ensure data integrity and availability, and check if they are properly aligned with the business's overall goals. This includes both technical controls and physical security controls.

Explain the importance of dynamic data masking (DDM).   DDM is a technique for limiting sensitive data exposure by masking that data to nonprivileged users. DDM helps improve the security of an application by limiting the data that nonauthorized users can access.

Know what Azure Cosmos DB is used for.   Azure Cosmos DB is a fully managed NoSQL database designed for modern app development. It allows for single-digit-millisecond response times, automatic and instant scalability, and guaranteed speed at scale. Cosmos provides business continuity through SLA-backed availability and a promise of enterprise-grade security. It supports fast app development thanks to turnkey multiregion data distribution to anywhere in the world, open-source APIs, and SDKs for commonly used programming languages.

Explain the function of Azure Synapse Link for Azure Cosmos DB.   Azure Synapse Link for Azure Cosmos DB is a cloud-based analytics processing capability tool. It provides near-real-time analytics over operational data in Azure Cosmos DB. The Azure Synapse Link makes this possible by creating a seamless integration between Azure Cosmos DB and Azure Synapse Analytics. Azure Synapse Link utilizes Azure Cosmos DB Analytical Stores. This is a fully isolated column store that enables wide-scale analytics against operational data in your Azure Cosmos DB without causing any negative impact to your workloads.

Be able to define what Azure Key Vault is.   Azure Key Vault is a cloud service for securely storing and accessing secrets. Microsoft defines a secret as anything to which you want to tightly control access. Some common examples are API keys, passwords, certificates, and cryptographic keys.

Explain the function of a Key Vault access policy.   A Key Vault access policy determines whether a given security principal can perform different operations on Key Vault secrets, keys, and certificates. Security principals in this context will primarily be users, applications, or user groups. Currently, Key Vault supports up to 1,024 access policy entries. Each of these entries grants a distinct set of permissions to a particular security principal.

Be able to list the types of secrets. Certificates: Certificates are tools that are used to authenticate a principal. For example, server certificates (SSL certificates) are used to authenticate the identity of a server.

Secret: A secret is any piece of sensitive information that shouldn't be shared with unauthorized users. A common example is user passwords or access tokens.

Keys: These are typically encryption keys that are used to encrypt and decrypt information. But they can also be things like access keys that allow you to access different types of resources. As the name suggests, keys simply provide you with access to some type of resource.

Review Questions

1. What facilitates data storage in Azure?

   A. Azure storage accounts

   B. File shares

   C. Disks

   D. Data blobs

2. What is a storage account access key?

   A. A key that provides authorization to access data in a storage account

   B. A root password

   C. An encryption key

   D. Part of public key encryption within Azure

3. What is the recommended authorization option for data in storage accounts?

   A. Azure Active Directory Domain Services Authentication

   B. On-premises Active Directory Domain Services Authentication

   C. Azure Active Directory Integration

   D. SAS

4. What is SAS?

   A. A means of signing a contract

   B. A signature to provide delegated access

   C. A check for data integrity

   D. A Microsoft means of authentication

5. Which of the following is not a type of shared access signature (SAS)?

   A. User Delegation SAS

   B. Service SAS

   C. Account SAS

   D. Delegated SAS

6. What is a URI?

   A. An identifier that points to one or more storage resources

   B. A type of URL

   C. A type of authentication

   D. A communication protocol in Azure

7. What is a SAS token used for?

    A. Authenticating users

    B. Encrypting communications between Azure apps

    C. Giving applications access to your network

    D. Giving applications access to resources

8. What is a key expiration policy?

    A. It defines when a key expires.

    B. It creates reminders for the rotation of your account access keys.

    C. It automates the rotation of access keys.

    D. It's a document outlining the standards around key rotation.

9. What is dynamic data masking (DDM)?

    A. A tool for hiding data from users

    B. A tool for encryption in Azure SQL Databases

    C. An obfuscation technique for applications in Azure

    D. A technique for limiting sensitive data exposure in Azure SQL databases

10. What is the Azure Cosmos DB?

    A. A version of SQL databases

    B. A managed NoSQL database primarily for mobile app development

    C. An analytics platform for database data

    D. A security platform for databases

11. What is Azure Key Vault?

    A. A tool for storing company passwords

    B. A tool for storing sensitive company information

    C. A service for securely storing and accessing secrets

    D. A tool for storing encryption keys in Azure

12. What is a secret in Azure?

    A. Any piece of sensitive information

    B. A piece of authentication information

    C. A combination of usernames and passwords

    D. Cryptographic information

13. What is the goal of an audit?

    A. To ensure compliance with industry standards

    B. To document deficiencies in technology

    C. To be a routine part of business

    D. To determine if the IT controls are working correctly

14. What is Azure Synapse?

   A. It's a transactional and analytical processing capability tool.

   B. It's an analytics platform for Azure Cosmos DB.

   C. It's a feature within Azure SQL databases.

   D. It's an integration of multiple VNets in Azure.

15. What does TDE do in Azure SQL database?

   A. It allows for encryption of communications to your database.

   B. It provides you with analytics for your data's usage.

   C. It provides real-time encryption and decryption of log files.

   D. It allows for effective data backups.

16. Which of the following is not a key rotation policy setting?

   A. Expiry time

   B. Rotation type

   C. Rotation time

   D. Encryption type

17. What is the risk of creating backups in Key Vault?

   A. It uses up storage on your servers.

   B. It can be expensive.

   C. It can create operational challenges.

   D. It can be time-consuming.

18. Which of the following is not a user account in Azure Key Vault?

   A. Vault owner

   B. Vault consumer

   C. Managed HSM Administrator

   D. Vault administrator

19. What is the purpose of database auditing in Azure SQL Database?

   A. Recording database events and writing them to an audit log

   B. Checking the database for vulnerabilities

   C. Recording any events related to a user's login

   D. Checking for any unmasked sensitive information

20. What is delegated access?

   A. A form of authentication

   B. The granting of user access to a resource owned by someone else

   C. Temporary access to a resource

   D. A form of access for services in Azure

Appendix A

An Azure Security Tools Overview

✓ **Chapter 2, "Managing Identity and Access on Microsoft Azure"**

- Azure AD
- Windows Hello for Business
- Microsoft Authenticator App
- Azure API Management

✓ **Chapter 3, "Implementing Platform Protections"**

- Azure Firewall
- Azure Application Gateway
- Azure Front Door
- Web Application Firewall
- Azure Service Endpoints
- Azure Private Links
- Azure DDoS Protection
- Microsoft Defender for Cloud
- Azure Container Registry
- Azure App Service

✓ **Chapter 4, "Managing Security Operations"**

- Azure Policy
- Microsoft Threat Modeling Tool
- Microsoft Sentinel

✓ **Chapter 5, "Securing Data and Applications"**

- Azure Storage Platform
- SQL Databases
- Azure Cosmos DB
- Azure Synapse Analytics
- Azure Key Vault

This appendix does not focus on the individual Azure chapter objectives. It does, however, serve as an overview that outlines all of the most important tools in Azure that you need to know for the exam. The exam focuses heavily on how to use these tools to accomplish different security objectives, so it's critical that you understand what these tools are, how they differ, and what services they provide from a security perspective.

Let's begin our overview with Chapter 2.

Chapter 2, "Managing Identity and Access on Microsoft Azure"

Chapter 3 focuses on identity and access management on the Azure platform. The tools discussed in Chapter 2 focus on how to create and manage identities that are used in controlling access to the Azure resources. By the end of this chapter overview, you should understand how these tools contribute to access control within the Azure environment.

Azure Active Directory (AD)

Azure AD is a cloud-based identity and access management service. While it's similar to the traditional Windows AD, Azure AD is not a cloud version of that service—it is an independent service. Azure AD allows employees (or anyone on the on-premises network) to access external resources, including Microsoft 365, the Azure portal, and software-as-a-service (SaaS) applications. It can help users in Azure's cloud environment to access resources on your corporate network and intranet. You can also integrate this service with your on-premises Windows AD server, connect it to Azure AD, and extend your on-premises directories to Azure. Doing so allows users to use the same login credentials to access local and cloud-based resources.

Who Uses Azure AD?

According to Microsoft, there are three main groups that Azure AD is intended for:

- **IT Admins:** IT admins can use Azure AD to control access to their applications and application resources based on your business requirements. A common use case is using

Azure AD to require multifactor authentication (MFA) when accessing important organizational resources. Overall, it's a tool for securing the authentication of your users within the Azure platform.

- **Application developers:** App developers can use Azure AD as a means for adding single sign-on (SSO) to their applications. This way, users can use their preexisting credentials to log in, as SSO both is secure and adds convenience to their applications. Finally, Azure AD has application program interfaces (APIs) that allow you to build a personalized app experience using existing organizational data about that user.

- **Subscribers to Microsoft 365, Office 365, Azure, or Dynamics CRM Online:** It allows you to manage access to any of your integrated cloud applications.

Most Important Features of Azure AD

The following are the most important features of Azure AD:

- **Application management:** The ability to manage your cloud and on-premises applications, including configuring Application Proxies and user authentication, and implementing SSO.

- **User authentication:** The facilitation of user authentication by allowing self-service password resets, enforcing MFA, using custom-banned password lists, and using smart lockout features.

- **Conditional access:** This ability provides users with access to resources *only* when certain conditions are met. These are facilitated by conditional access policies, which in simple terms are if-then statements that control whether a user is able to access a resource or complete an action. This feature provides users with very granular access control to Azure resources.

- **Identity protection:** This feature automatically detects potential vulnerabilities that might affect your organization's identities, configures policies that respond to suspicious actions, and can automatically take action to remediate such actions.

- **Managed identities for Azure resources:** A managed identity provides your Azure services with an identity that they can use to authenticate to any Azure AD-supported authentication service. Developers can use managed identities in their applications to access resources and to avoid having to manage secrets and credentials themselves.

- **Privileged Identity Management (PIM):** Azure AD contains special features for managing, controlling, and monitoring access to your organization's most privileged accounts, thus adding an extra layer of security for these accounts.

- **Reports and monitoring:** Azure AD collects insights into your security and usage patterns for your environment. It then allows you to visualize these insights easily and export them for integration with a third-party solution like security information and event management (SIEM).

- **Windows Hello for Business:** This tool replaces a traditional password with strong two-factor authentication on devices. Two-factor authentication is a type of user credential that includes the verification of a biometric or PIN and is meant to address the following common issues related to password-based authentication:

- **Difficulty associated with remembering strong passwords:** This issue results in users having to constantly reset their passwords or choosing to reuse passwords on multiple sites, which reduces the security of the password.

- **Server breaches:** A server breach can expose passwords, making them obsolete for ensuring authentication.

- **Password exploitation:** Passwords can be exploited using replay attacks, such as the reuse of a password hash to compromise an account.

- **Password exposure:** Users can accidentally expose their passwords when targeted by a phishing attack.

How Does Windows Hello for Business Work?

Windows Hello is set up on a user's device. During that setup, Windows asks the user to set a gesture, which typically is a biometric like a fingerprint or possibly a PIN. The user provides the biometric to verify their identity and Windows then uses Windows Hello to authenticate the user.

The biggest reason that Windows Hello is such a reliable form of authentication is because it allows fully integrated biometric authentication based on facial recognition or fingerprint matching. Windows Hello uses a combination of infrared cameras and software, which results in high accuracy of their biometric authentication while guarding against spoofing. Most major hardware vendors build devices that have Windows Hello–compatible cameras, so compatibility is rarely an issue. Most devices already have fingerprint reader hardware, and it can be added to those devices that don't have it fairly easily.

Difference between Windows Hello and Windows Hello for Business

Windows Hello and Windows Hello for Business varies as follows:

- **Windows Hello:** Windows Hello allows individuals to create a PIN or biometric gesture on their personal device for convenient sign-ins. The standard Windows Hello is unique to the device that it is set up on. It is not backed by asymmetric or certificate-based authentication.

- **Windows Hello for Business:** Windows Hello for Business is configured by a Group Policy or mobile device management policy. This affects multiple devices in an environment and always uses key-based or certificate-based authentication, making it much more secure than Windows Hello, which only uses a PIN.

Microsoft Authenticator App

This application helps you sign into your accounts when you're using two-factor verification, which helps you to use your accounts more securely, since passwords can be forgotten, stolen, and so on. Using two-factor verification that employs verification via your phone makes it much harder for your account to be compromised.

Authenticator is simple to use. The standard verification method is where one factor is a password. After you sign in using your username and password, you would need to either approve the notification or enter the provided verification code, usually via your smartphone.

Azure API Management

Azure API Management is a management platform for all APIs across all your Azure environments. APIs are important for simplifying application integrations and making data and services reusable and universally accessible to users. The Azure API is designed to make API usage easy for applications on the Azure platform.

Azure API Management consists of three elements: an API gateway, a management plane, and a developer portal. All these components are hosted in Azure and are fully managed by default.

API Gateway

Whenever a client application makes a request, it first reaches the API gateway, which then forwards the request to the proper backend services. The gateway acts as a proxy for the backend services and provides consistent configuration for routing, security, throttling, caching, and observability.

Using a self-hosted gateway, an Azure customer can deploy the API gateway to the same environments that host their APIs. Doing so allows them to optimize API traffic and ensures compliance with the local regulations and guidelines. The API gateway can perform the following actions:

- It can accept API calls and route them to preconfigured backends.
- It verifies API keys, JWT tokens, certificates, and other access credentials.
- It can enforce usage quotas and rate limits for your applications and resources.
- It can perform transformations to optimize requests and responses.
- It improves your caches' responses to enhance response latency and minimize the load on your backend services.
- It creates logs, metrics, and traces for monitoring, reporting, and troubleshooting.

Management Plane

The management plane is how you interact with the service; it provides you with full access to the API Management service. You can interact with it via the Azure portal, Azure PowerShell, the Azure command-line interface (CLI), a Visual Studio Code extension, or client software development kits (SDKs) in most programming languages. You can use the management plane to perform the following actions:

- Manage Azure users.

- Provision and configure API Management settings.

- Get insights on your applications and APIs from analytics.

- Set up policies like quotas or transformations for your APIs.

Developer Portal

The developer portal is an automatically generated and fully customizable website that holds the documentation for your APIs. An API provider can customize the look and feel of their developer portal. Some common examples include adding custom content to the site, changing its styles, or adding your branding.

The developer portal allows developers to discover APIs, onboard them for use, and learn how to consume them in their applications. Here are some actions you can perform in the developer portal:

- Read API documentation

- Call an API using the console

- Create and access API keys

- View analytics on your API usage

- Manage API keys

Chapter 3, "Implementing Platform Protections"

Chapter 3 focuses on how to implement platform protection in Azure. In this overview, we will review the security tools that you can use to secure your environment from outside attacks and ensure proper network segmentation.

Azure Firewall

Azure Firewall is a cloud-native and intelligent network firewall service designed to protect against threats to your cloud workloads. It's a stateful firewall since it's a service with high availability and unrestricted scalability. You can obtain it in either the standard or premium editions.

Azure Firewall Standard

The standard edition of Azure Firewall provides filtering and threat intelligence feeds directly from Microsoft's cybersecurity team. The firewall's threat intelligence-based filtering will alert you of and deny traffic to/from malicious Internet protocol (IP) addresses and domains. The firewall's database for malicious IP addresses and domains is consistently updated in real time to protect against new threats.

Azure Firewall Premium

The premium version of this firewall has quite a few improvements over the standard edition. First, it allows for a signature-based intrusion detection and protection system (IDPS) that allows for the rapid detection of attacks by looking for specific patterns of byte sequences in network traffic and known malicious instruction sequences used by known malware. The premium version has more than 58,000 signatures in over 50 categories that are constantly being updated in real time to protect against new and emerging exploits.

Azure Firewall Manager

Azure Firewall Manager is a security management service that allows you to create central security policies and enforce route management for cloud-based security. You can use it to provide security management for the following two types of network architectures:

- **Secured Virtual Hub:** The Azure Virtual WAN Hub is a managed resource that allows you to create hub-and-spoke architectures. When security and routing policies become associated with one of these hubs, it is then referred to as a *secured virtual hub*.

- **Hub Virtual Network:** This hub is the normal Azure VNet that you will create and manage for your cloud environment.

Now that you understand what Azure Firewall Manager is, let's look at some of its key features:

- **Azure Firewall deployment and configuration:** The first feature allows you to deploy and configure instances of Azure Firewall across different regions and subscriptions, which is important for enforcing proper network segmentation. These firewall instances allow you to control traffic between subnets and between your cloud environment and the Internet. Azure Firewall Manager gives you one central hub from which you can deploy and manage these firewall instances.

- **Ability to create global and local firewall policies:** You can use Azure Firewall Manager to create global and local firewall policies. It's important to understand the difference between a firewall and a firewall policy. While a firewall is a logical/physical device that filters traffic, a firewall policy is a top-level resource that contains the security and operational settings for Azure Firewall. You can think of a policy as the rules that govern how a firewall functions in Azure. The firewall policy organizes, prioritizes, and processes the rule sets based on a hierarchy of subcomponents of rule collection groups, rule collections, and rules. See Figure A.1.

FIGURE A.1 Components of a firewall policy

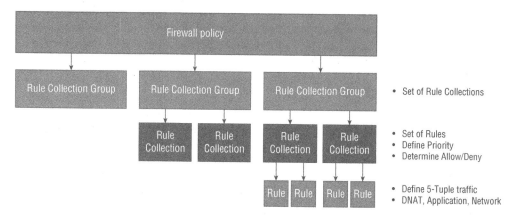

- **Rule collection groups:** This rule set is the highest in the hierarchy and is used to group rule collections. They are the first unit to be processed by Azure Firewall and follow a priority order based on their associated values. By default, there are three rule collection groups with a preset priority value for each (see Table A.1).

TABLE A.1 Rule collection groups

Rule collection group name	Priority
Default DNAT (Destination Network Address Translation) rule collection group	100
Default Network rule collection group	200
Default Application rule collection group	300

By default, you can't delete a default group or change their priority values, but you can add new groups and give them the priority value of your choice.

- **Rule collections:** A rule collection falls under a rule collection group and contains one or more rules. These rules are processed second by the firewall and follow a priority order based on values (similar to those listed previously). All rule collections must have a defined action that either allows or denies traffic and a priority value. The defined action will apply to all rules within that rule collection. Same as the previous rule, the priority values will determine the order in which the rule collections are processed. There are three types of rule collections:

  - DNAT
  - Network
  - Application

  Each of the rule collection types must match their parent rule collection group category. For example, DNAT rule collection must be part of the DNAT rule collection group.

  - **Rules:** Last on the list are rules, which belong to a rule collection that specifies that traffic is allowed or denied in your network. Unlike the past elements, these do not follow a priority order based on values. Instead, they follow a top-down approach where all traffic that passes through the firewall is evaluated by defined rules for an allow or deny match. If there is no rule allowing the traffic, it will be denied by default.

- **Integration with a third-party security-as-a-service (SaaS):** Azure Firewall Manager supports the integration of third-party security providers, allowing you to bring in many of your favorite security solutions into your Azure environment. Currently, the supported security partners are Zscaler, Check Point, and iboss.

  Integration is done through the use of automated route management, which doesn't require the setting up or managing of user-defined routes (UDRs). You can deploy secure hubs that are configured with the security partner of your choice in multiple Azure regions to get connectivity and security for your users. See Figure A.2.

- **Route management:** Route management is the ability to route traffic through your secured hubs for filtering or logging without needing to set up UDRs.

Azure Application Gateway

The Azure Application Gateway is Azure's web traffic load balancer that enables you to manage the amount of traffic going to your application, thus preventing it from becoming overloaded. Azure's Application Gateway is more advanced than a traditional load balancer. Traditionally, load balancers operate at the Transport layer of the OSI model (i.e., Layer 4 TCP and UDP) and can only route traffic based on the source IP address and port to a destination IP address and port. However, Azure's Application Gateway operates at

Layer 7 of the OSI model and can make decisions based on additional attributes found in an HTTP request, such as URL-based routing. From a security viewpoint, this is very important for protecting against DDoS attacks and ensuring high uptimes for all of your network resources. In addition to load balancing, this tool comes with other useful features for security and scalability. Here are some of the most important features to remember:

FIGURE A.2 Secure hubs configuration

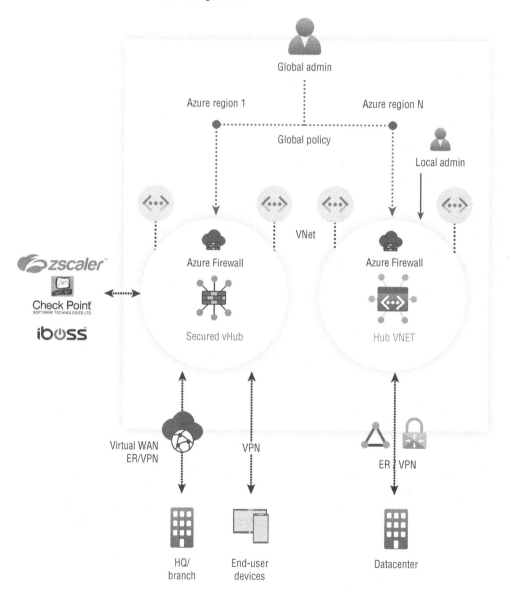

- **Secure Sockets Layer (SSL/TLS) termination:** To ensure that information is transported securely over the Internet, it's common to use encryption protocols like SSL/TLS. However, doing the encryption and decryption is extra overhead for the web server. Azure Application Gateway handles the encryption/decryption and allows data to flow unencrypted to the backend servers, thus reducing the work that the backend servers must do.

- **Autoscaling:** Azure Gateway supports autoscaling, which means it can scale up or down in the number of instances depending on your environment's traffic needs. This saves your company money because you won't have more resources provisioned than you actually need. You must specify a minimum and optionally maximum instance count, though, which will ensure that the application gateway doesn't fall below the minimum instance count, even without traffic.

- **Zone redundancy:** Azure Gateway can span across multiple availability zones, so there's no need to provision separate application gateways for different zones. This also means that you have zone redundancy because all of your gateway instances can be used to handle traffic in other zones as needed.

- **Static VIP:** This static virtual IP address enables the IP address connected to the application gateway to remain static (i.e., not change) over its lifetime, thus reducing the chances of misconfigurations and misdirection due to a change in IP addresses.

- **Web Application Firewall (WAF):** This feature gives you centralized protection for your web application from publicly known exploits. For example, it will filter out SQL injection attacks, cross-site scripting, directory traversals, and other attacks that come in through the web application itself. The WAF solution can also react by patching a known vulnerability once it is discovered. A single instance of Application Gateway can host up to 40 websites that are protected by a WAF.

  The WAF also offers monitoring to detect any potentially malicious activity. It uses real-time WAF logs, which are integrated with Azure Monitor to track WAF alerts and monitor trends. It also integrates with Defender for Cloud, which gives you a central view of the security state of all your Azure, hybrid, and multicloud resources. See Figure A.3.

  - **Ingress controller for AKS:** This feature allows you to use the application gateway as an ingress for an Azure Kubernetes Service (AKS). AKS is a service that allows you to deploy a managed Kubernetes cluster in Azure to offload the operational overhead to Azure.

  - **URL-based routing:** This feature allows you to route traffic to backend server pools based on the URL paths in the request.

  - **Multiple-site hosting:** Using this feature, you can configure routing based on a host or domain name for multiple web applications on the same application gateway.

  - **Redirection:** This feature allows you to support automatic HTTP to HTTPS redirection. It ensures that all communications between an application and its users will be encrypted.

FIGURE A.3   Web Application Firewall

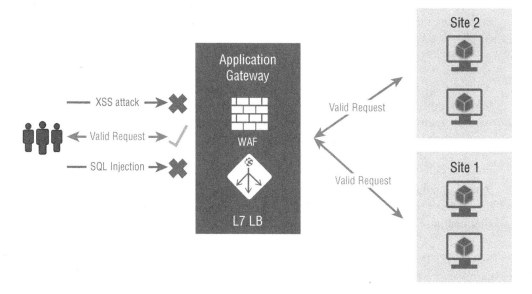

- **Session affinity:** When using this feature, you can use gateway-managed cookies that allows the application gateway to direct traffic from a user session to a server and maintain user sessions on the same server.

  - **WebSocket and HTTP/2 traffic:** Azure's Application Gateway provides support for WebSocket and HTTP/2 protocols over ports 80 and 443.

  - **Connection draining:** If you ever have a need to change the backend servers that your application uses (the backend pool), this feature ensures that all deregistering instances won't receive any new requests while allowing the existing requests to be sent to the appropriate servers for completion within the configured time limit. This includes instances that have been explicitly removed and those that have been reported as unhealthy by Azure's health probes.

  - **Custom error pages:** Azure's Application Gateway allows you to display custom error pages instead of the defaults, which prevents you from displaying information that should be kept confidential. Also, it gives you the chance to use your own branding and layout in the custom error page.

  - **Ability to rewrite HTTP headers and URL:** HTTP headers are used to allow the client and server to pass additional information with a request or response. By rewriting HTTP headers, you can add security-related information protection. You can remove header fields that may contain sensitive information and strip port information from the header. You can also rewrite URLs, and when you combine this with URL path-based routing, you can route requests to your desired backend pool of servers.

Azure Front Door

Azure Front Door is great for building, operating, and scaling out your web applications. It is a global, scalable entry point used to create fast, secure, and widely scalable web applications using Microsoft's global network. It's not limited to just new applications; you can use Azure Front Door with your existing enterprise applications to make them widely available on the web. Azure Front Door providers have a lot of options for traffic routing, and it comes with backend health monitoring so that you can identify any backend instances that may not be working correctly. Here's some of the key features that come with Azure Front Door:

- Better application performance using split TCP-based anycast protocol
- Intelligent health monitoring for all backend resources
- URL path-based routing for application requests
- Hosting of numerous websites via an efficient application infrastructure
- Cookie-based session affinity
- SSL/TLS offloading and certificate management
- Ability to define a custom domain
- Application security via an integrated web application firewall (WAF)
- Ability to redirect HTTP traffic to HTTPS seamlessly with a URL redirect
- A custom-forwarding path with an URL rewrite
- Native support for end-to-end IPv6 connectivity and support for HTTP/2 protocol

Web Application Firewall

A web application firewall (WAF) is a specific type of application firewall that monitors, filters, and, if necessary, blocks HTTP traffic to and from a web application. Azure's WAF uses Open Web Application Security Project (OWASP) rules to protect applications against common web-based attacks, such as SQL injection, cross-site scripting, and hijacking attacks. In Azure, WAFs are part of your Application Gateway, which we just discussed in the last section. All of WAF's customizations are contained in a WAF policy that must be associated with your Application Gateway. There are three types of WAF policies in Azure: global, per-site, and per-URI policies. Global WAF policies allow you to associate the policy with every site behind your Application Gateway with the same managed rules, custom rules, exclusions, or any other rules you define. A per-site policy allows you to protect multiple sites with different security needs. Lastly, the path-based rule (per URI) allows you to set rules for specific website pages. It's also important to know that a more specific policy will always override a more general one in Azure. That means you can have a global policy that applies to all machines and have per-site policies for specific instances, and the per-site policy will override the global policy.

Azure Service Endpoints

VNet service endpoints provide secure and direct connectivity to Azure services over an optimized route via the Azure backbone network. This network is a connection of hundreds of datacenters located in 38 regions around the world that are designed to provide near-perfect availability, high capacity, and the flexibility required to respond to unpredictable demand spikes, which provides you with a more secure and efficient route for sending and receiving traffic. It allows private IP addresses on a VNet to reach the endpoint of an Azure service without needing a public IP address on the VNet.

Azure Private Links

Azure Private Links allow you to access Azure PaaS services and Azure hosted customer-owned/partner services over a private endpoint. A *private endpoint* is simply any network interface that uses a private IP address from your virtual network. It simplifies network architecture and secures the connection between endpoints by keeping the traffic on the Microsoft global network and eliminating the potential for data exposure over the Internet. Here are the key benefits of using Azure Private Links:

- **Ability to privately access services on Azure:** Using a private link ensures that traffic between your virtual network and the service will occur along Microsoft's backbone network rather than exposing the service to the public Internet. Service providers can host their services in their own virtual network and consumers will be able to access those services in their local virtual network, which helps to ensure that their communications remain private and protected against potential eavesdropping attacks from people on the Internet.

- **On-premises and peered networks:** You can also access services running in Azure from your on-premises network over ExpressRoute private peering, VPN tunnels, and peered virtual networks. This structure gives you a secure way to migrate workloads from on-premises to Azure without needing to traverse the Internet to reach that service, helping to prevent any potential attacks or data leakages by keeping all communications on networks that you trust.

- **Prevent data leakage:** When using a private endpoint with a private link, consumers will be mapped to an instance of the PaaS resource instead of the whole service. Access to any other resource is blocked, which helps to prevent data leakage because you are only providing the access needed by the customer and nothing extra. See Figure A.4.

- **Global reach:** Using private links, you can connect to the services running in other regions, which allows you to provide secure connectivity to resources/services anywhere in the world.

FIGURE A.4   Preventing data leakage

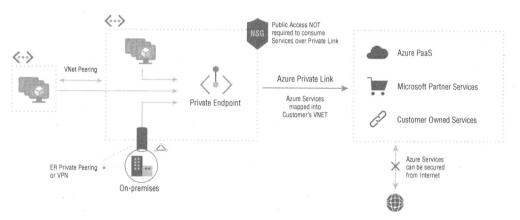

Azure DDoS Protection

Azure DDoS Protection is Azure's default DDoS protection service. Unlike other tools in the list, this tool doesn't need to be configured by an administrator; every endpoint in Azure is protected by Azure's DDoS Protection basic version, free of cost. The important thing is to understand is the difference in features among the basic version and the paid version of DDoS Protection, which comes with two main features:

- **Always-on traffic monitoring:** This tool monitors your application traffic patterns 24 hours a day, 7 days a week, looking for indicators of DDoS attacks. Once an attack is detected, DDoS Protection Basic instantly and automatically mitigates the attack, with no actions required by the end user.

- **Extensive mitigation scale:** The basic version of this tool can detect over 60 different attack types and mitigate those attacks with global capacity, meaning that it can defend against attacks that come from/target resources in any part of the globe. This ability lends your applications protection against the largest known DDoS attacks.

Now, let's look at the features of the standard Azure DDoS protection tool, which is a paid-for resource:

- **Native platform integration:** Azure DDoS protection is natively integrated into Azure, which makes it extremely easy to use. You apply configurations through the Azure portal. DDoS Protection Standard also has the ability to understand your resources and resource configurations without the need for user input.

- **Turnkey protection:** As soon you enable DDoS Protection Standard, it automatically begins to protect all resources on your virtual network without any need for user intervention.

- **Adaptive tuning:** This allows for Azure DDoS protection to learn your application's traffic profile over time and then select the profile that best suits your service. A *traffic profile* is simply a set of measures over a specific period of time that allows Azure DDoS to understand what type of traffic is normal for your application and what isn't. Azure DDoS continues to observe your traffic and changes the profile accordingly over time so that it flags fewer false positives and misses fewer false negatives.

- **Multilayered protection:** Whenever you deploy a WAF, Azure DDoS Protection Standard provides additional security protection at Layers 3, 4, and 7 of the OSI model (i.e., the Network, Transport, and Application layers), helping to ensure that your application is protected by multilayers of security and a defense-in-depth approach.

- **Attack analytics:** Once the DDoS protection tool determines that an attack has started, it provides you with a detailed report every 5 minutes during the attack and a complete summary of the attack once it has completed. This way, you have documentation of what has occurred without having to do any manual work. Also, you can stream the flow logs that are created into Azure Sentinel or an offline SIEM for near-real-time monitoring of the attack against your systems.

- **Attack metrics:** This feature allows you to view summarized metrics for every attack against your resources via the Azure Monitor dashboard.

- **Attack alerting:** With this feature, you can configure alerts to be created at the start, at the stop, or over the duration of an attack using built-in metrics, which tell DDoS protection what the thresholds are for considering traffic to be an attack, allowing for customization on your end. These alerts can be integrated into an operational software of your choosing, such as Azure Monitor logs or Splunk for further analysis/monitoring.

- **DDoS Rapid Response:** You have the option of engaging the DDoS Protection Rapid Response (DRR) team to aid you with an attack investigation if the standard features aren't sufficient. This dedicated team of security experts within Microsoft can provide you with personalized support in an emergency situation.

- **Cost guarantee:** You can receive data transfer and application scale-out service credits for resource costs incurred due to documented DDoS attacks. So, in the event that DDoS protection doesn't deliver on its promised protection, you can obtain financial reimbursement from Microsoft to cover the costs of the attack, giving you another line of defense behind just the software itself.

Microsoft Defender for Cloud

Azure's endpoint protection feature has been integrated into a tool called Microsoft Defender for Cloud, which provides antimalware protection to Azure VMs in three primary ways:

- **Real-time protection:** In this way, endpoint protection acts similar to any other antimalware solution that alerts when you attempt to download a piece of software that might be malware or when you attempt to change important Windows security settings.

- **Automatic and manual scanning:** Endpoint protection comes with an automatic scanning feature that alerts you of any detected malware on your VMs. This feature can be turned on or off at your discretion.

- **Detection/remediation:** For severe threats, some actions will automatically be taken in an attempt to remove the malware and to protect your VMs from a potential or further infection. It can also reset some Windows settings to more secure settings.

Defender for Cloud also generates a secure score for all of your subscriptions, based on its assessment of your connected resources compared to the Azure security benchmark. This secure score helps you to understand at a quick glance how good your security is, and it provides a compliance dashboard that allows you to review your compliance using the built-in benchmark. Using the enhanced features, you can customize the standards used to assess compliance and add other regulations that your organization is subject to, such as NIST, Azure Center for Information Security (CIS), or other organization-specific security requirements.

Defender for Cloud also gives you hardening recommendations based on the security misconfigurations and weaknesses that it has found. You can use these recommendations to improve your organization's overall security.

Azure Container Registry

A *container* is a form of operating system virtualization. Think of this container as a package of software components. A container houses all of the necessary executables, code, libraries, and configuration files to run an application. However, a container doesn't house the operating system images, which makes it more lightweight and portable with less overhead. To support larger application deployments, you must combine multiple containers to be deployed as one or more container clusters.

The Azure Container Registry is a service for building, storing, and managing container images and their related artifacts and allows for the easy and quick creation of containers. When it comes to security, the Azure Container Registry supports a set of built-in Azure roles. These roles enable you to assign various permission levels to an Azure Container Registry, which allows you to use RBAC to assign specific permissions to users, service principals, or other identities that may need to interact with a container in that particular registry or the service itself. You can also create custom roles with a unique set of permissions. Here are some specific features of Azure Container Registry:

- **Registry service tiers:** This feature allows you to create one or more container registries in your Azure subscription and comes in three tiers: Basic, Standard, and Premium. It provides local, network-close storage of your container images by creating registries in the same Azure location as your deployments.

- **Security and access:** You can log into a registry via the Azure CLI or the standard Docker `login` command. To ensure good security, Azure Container Registry transfers container images over HTTPS and supports TLS to provide secure client connections.

When it comes to access control for container registries, you can use an Azure identity, an Azure Active Directory–backed service principal, or a provided admin account. Use Azure role-based access control (RBAC) to assign users or systems fine-grained permissions to a given registry.

- **Content trust feature:** In the premium version of Registry, you can use the Content Trust feature, which is a tool for verifying the source and integrity of data entering the system to ensure that it hasn't been improperly modified. There's also the option of integrating Defender for Cloud to allow for scanning of images whenever they are pushed to a registry to ensure they are safe before use.

- **Supported images and artifacts:** Azure Container Registries can include both Windows and Linux images. You can use Docker commands to push or pull images from a repository.

- **Automated image builds:** Azure allows you to automate many of the tasks related to building containers. You can use Azure Container Registry Tasks to automate building, testing, pushing, and deploying images in Azure. This is done through the use of task steps, which define the individual container image build and operations needed.

Azure App Service

Azure App Service quickly and easily creates enterprise-grade web and mobile applications for any platform or device and then deploys them with a reliable cloud infrastructure. Azure App Service Environment (ASE) allows you to have an isolated and dedicated hosting environment to run your functions and web applications. There are two ways to deploy an ASE: you can use an external IP address (External ASE), or you can use an internal IP address (ILB ASE). Doing so allows you to host both public and private applications in the cloud. It's important that you understand the following security features that Azure App Service offers for securing your cloud-hosting applications:

- **App Service Diagnostics:** This interactive tool helps with troubleshooting your application with no required configuration. When you run into application issues, you can use App Service Diagnostics to identify what went wrong, troubleshoot, and resolve the issue.

- **Integration with Azure Monitor and Application Insights:** This feature allows you to view the application's performance and health to make quick decisions about your application.

- **Azure Autoscale and Azure Front Door:** This feature allows your application to automatically react to traffic loads and perform traffic routing and load balancing.

- **Azure Content Delivery Network:** This feature reduces latency to your applications by moving your content assets closer to your customers.

- **Azure Web Application Firewall:** Azure App Service integrates with Azure Web Application Firewall to protect your applications against common web-based attacks.

Chapter 4, "Managing Security Operations"

This section focuses on the tools that automate and manage security operations in Azure. These tools help you to monitor and enforce your security standards in your organization.

Azure Policy

Azure Policy is a tool that helps enforce the standards of your organization and ensures the compliance of your Azure resources. An Azure Policy gives you the ability to define a set of properties that your cloud resources should have, and then it compares that defined list of properties to your resource's actual properties to identify those that are noncompliant. When defining these rules in an Azure policy, you describe them using the JavaScript Object Notation (JSON) format; the policy rules are known as *policy definitions*. You can assign policy definitions to any set of resources that Azure supports. These rules may use functions, parameters, logical operators, conditions, and property aliases to match the exact standards you want for your organization.

You can also control the response to a noncompliant evaluation of a resource with those policy definitions. For example, if a user wants to make a change to a resource that will result in it being noncompliant, you have multiple options: you can deny the requested change, you can log the attempted/successful change to that resource, and you can alter the resource *before/after* the change occurs, among other options. All these options are possible by adding what's called an *effect* in the policies in which you create.

You can create the policies from scratch, or you can use some of Azure's prebuilt policies that are created and available by default:

- **Allowed Storage Account SKUs (Deny):** This policy determines whether a storage account being deployed is within a predetermined set of stock keeping unit (SKU) sizes that's defined by your organization. It will deny all storage accounts that do not meet the set of defined SKU sizes.

- **Allowed Resource Type (Deny):** This policy defines the resource types that you are allowed to deploy. Any resources that aren't on this list will be denied.

- **Allowed Locations (Deny):** This policy allows you to restrict the location that your organization can select when deploying new resources and allows you to enforce geo-compliance for all new resources.

- **Allowed Virtual Machine (VM) SKUs (Deny):** This policy allows you to specify a set of VM SKUs that you are able to deploy in your organization. All others will be blocked.

- **Add a Tag to Resources (Modify):** This policy adds a required tag and its value to any resource that's created.

- **Not Allowed Resource Types (Deny):** This policy prevents a specified list of resource types from being deployed.

Creating a Custom Security Policy

To create individual policies, the easiest method to use is Azure Policy, a service that allows you to create, assign, and manage the policies that control or audit your cloud resources. You can use Azure Policy to create individual policies, or you can create initiatives, which are combinations of individual policies. There are three steps to implementing a policy in Azure Policy:

1. **Create a policy definition.** A *policy definition* defines what you want your policy to evaluate and what actions it should take on each resource to which it is assigned. For example, say you want to prevent VMs from being deployed in certain Azure regions; just create a policy that prevents VM deployment in that region.

2. **Assign the definition to your target resources.** Next, you need to assign the policy definition to the resources that you want them to affect. Referred to as a *policy assignment*, this step involves assigning a policy definition to a specified scope. For example, you may want the policy to affect all VMs in a certain geographical region. Policy assignments are inherited by all child resources within the scope by default. Therefore, any new resources created within that scope will automatically be assigned that same policy assignment.

3. **Review the evaluation results.** Once a condition is evaluated against a resource, the resource is marked as either compliant or noncompliant. You then have the option to review the results and decide what action needs to be taken. Policy evaluations occur approximately once per hour.

Effects in Azure Policy

Every policy definition that you create in Azure Policy has an evaluation called an *effect*, which determines what will happen when a policy rule is evaluated for matching. The effect can be applied whether it's the creation of a new resource, an updated resource, or an existing resource. Here are the various effect types that you can create in Azure:

- **Append:** This effect is used to add extra fields to a resource during its creation or update. For example, let's say that you have a policy for all the storage resources in your environment. You can add an append effect that will specify what IP addresses are allowed to communicate with your storage resources, and it will be applied during the creation of any storage resource.

- **Audit:** This effect is used to create a warning event, which is stored in the activity logs when your policy evaluates a noncompliant resource. Note, however, that an audit will not stop the request. For example, if you have a policy that states all VMs must have the latest software patch applied and a VM exists that doesn't have that patch applied when the policy is evaluated, then it will create an event in the activity log that details this information.

- **AuditIfNotExists:** This effect goes a step further by allowing the effect to have *if* and *then* conditions. If you've programmed before, it works similar to an if/then statement. This effect allows you to audit resources related to the resource that matches the *if* condition but fails to match the *then* condition. For example, you can use this effect if you want to determine whether VMs have an antimalware extension installed, and then audit the VMs for a separate condition if the antimalware extension is missing.

- **Deny:** As the name suggests, this effect allows you to prevent a resource create/update request from being fulfilled if it doesn't match the standards outlined in the policy definition that you created.

- **DeployIfNotExists:** This effect executes a template deployment when a certain condition is met. Typically, that condition is the absence of a property. For example, you may have a policy that evaluates a Structured Query Language (SQL) server database to see whether or not TransparentDataEncryption is enabled. If it isn't, then a deployment is executed based on a predetermined template.

- **Disable:** This effect allows you to disable individual assignments when a policy is evaluated. Whereas Deny would prevent a resource create/update request from being fulfilled in its entirety, Disable allows you to remove individual assignments that might be causing the noncompliance.

- **Modify:** This effect is used to add, update, or remove properties/tags on a subscription or resource during its creation or update. Existing resources can be remediated with a remediation task. For example, you might want to add a tag with the value `test` to all VMs that are created for testing purposes so that they don't get confused with production VMs.

Order of Evaluation

If you have multiple effects attached to a policy definition, there's a certain order in which the effects will be evaluated. This order of evaluation is as follows:

1. **Disabled:** This effect is checked first to determine if a policy rule should be evaluated.

2. **Append and Modify:** This effect is evaluated next. Because either one of these effects can cause a change in the request, it's possible that neither Deny or Audit will be evaluated at all.

3. **Deny:** The next effect to be evaluated is Deny. It is important because by evaluating Deny now, the double-logging of an undesired resources is prevented.

4. **Audit:** The Audit effect is *always* evaluated last.

Microsoft Threat Modeling Tool

Threat modeling is the process of identifying risks and threats that are likely to affect an organization. Microsoft has created its own threat modeling tool to allow for the easy creation of threat-modeling diagrams. This tool helps you plan your countermeasures and security controls to mitigate threats. When you are threat modeling, you need to consider multiple elements in order to obtain a good overview of your company's complete threat landscape, which consists of all threats pertaining to your organization.

Elements of Threat Modeling

There are three primary elements of threat modeling: threat actors, threat vectors, and the countermeasures you plan to use.

Threat Actors

The first element you must identify as part of your threat modeling process is the threat actors who will be targeting your organization. A *threat actor* is a state, group, or individual who has malicious intent. In the cybersecurity field, malicious intent usually means a threat actor is seeking to target private corporations or governments with cyberattacks for financial, military, or political gain. Threat actors are most commonly categorized by their motivations, and to some extent, their level of sophistication. Here are some of the most common types of threat actors:

Nation-State   Nation-state threat actors are groups who have government backing. Nation-state actors are typically the most advanced of the threat actors, with large amounts of resources provided by their governments; they have relationships with private sector companies and may leverage organized crime groups to accomplish their goals. They are likely to target companies that provide services to the government or that provide critical services like financial institutions or critical infrastructure businesses do. Their goal might be to obtain information on behalf of the government/crime syndicate backing them, to disable their target's infrastructure, and, in some cases, to seek financial gain.

Organized Crime Groups/Cybercriminals   These threat actors are organized crime groups/hackers who are working together or individually to commit cybercrimes for financial gain. One of the most common attack types that this group performs are ransomware attacks, where they hope to obtain a big payout from the company they are attacking. Generally, they will target any company with data that can be stolen or resold as well as companies with enough money to pay a high ransom to retrieve their data.

Hacktivist   A *hacktivist* is someone who breaks into a computer system with a political or socially motivated purpose. They disrupt services to bring attention to their cause, and typically don't target individual civilians or businesses for financial gain. Their main goal is to instigate some type of social change, and they will target companies whose actions go against what they believe is the correct conduct.

Thrill Seekers   This type of threat actor simply hacks for the thrill of the hack. While they don't intend to do any damage, they will hack into any business that piques their interest with the goal of testing their skills or gaining notoriety.

Script Kiddies   These individuals are the lowest level of hackers—they don't have much technical expertise and rely primarily on using prewritten hacking tools to perform attacks. Because they cannot target companies with customized exploits, they typically only target companies with vulnerabilities that can be easily detected by outside scans. Due to their inability to customize or create hacking tools of their own, script kiddies can be defended against by simply being up to date with patching and standard information security best practices.

Insider Threats   Known as insider threats, these individuals work for a legitimate company and are usually disgruntled employees seeking revenge or a profit. They can also be associated with any of the groups previously mentioned and work as an insider by providing them with company information and getting them access to the company's network from within.

Threat Vectors

A *threat vector* is the path or means by which a threat actor gains access to a computer by exploiting a certain vulnerability. The total number of attack vectors that an attacker can use to compromise a network or computer system or to extract data is called your company's *attack surface*. When threat modeling, your goal is to identify as many of your threat vectors as possible, and then to implement security controls to prevent these attackers from being able to exploit those threat vectors. Here are some common examples of threat vectors:

Compromised Credentials   These include stolen or lost usernames, passwords, access keys, and so forth. Once these credentials are obtained by attackers, they can be used to gain access to company accounts, and therefore, the company network.

Weak Credentials   Typically, these credentials are easily guessable or weak passwords that can be obtained using brute force or that can be cracked using software.

Malicious Insiders   Such insiders are disgruntled or malicious employees who may expose information about a company's specific vulnerabilities.

Missing or Poor Encryption   Missing or poor encryption can allow attackers to eavesdrop on a company's electronic communications and gain unauthorized access to sensitive information.

Misconfiguration   Having incorrect configurations gives users access that they should not have, or it creates security vulnerabilities that shouldn't exist. For example, if you have insecure services running on your Internet-facing machines, a threat actor may be able to exploit that vulnerability by scanning the machine.

Phishing Emails   Most malware is spread via email attachments in phishing emails. Such emails continue to be one of the most popular threat vectors used by hackers to get malware on corporate machines.

Unpatched Systems   Unpatched systems are one of the biggest entry points for attackers to gain entry into an organization. Most cyberattacks do not exploit zero-day vulnerabilities, which means most vulnerabilities are old and known. Most often, hackers exploit machines with vulnerabilities that haven't yet had patches applied.

Poor Input Validation   Having poor input validations allows attackers to perform many injection-based attacks, such as cross-site scripting (XSS), SQL injection attacks, and so on. This type of vulnerability is commonly exploited on web applications and websites.

Third- and Fourth-Party Vendors   Third- and fourth-party vendors play a big part in your company's security posture. Vendors typically have trusted relationships with your company where you open up aspects of your network, share information and client data, and use their products in your business. Attackers can then take advantage of this trust relationship to gain access to your company's internal environment. SolarWinds's attack in December 2020 is a good example. Hackers were able to hack into SolarWinds and place malware into the software update they pushed out to their clients. Because the clients already trusted SolarWinds, they downloaded the software update without performing any security checks, which resulted in hundreds of clients being infected with malware.

Threat Surface

Your *cyberthreat surface* consists of all the endpoints that can be exploited, which give an attacker access to your company's network. Any device that is connected to the Internet, such as smartphones, laptops, workstations, and even printers, is a potential entry point to your network and is part of your company's overall threat surface. It's important to map out your threat surface so that you understand what needs to be protected to prevent your business from being hacked. To map out this threat surface, it's extremely important that you have a complete inventory of all of your company's digital assets.

Countermeasures

Now that you have identified your threat surface, the most relevant threat actors for your business, and the threat vectors they will likely use, you can start planning your appropriate attack *countermeasures*. Countermeasures consist of a wide range of redundant security controls you can use to ensure that you have *defense-in-depth* coverage. Defense-in-depth simply means that every important network resource is protected by multiple controls so that no single control failure leaves the resource exposed. The key here is not only to have multiple layers of controls, but to also ensure that you use all the appropriate categories and multiple types of security controls to defend your company against attacks.

Control Categories

You must ensure that you have coverage for all of the following control categories so that your company is properly protected:

Physical Controls   These controls include all tangible/physical devices used to prevent or detect unauthorized access to company assets. They include fences, surveillance cameras, guard dogs, and physical locks and entrances.

Technical Controls   These controls include hardware and software mechanisms used to protect assets from nontangible threats. They include the use of encryption, firewalls, antivirus software, and intrusion detection systems (IDSs).

Administrative Controls   These controls refer to the policies, procedures, and guidelines that outline company practices in accordance with the company's security objectives. Some common examples of administration controls are employee hiring and termination procedures, equipment and Internet usage, physical access to facilities, and the separation of duties.

Control Types

In addition to having coverage for all the control categories to protect your company, you must ensure that you have coverage for all the following control types:

Preventive Controls   A *preventive security control* is what you use to prevent a malicious action from happening. It typically is the first type of control you want, and when working correctly, it provides the most effective overall protection. Preventive controls are part of all the control categories. Here are some examples, along with their control category:

> Computer Firewalls (Technical)   A *firewall* is a hardware or software device that filters computer traffic and prevents unauthorized access to your computer systems.

> Antivirus (Technical)   *Antivirus software* is software programs that prevent, detect, and remove malware from your organization's computer systems.

> Security Guards (Physical)   *Security guards* (i.e., people) are typically assigned to specific areas and are responsible for ensuring that people do not enter restricted areas unless they can prove they have a right to be there.

> Locks (Physical)   *Locks* refer to any physical lock on a door that prevents individuals from entering without having the proper entrance key.

> Hiring and Termination Policies (Administrative)   During the hiring process, *hiring policies* like background checks help to prevent people with a history of bad behavior (e.g., sexual violence) from being hired by a company. *Termination policies* are policies that allow managers to get rid of people who are causing problems for the company.

> Separation of Duties (Administrative)   The *Separation of Duties* is a company policy that requires more than one person to complete any given task. It prevents people from committing fraud, because every process requires multiple people for process completion, and any individuals trying to commit fraud would be noticeable by those responsible for carrying out said processes.

Detective Controls   *Detective controls* are meant to find any malicious activities in your environment that have snuck past the preventive measures. Realistically, you're not going to stop all the attacks against your company before they occur, so you must have a way to discover when something has failed in order to be able correct it. Here are some examples, along with their control category:

Intrusion Detection Systems (Technical)   *Intrusion detection systems* monitor a company's network for any signs of malicious activities and send out alerts whenever any abnormal activity is found.

Logs and Audit Trails (Technical)   *Logs* and *audit trails* are records of activity on a network or computer system. By reviewing these logs or trails, you can discover if malicious activity occurred on the network or computer system.

Video Surveillance (Physical)   *Video surveillance* includes setting up cameras to video important areas of a company, and then having security monitor those video feeds to see if anyone who isn't supposed to be there is able to obtain access.

Enforced Staff Vacations (Administrative)   *Enforced staff vacations* help to detect fraud by forcing individuals to leave their work and have someone else pick up that work in their absence. If someone has been taking part in fraudulent activity, it will become apparent to the new person performing their work.

Review Access Rights Policies (Administrative)   By reviewing an individual's *access rights policies*, you can see who has access to resources they shouldn't, and you can review who has been accessing those resources.

Deterrent Controls   *Deterrent controls* attempt to discourage people from performing activities that are harmful to your company. By incorporating deterrent controls, your company will have fewer threats to deal with, because it becomes harder to perform the fraudulent action and the consequences for getting caught are well-known. Here are some examples, along with their control category:

Guard Dogs (Physical)   Having *guard dogs* patrolling the company property can intimidate potential trespassers and help deter crime.

Warning Signs (Physical)   Advertising that your property is under video surveillance and has security alarms deters people from trying to break in.

Pop-up Messages (Technical)   By displaying messages on users' computers or corporate homepages, your company can warn people of certain bad behaviors (e.g., no watching porn on a company laptop).

Firewalls (Technical)   You may have experienced a *firewall* when you try to browse certain sites on a corporate laptop and are blocked from so doing and a warning message then pops up, stating that certain sites are not permitted on the laptop. These messages help to deter people from trying to browse certain sites on company laptops.

Advertise Monitoring (Administrative)   Many companies make it known that administrative account activities are logged and reviewed, which helps deter people from using those accounts with malicious intent.

Employee Onboarding (Administrative)   During *employee onboarding*, the company's representative can highlight the penalties for misconduct in the workplace, which helps deter employees from engaging in malicious behavior.

Recovery Controls   *Recovery controls* are controls that try to return your company's systems back to a normal state following a security incident. Here are some examples of recovery controls, along with their control categories:

Reissue Access Cards (Physical)   In the event of a lost or stolen access card, the access card will need to be deactivated and a new access card reissued.

Repair Physical Damage (Physical)   In the event of a damaged door, fence, or lock, you will need a process in place for repairing it very quickly.

Perform System and Data Backups (Technical)   Your company should be performing regular backups of important data and have a process in place for quickly restoring the last known good backup in the event of a security incident.

Implement Patching (Technical)   In the event of a possible vulnerability that places your company at risk, you should have a process in place for quickly implementing a patch on your company's systems in order to return your company's network to a "secure state."

Develop a Disaster Recovery Plan (Administrative)   A *disaster recovery plan* outlines how to return your company back to a normal state of operations following a natural or human-made disaster (e.g., a fire or earthquake). It includes instructions on repairing both the physical buildings and the company's computing network.

Develop an Incident Response Plan (Administrative)   An *incident response plan* outlines the steps you can take to return to normal business operations following a cybersecurity breach.

Microsoft Sentinel

Microsoft Sentinel is the cloud-native security information and event management (SIEM) and security orchestration, automation, and response (SOAR) technology that leverages AI to provide advanced threat detection and response based on the information collected across your company's environment. First, let's look at the SIEM aspect of it.

A SIEM is responsible for collecting and analyzing security data, which is collected from the different systems within a network to discover abnormal behavior and potential cyber-attacks. Some common technologies that feed data into a SIEM for analysis are firewalls, endpoint data, antivirus software, applications, and network infrastructure devices. The second aspect of Microsoft Sentinel is that it acts as a SOAR, which is designed to coordinate, execute, and automate tasks between different people and tools within a single platform. For example, using SOAR, you can define an automated playbook that tells the system what actions it should take when a certain condition is met. If it suspects a file is malicious, it may automatically quarantine or delete that file. In the following sections, we will look at the features of Azure Sentinel broken down into its SIEM and SOAR features:

How Does a SIEM Work?

A SIEM works in the following ways:

- **It collects data from different sources:** First, you must configure your SIEM to obtain data from all the data sources of interest to you. These sources include network devices, endpoints, domain controllers, and any other device or service that you want to monitor and perform an analysis on.

- **It aggregates the data:** Once all the devices and services you care about are connected to the SIEM, the SIEM must *aggregate* and *normalize* the data coming from all those various sources so the data can be analyzed. *Aggregation* is the process of moving data from different sources into a common repository; think of it as collecting data from all the devices and putting it in one centralized location. *Normalization* means taking different events from several different places and putting them into common categories so that analysis can begin. For example, if you have multiple devices in various time zones, the SIEM can convert them all to one time zone so that a consistent timeline can be created. Finally, the SIEM can perform *data enrichment* by adding supplemental information, such as geolocations, transaction numbers, or application data, which allows for better analysis and reporting.

- **It create policies and rules:** SIEMs allow you to define profiles that specify how a system should behave under normal conditions. Some SIEMs use machine learning to automatically detect anomalies based on this normal behavior. However, you can also manually create rules and thresholds that determine which anomalies are considered a security incident. Then when the SIEM is analyzing the data that comes in, it can compare it to your normal profile and the rules you created to determine if something is wrong with your systems that requires investigation.

- **It analyzes the data:** The SIEM looks at the data gathered to determine what has happened among the various data sources, and then it identifies trends and discovers any threats based on the data. In addition, if you create rules for a certain threshold like five failed login attempts in a row, then the SIEM will raise an alert when that rule is violated.

- **It assists in the investigation:** Once an investigation begins, you can query the data stored in the SIEM to pinpoint certain events of interest. This allows you to trace back in the events to find an incident's root cause and to provide evidence to support your conclusions.

The next aspect to Microsoft Sentinel is security orchestration, automation, and response (SOAR). SOAR is a combination of software that enables your organization to collect data about security threats and to respond to those security events without the need for human intervention.

Security Orchestration

Security orchestration focuses on connecting and integrating different security tools/systems with one another to form one cohesive security operation. Some of the common systems that might be integrated are vulnerability scanners, endpoint security solutions, end-user behaviors, firewalls, and IDS/IPS. This aspect can also connect external tools like an external threat intelligence feed. By collecting and analyzing all this information together, you can gain insights that might not have been found if you'd analyzed all that information separately. However, as the datasets grow larger, more and more alerts will be issued—and ultimately a lot more false positives and noise will be created that must be sorted through in order to get to the useful information.

Security Automation

The data and alerts collected from this security orchestration are then used to create automated processes that replace manual work. Traditional tasks, which would need to be performed by analysts—tasks such as vulnerability scanning, log analysis, and ticket checking—can be standardized and performed solely by a SOAR system. These automated processes are defined in *playbooks*, which contain the information required for the automated processes. The SOAR system can also be configured to escalate a security event to humans if needed. As you can imagine, this automated system will save your company a lot of money and time on human capital. Also, machines tend to be more reliable and consistent than humans, which leads to fewer mistakes in your security processes.

Security Response

As the name suggests, security response is all about providing an efficient way for analysts to respond to a security event. It's where a SOAR creates a single view for analysts to provide planning, managing, monitoring, and the reporting of actions once a threat is detected. In addition to providing a single view of information for the analyst, a SOAR can respond to potential incidents on behalf of an analyst through automation.

Threat Hunting

Microsoft Sentinel also offers *threat-hunting* capabilities. Sentinel's threat-hunting search and query tools are based on the MITRE framework, and they enable you to proactively hunt for threats across your Azure environment. You can use Azure's prebuilt hunting queries, or you can create your own custom detection rules during threat hunting.

How Does Microsoft Sentinel Work?

Microsoft Sentinel ingests data from services and applications by connecting to the service and forwarding the events and logs of interest to itself. To obtain data from physical and virtual machines, you can install a log analytics agent to collect the logs and to forward them to Microsoft Sentinel. For firewalls and proxies, you will need to install the log analytics agency agent on a Linux syslog server, and from there the agent will collect the log files and forward them to Microsoft Sentinel.

Once you have connected all of the data sources you want to Microsoft Sentinel, you can begin using it to detect suspicious behavior. You can do this in two ways: you can either use

Microsoft's prebuilt detection rules, or you can create custom detection rules to suit your needs. Microsoft recommends that people leverage their prebuilt rules because they have been created to allow for the easy detection of malicious behavior and are regularly updated on Microsoft's security teams. These templates were designed by Microsoft's in-house security experts and analysts and are based on known threats and patterns of suspicious activity and common attack vectors. You also have the option of customizing them to your liking, which is usually easier than creating a new one from scratch.

Automation

Automated responses in Microsoft Sentinel are facilitated by automation rules. An *automation rule* is a set of instructions that allow you to perform actions around incidents without the need for human intervention. For example, you can use these rules to automate processes like assigning incidents to certain people, closing noisy incidents/false positives, and changing an incident's severity or adding tags to incidents based on predetermined characteristics. Automation rules also allow you to run playbooks in response to incidents.

A *playbook* is a set of procedures that can be executed by Sentinel as an automated response to an alert or an incident. Playbooks are used to automate and orchestrate your response and can be configured to run automatically in response to specific alerts or incidents. This automated run is configured by attaching the playbook to an analytics rule or an automation rule. Playbooks can also be triggered manually if need be.

Chapter 5, "Securing Data and Applications"

This section focuses on how you can secure your data and applications within the Azure platform. Primarily this refers to database security, using secure data storage, creating data backups, and ensuring proper encryption throughout your environment. Your goal should be to understand all of the different Azure tools that you can use to achieve each of these goals.

Azure Storage Platform

Azure's Storage platform is Microsoft's cloud storage solution for data storage. Azure Storage is designed to offer highly available, scalable, secure, and reliable storage of data objects in the cloud. In Azure, data storage is facilitated through an Azure Storage account. You can find the complete list of Azure Storage account types at `https://docs .microsoft.com/en-us/azure/storage/common/storage-account-overview`, but it's important to note that each account supports one or more type of Azure Storage data service. These services are as follows:

Azure Blobs: These are large scalable objects that store text and binary data.

Azure Files: These are managed file shares for cloud or on-premises deployments.

Azure Queues: This a service for storing large numbers of messages, particularly the messages between application components.

Azure Tables: This is a NoSQL store for the storage of structured data.

Azure Disks: These provide block-level storage volumes for Azure VMs.

Table A.2 contains a breakdown of the different storage accounts that Azure supports.

TABLE A.2 Various Azure-supported storage accounts and their breakdown

Type of storage account	Supported storage services	Redundancy options	Usage
Standard general-purpose v2	Blob (including Data Lake Storage), Queue, Table storage, Azure Files	LRS/GRS/RA-GRS ZRS/GZRS/RA-GZRS	This is the standard storage account for blobs, file shares, queues, and tables. You will want to use this standard for the majority of scenarios in Azure Storage.
Premium block blobs	Blob storage (including Data Lake Storage)	LRS ZRS	This is the premium storage account for blobs and appended blobs. It should be used in scenarios where there are high transaction rates, where smaller objects are being used, or in situations that require consistently low storage latency.
Premium file shares	Azure Files	LRS ZRS	This is a premium storage account for file shares. It should be used for enterprise or high-performance applications. It is a storage account that can support both SMB and NFS file shares.
Premium page blobs	Page blobs only	LRS	This is a premium storage account for page blobs only.

Benefits of Azure Storage

The benefits of Azure Storage are as follows:

- **Secure:** All data written to an Azure Storage account is automatically encrypted to protect the data for unauthorized access. Azure Storage also provides you with very detailed control over who can access your data using RBAC.

- **Scalable:** Azure Storage is designed to be scalable to accommodate for the storage and performance needs of today's applications.

- **Automatically managed:** Azure handles hardware maintenance, updates, and critical issues on behalf of the user.

- **Worldwide accessibility:** Azure Storage data is accessible from any location in the world over HTTP or HTTPS.

- **Highly resilient and available:** Azure creates redundancy to ensure that your data is safe and available in the event of hardware failures. You can also choose to replicate data across data centers for additional protection from a potential catastrophe.

Azure SQL Database

Azure SQL Database is a platform as a service (PaaS) database engine that handles the majority of Azure's database management functions. Most of these functions can be performed without user involvement, including upgrading, patching, backups, and monitoring.

Azure SQL allows you to create data storage for applications and solutions in Azure while providing high availability and good performance. It allows applications to process both relational data and nonrelational structures, such as graphs, JSON, and XML.

Deploying SQL Databases

When deploying an Azure SQL database, you have two options:

- **Single Database:** In this deployment, this fully managed and isolated database will have its own set of resources and its own configuration.

- **Elastic Pools:** This collection of individual databases shares a set of resources like memory. You can move an individual database in and out of an elastic pool after its creation.

Resource Scaling in Azure SQL Databases

In Azure, you can define the amount of resources allocated to your databases as follows:

- **Single Databases:** For a single database, each will have its own amount of computer memory and storage resources. You can dynamically scale these resources up or down, depending on the needs of that single database.

- **Elastic Pools:** In this case, you can assign resources to a pool of machines that are shared by all databases in that pool. To save money, you will need to move existing single databases into the resource pool to maximize the use of your resources.

Databases can scale the resources being used in two ways: via dynamic scalability and autoscaling. *Autoscaling* is when a service automatically scales based on certain criteria, whereas *dynamic scalability* allows for the manual scaling of a resource with no downtime.

Monitoring and Alerting

Azure SQL Database comes with built-in monitoring and troubleshooting features to help you determine how your databases are performing and to help you monitor and trouble-shoot database instances. Query Store is a built-in SQL Server monitoring feature that records the performance of your queries in real time. It helps you find potential performance issues and the top resources for consumers. It uses a feature called *automatic tuning*, an intelligent performance service that continuously monitors queries that are executed on a database, and it uses the information it gathers to automatically improve their performance. Automatic tuning in SQL Database gives you two options: you can manually apply the scripts required to fix the issue, or you can let SQL Database apply the fix automatically. In addition, SQL Database can test and verify that the fix provides a benefit. Based on its evaluation, it then will either retain or revert the change.

In addition to the performance monitoring and alerting tools, Azure SQL Database gives you performance ratings that let you monitor the status of thousands of databases as you scale up or down. This allows you to see the effect of making these changes based on your current and projected performance needs. You can also generate metrics and resource logs for further monitoring of your database environment as well.

Database Resiliency in SQL Database

Azure SQL Database contains several features to help continue business operations during disruptions. In traditional SQL server environments, you have at least two machines set up locally that have exact, synchronously maintained data copies to prevent against the failure of one machines. While this provides good availability, it doesn't protect against a natural disaster that destroys both physical machines.

Azure SQL therefore provides options for ensuring that you have your data stored in locations far enough away that no single catastrophic event can bring down your services. This is primarily done by spreading replicas of your database in different availability zones. *Azure availability zones* are physically separated and stored in different locations within each Azure region, which allows them to be tolerant to local "failures." Azure defines these *failures* as issues that can cause outages, such as software and hardware failures, earthquakes, floods, and fires. Azure ensures that a minimum of three separate availability zones are present in all available zone-enabled regions. These datacenter locations are selected using vulnerability risk assessment criteria created by Microsoft, which has identified all significant datacenter-related risks. Microsoft also considers risks that may be shared between availability zones. You can use availability zones to design and operate databases that will automatically transition between zones as needed without interrupting any of your services.

Azure's service level agreement (SLA) helps to maintain ongoing service 24/7 by mandating that Azure takes certain actions on behalf of its customers. The Azure Platform completely manages every database, and it guarantees no data loss with a high percentage of data availability. Azure also guarantees it will handle patching; backups; replication; failure detection; underlying potential hardware, software, and network failures; bug fixes; failovers; database upgrades; and a few other maintenance tasks.

The last notable features for SQL Databases are its built-in business continuity and global scalability features. These include the following:

- **Automatic backups:** SQL Database will automatically create full, differential, and transaction log backups of your databases, allowing you to restore your data up to any point in time. You may also configure SQL databases to store full database backups in Azure Storage for long-term retention.

- **Point-in-time restores:** All SQL database deployment options allow for data recovery to any point in time within the automatic backup retention period for a database.

- **Active geo-replication:** For both single and pooled databases, you can configure up to four readable secondary databases in the same or globally distributed datacenters, which helps to prevent an overload on the primary databases due to read requests and allows for the use of auto-failover groups in the event of an issue with the primary databases.

- **Auto-failover groups:** These groups are a means for ensuring high availability and load balancing at scale. SQL Database handles all of the monitoring, routing, and failover orchestration to databases distributed globally.

- **Zone-redundant databases:** SQL Database allows you to provision critical databases or elastic pool replicas across your availability zones to give you the ability to recover automatically from a datacenter failure without data loss.

Database Authentication Using Azure AD

Azure Active Directory (Azure AD) authentication is a method for connecting to Azure SQL Database, Azure SQL Managed Instance, and Synapse SQL in Azure Synapse Analytics using identities in Azure AD. The benefit of Azure AD authentication is that you can centrally manage the identities of database users and Microsoft services in one central location. Here are some of the benefits of using Azure AD for database authentication:

- It's an alternative to SQL Server authentication.

- It allows all password rotation to occur in a single place.

- It eliminates the need for storing passwords by enabling integrated Windows authentication and other types of authentication supported by Azure AD.

- Azure AD supports token-based authentication for applications that need to connect to SQL Database and SQL Managed Instances.

- Azure AD supports multifactor authentication, which adds an extra layer of strong authentication using easy verification options, such as phone calls, text messages, and smart cards with PIN or mobile app notification.

Azure Cosmo DB

Azure Cosmos DB is a fully managed NoSQL database designed for modern app development. It allows for single-digit millisecond response times, automatic and instant scalability, and guaranteed speed at scale. Cosmos provides business continuity through the SLA-backed availability of 99.99 percent and a promise of enterprise-grade security. Table A.3 contains a summary of the benefits and features of Azure Cosmo.

TABLE A.3   Summary of Azure Cosmo's benefits and features

Benefit	Features
Guarantees speed at scale	■ Real-time access with fast read-and-write latencies globally; throughput and consistency all backed by SLAs. ■ Multiregion writes and data distribution to any Azure region with the click of a button. ■ Independently and elastically scale storage and throughput across any Azure region—even during unpredictable traffic bursts—for unlimited scale worldwide.
Simplified application development	■ Deeply integrated with key Azure services used in modern (cloud-native) app development, including Azure Functions, IoT Hub, Azure Kubernetes Service (AKS), App Service, and more. ■ Choose from multiple database APIs, including the native Core (SQL) API, API for MongoDB, Cassandra API, Gremlin API, and Table API. ■ Build apps on the Core (SQL) API using the languages of your choice with SDKs for .NET, Java, Node.js, and Python. Or you have your choice of drivers for any of the other database APIs. ■ Change feed makes it easy to track and manage changes to database containers and create triggered events with Azure Functions. ■ Azure Cosmos DB's schema-less service automatically indexes all your data, regardless of the data model, to deliver blazingly fast queries.

TABLE A.3   Summary of Azure Cosmo's benefits and features *(continued)*

Benefit	Features
Guaranteed business continuity and availability	▪ Azure Cosmos DB offers a comprehensive suite of SLAs, including industry-leading availability worldwide. ▪ Easily distribute data to any Azure region with automatic data replication. Enjoy zero downtime with multiregion writes or RPO 0 when using Strong consistency. ▪ Enjoy enterprise-grade encryption-at-rest with self-managed keys. ▪ Azure role-based access control keeps your data safe and offers fine-tuned control.
Fully managed and cost-effective	▪ Fully managed database service, including automatic, no-touch maintenance; patching; and updates, saving developers time and money. ▪ Cost-effective options for unpredictable or sporadic workloads of any size or scale, enabling developers to get started easily without having to plan or manage capacity. ▪ Serverless model offers spiky workloads automatic and responsive service to manage traffic bursts on demand. ▪ Autoscale provisioned throughput automatically and instantly scales capacity for unpredictable workloads while maintaining SLAs. This service offers a comprehensive 99.99% SLA for both read-and-write availability.
Azure Synapse Link for Azure Cosmos DB	▪ Reduced analytics complexity with no ETL jobs to manage. ▪ Near-real-time insights into your operational data. ▪ No impact on operational workloads. ▪ Optimized for large-scale analytics workloads. ▪ Cost effective. ▪ Analytics for locally available, globally distributed, multiregion writes. ▪ Native integration with Azure Synapse Analytics.

Azure Synapse Analytics

Azure Synapse Analytics is an analytics service that combines three services: data integration, enterprise data warehousing, and big data analytics. It's designed to give you the ability to freely query data to generate new business insights. See Figure A.5.

FIGURE A.5   Azure Synapse

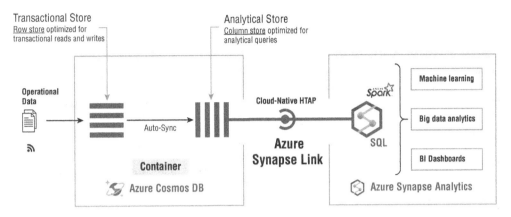

Table A.4 lists some of its most important features.

TABLE A.4   Azure Synapse Analytics Features

Feature Name	Description
Unified analytics platform	It provides a single unified environment for data integration, data exploration, data warehousing, big data analytics, and machine learning tasks.
Serverless and dedicated options	It supports both data lake and data warehousing use cases.
Enterprise data warehousing	It allows you to create data warehouses on the foundation of a SQL engine.
Data lake exploration	It combines relational and nonrelational data to easily query files in the data lake.
Choice of language	Synapse supports multiple languages, allowing you to use the programming language of your choice.

To make the most of Azure Cosmos, you need to leverage a tool called Azure Synapse Link, which allows you to obtain real-time analytics for your operational data in Azure Cosmos. The Azure Synapse Link makes this possible by creating a seamless integration between Azure Cosmos DB and Azure Synapse Analytics. Azure Synapse Link utilizes the Azure Cosmos DB Analytical Store, which is a fully isolated column store that enables large-scale analytics against operational data in your Azure Cosmos DB without any impact to your workloads. Table A.5 lists the key benefits to using Azure Synapse links.

TABLE A.5 Key benefits of using Azure Synapse Links

Benefits	Description
Reduced complexity	With Synapse Link, you can directly access the Azure Cosmos DB analytical store using Azure Synapse Analytics without the need for complex data movements. Any changes made to the operational data will be visible in near real time without the need for extraction, transformation, or loading (ETL) jobs. This allows you to run analytics against the analytical store without the need for additional data transformation.
Near real-time insights into your operational data	You can get quality data insights in near real time.
No impact on operational workloads	When you use Azure Synapse Link, you can run queries against an Azure Cosmos DB analytical store, which is a representation of your real data. The analytical workload is separate from your transactional workload traffic, and therefore doesn't have any negative impact on your operational data.
Optimization for large-scale analytics	Azure Cosmos DB is optimized to provide scalability, elasticity, and performance for analytical workloads. Using Azure Synapse Analytics, you can access Azure Cosmos's storage layer with simplicity and high performance.
Cost-effectiveness	Using Azure Synapse Link gives you a cost-optimized, fully managed solution for generating operational analytics. It eliminates extra storage and compute layers that are used in traditional ETL pipelines for analyzing operational data. It uses a consumption-based pricing model that is based on data storage, analytical read/write operations, and queries that are executed.
Analytics for local, global, and multiregional data	Copies of your data will be created and distributed to nearby datacenters, allowing you to run analytical queries effectively against the nearest regional copy of your data in Cosmos.
Allows for hybrid transaction/ analytics processing (HTAP) scenarios for your operational data	HTAP is a solution that generates insights based on real-time updates to your operational data. It allows you to raise alerts based on live trends and create near-real-time dashboards and business experiences based on user behavior.

Azure Key Vault

Azure Key Vault is a cloud service for securely storing and accessing secrets. Microsoft defines a *secret* as anything to which you want to tightly control access. Some common examples of this are API keys, passwords, certificates, and cryptographic keys. The compromise of company secrets could provide an attacker with highly privileged access to your company's environment and cause major data breaches, which is why you want to ensure that they are properly protected. Here is a summary of the security features of Azure Key Vault:

- **Encryption of Data:** Azure Key Vault enforces the Transport Layer Security (TLS) protocol to protect data when it's traveling between Azure Key Vault and any client. TLS is the successor of SSL and is a cryptographic protocol designed to provide communications security over a computer network. TLS provides strong authentication, message privacy, and integrity, combined with the fact that it's easy to deploy and use. Another aspect of encryption is perfect forward secrecy (PFS), specific key agreement protocols that give assurances that session keys will not be compromised. PFS protects data on the Transport layer of a network that uses TSL protocols. When PFS is used, encrypted communications and sessions that occurred in the past cannot be retrieved or decrypted even if long-term secret keys or passwords are compromised in the future. This protection significantly reduces the risk associated with hackers compromising keys.

- **Secure Authentication:** Azure Key Vault allows you to store your secrets and securely access them by authenticating in one of three ways:

  1. **Managed identities for Azure resources:** When you deploy an app on a virtual machine in Azure, you can assign an identity to your virtual machine that has access to Key Vault. You can also assign identities to other Azure resources. The benefit of this approach is that the app or service isn't managing the rotation of the first secret. Instead, Azure automatically rotates the identity. Microsoft recommends this approach as a best practice.

  2. **Service principal and certificate:** You can use a service principal and an associated certificate that has access to Azure Key Vault. Microsoft doesn't recommend this approach, however, because the application owner or developer must rotate the certificate.

  3. **Service principal and secret:** Although you can use a service principal and a secret to authenticate to Azure Key Vault, Microsoft doesn't recommend it. It's hard to automatically rotate the bootstrap secret used to authenticate to Azure Key Vault.

     - **Key Vault access policies:** A Key Vault access policy determines whether a given security principal can perform different operations on Azure Key Vault secrets, keys, and certificates. Security principals, in this context, will primarily be users, applications, or user groups. Currently, Azure Key Vault supports up to 1,024 access policy entries. Each of these entries grants a distinct set of permissions to a particular security principal. Due to these restrictions, it's advised that you assign access policies to groups of users when possible, rather than assigning them to individuals, to preserve as many of these access policies as you can. Using groups also makes it much easier to manage permission for multiple people in your organization.

- **Network security:** You can reduce the exposure of your vaults by specifying what IP addresses can have access to them. You can also reduce access to Azure Key Vault to a specified virtual endpoint or address range. Once configured, only the users whose requests originate from the allowed virtual networks or IP addresses can read/access data.

- **Central management of your vaults:** You can control access to a key vault through two interfaces: the management plane and the data plane. The *management plane* is what you use to manage Azure Key Vault itself. Here you can do things like creating and deleting key vaults, retrieving Key Vault properties, and updating your access policies. The *data plane* is where you will interact with data that is stored in a key vault. You can add, delete, and modify keys, secrets, and certificates there. Authentication to the planes themselves is managed by Azure Active Directory. Authorization to the management plane uses Azure RBAC, while the data plane uses a Key Vault access policy *and* Azure RBAC, which helps to ensure that it's very difficult for someone to gain unauthorized access to the management console.

- **Logging and monitoring:** Key Vault logging saves information about the activities performed on your vaults. It also allows you to monitor the health of your key vault to ensure that they are running as intended by setting up monitoring and alerts for your key vaults.

- **Backup and Recovery:** Azure Key Vault has a feature called soft-delete and purge protection that both give you the ability to recover deleted vaults and vault objects.

Appendix

B

Answers to Review Questions

Chapter 1: Introduction to Microsoft Azure

1. D. Nonrepudiation is a cybersecurity objective but not an element of the CIA triad.

2. D. Nonrepudiation is about making sure that once a user performs an action they can't deny having performed that action. It holds users accountable for their actions.

3. A. Confidentiality is the element of the CIA triad that focuses on ensuring that only authorized people have access to information.

4. B. Integrity is the element of the CIA triad that focuses on preventing unauthorized changes to data.

5. C. Availability is the element of the CIA triad that focuses on making sure data is available to users.

6. B. This principle seeks to limit users' access in order to prevent the misuse of access.

7. C. As the name suggests, zero-trust means that users inside and outside the network must be authenticated to access network resources.

8. B. Defense in depth is about having multiple layers of security so that one failure does not result in a compromise of a network resource.

9. D. While these are important for overall security, policies, procedures, and awareness training are not considered a layer of defense in depth for any particular resource.

10. B. Security through obscurity is reliant on hiding the workings of a system as its sole form of security.

11. C. Availability is a part of the CIA triad that focuses on making information available to users when needed.

12. C. The same key is used for encryption and decryption in symmetric encryption.

13. B. A different key is used for encryption and decryption in asymmetric encryption.

14. B. A DMZ is a means of protecting your internal network from exposure to the outside by isolating all network resources that need to communicate with untrusted networks.

15. B. Configuration management is about ensuring that the initial configuration of your devices is secure.

16. B. A DDoS floods a resource with requests, making it unavailable to other users.

17. D. Adware is malware that simply displays ads and is more of an annoyance than a legitimate security risk.

18. D. The type of software you use should not affect your compliance requirements.

19. C. Digital signatures are used to prove that messages haven't been altered by using hash algorithms and public key cryptography.

20. D. Web cookies are a normal part of browsing the Internet and are not considered malware.

Chapter 2: Managing Identity and Access in Microsoft Azure

1. A. A managed identity provides an identity for applications to use when connecting to resources that support Azure AD Authentication.

2. A. Azure AD is an Azure-native version of Windows AD.

3. C. RBAC works by assigning access to roles, then assigning roles to users to receive their access.

4. D. RBAC does not increase the amount of authentication for users; it requires users to authenticate less, which helps to reduce overhead.

5. C. Multifactor authentication (MFA) is not a feature of Azure AD Identity Protection.

6. B. The goal of PIM is to manage accounts that have higher access than normal.

7. A. Setting these conditions allows for more granular access control for Azure resources.

8. D. Conditional access policies cannot restrict access based on the type of resource.

9. D. Something you provide is not a type of MFA authentication.

10. D. You can't have an automated response to rerun a review.

11. D. Having more complex passwords isn't a benefit of SSO.

12. A. The Authenticator app is used for SSO.

13. D. API permissions can be controlled using the Azure API Manager.

14. B. Azure built-in AD roles are premade roles that you can use for RBAC.

15. A. A custom role is any role that you build in Azure.

16. D. While this is a legitimate authentication method, it is not available in Azure.

17. A. Something you know is anything that you memorize, such as passwords and PIN codes.

18. C. Something you are is a physical attribute you have such as fingerprints.

19. B. Something you have is a code or physical item that you must provide to authenticate.

20. D. User permissions are only usable by users and not applications.

Chapter 3: Implementing Platform Protections

1.   C. Azure Front Door allows you to easily create scalable applications.

2.   B. This tool is designed to protect your web applications.

3.   D. Azure DDoS Protection will not compensate you for your loss of business due to a DDoS attack.

4.   B. Tracking an IP address's origin of web traffic is not a feature of Azure DDoS Protection Premium.

5.   C. Azure Service Endpoints provide great connectivity over the Azure network.

6.   D. This service provides you with a private and secure connection to services via an Azure Private Link.

7.   C. Encryption in rest is the encryption of data that is not being used or moved.

8.   D. Encryption in transit is the encryption of data that is being moved from one place to another.

9.   C. A Database Administrator role is not a recommended role for access control.

10.   B. Resource groups makes it easier to assign roles to multiple resources at once.

11.   C. DNAT allows you to have one public IP address for your firewall and to mask the IP address of all devices behind it.

12.   B. ASGs are used for communications outside the network, whereas NSGs are used for communications between subnets.

13.   B. NSGs use flow logs to monitor performance and security.

14.   B. User-defined routes (UDRs) allow you to control how traffic moves within a network.

15.   A. Azure Firewall has no threat intelligence,

16.   A. The Azure Application Gateway load-balances web traffic to avoid overloading individual resources.

17.   D. The Azure Application Gateway itself does not provide web application protection—that's the role of the Web Application Firewall (WAF).

18.   D. A web application firewall (WAF) protects you from web-based attacks only, not unauthorized access.

19.   D. Web App Hijacking is not a common type of web application attack.

20.   B. Autoscaling means commissioning or decommissioning instances on the backend as demand increases or decreases.

Chapter 4: Managing Security Operations

1. B. Security operations includes preventing, detecting, assessing, monitoring, and responding to threats.

2. B. Threat modeling helps you to identify risks and threats that may affect your organization.

3. A. Azure Policy is a tool used to identify resources that are out of compliance with your organization's standards.

4. D. A policy defines what Azure Policy is looking for when scanning each resource and what it will do when a resource is not in compliance.

5. C. Alerts are simply notifications (informational), whereas incidents are designed to facilitate action toward remediation.

6. C. Encryption keys are not an entity in Sentinel.

7. A. Automated compliance assessments is not a feature available in Microsoft Defender.

8. B. An effect in Azure Policy is what should be done when a resource is found to be out of compliance.

9. D. There are multiple types of effects, but remediate is not an option. However, there is an effect called modify that lets you change the properties of a resource that is not in compliance.

10. B. This is the order in which a policy definition will execute effects for out-of-compliance resources.

11. A. Azure's vulnerability scanner integrates QualysGuard without any need for payment on your end.

12. D. The E in STRIDE stands for elevation/escalation of privilege, not enumeration.

13. C. This tool allows you to collect information from your environment and use it to make intelligence decisions.

14. A. The highest level of severity for a log alert is critical, not urgent.

15. C. Remediation is not a feature of Azure Monitor Logs.

16. D. You can't import into Azure Monitor Metrics, but you can export data/reports.

17. A. Simply put, filtering allows you to choose what information is displayed in your data visualizations (charts).

18. D. Splitting in Log Analytics allows you to choose how you display the information on your data visualizations—you can have separate lines for each dimension or aggregate them all into one line.

19. B. Sentinel is both a SIEM and a SOAR in one, allowing you to both detect and automate responses to potential security incidents.

20. A. Kusto Query Language (KQL) is the language for creating custom queries in Microsoft Sentinel. Sentinel also provides built-in queries that you can use without having to write any code in KQL.

Chapter 5: Securing Data and Applications

1. A. Azure storage accounts are where data storage is stored in Azure. These accounts contain all the storage artifacts, including files shares, disks, and data blobs.

2. A. This is similar to a root password key that provides access to data in a storage account via shared key authorization.

3. C. This option is recommended because it has good overall security and is relatively easy to use.

4. B. SAS is shared access signature, which provides limited delegated access to resources on a storage account.

5. D. This is not a valid type of SAS signature; all types of SAS provide delegated access.

6. A. This is a unique resource identifier, and it points to one or more storage resources in Azure.

7. D. It is a string that is distributed to client applications that need access to resources in your storage account.

8. B. It is a policy that allows you to set reminders for the rotation of your account access keys.

9. D. It is a technique that limits data exposure by masking data for nonprivileged users.

10. B. It is a database that you can use for mobile app development.

11. C. Azure Key Vault allows you to securely store all types of company secrets and access them directly or through applications.

12. A. Any piece of information that shouldn't be shared with unauthorized users is a secret in Azure.

13. D. An IT audit focuses on determining if the controls designed to protect your assets are working correctly.

14. A. It a transactional and analytical processing capability tool that provides near-real-time analytics over operational data.

15. C. Transparent Data Encryption (TDE) provides real-time encryption and decryption for SQL servers, Azure SQL Database, and Azure Synapse Analytics data files.

16. D. Encryption type is not a setting when creating a key rotation policy.

17. C. Creating backups of your secrets can create operational challenges, so it should only be done when there's a business justification.

18. D. There is no user called vault administrator in Azure Key Vault.

19. A. Database auditing records database events to an audit log that can be reviewed later to detect events of interest.

20. B. Delegated access is when someone grants access to a resource they control, usually through use of an SAS.

Index

S

Online Test Bank

Register to gain one year of FREE access after activation to the online interactive test bank to help you study for your MCA Azure Security Engineer certification exam—included with your purchase of this book! All of the chapter review questions and the practice tests in this book are included in the online test bank so you can practice in a timed and graded setting.

Register and Access the Online Test Bank

To register your book and get access to the online test bank, follow these steps:

1. Go to www.wiley.com/go/sybextestprep. You'll see the "How to Register Your Book for Online Access" instructions.
2. Click "here to register" and then select your book from the list.
3. Complete the required registration information, including answering the security verification to prove book ownership. You will be emailed a pin code.
4. Follow the directions in the email or go to www.wiley.com/go/sybextestprep.
5. Find your book on that page and click the "Register or Login" link with it. Then enter the pin code you received and click the "Activate PIN" button.
6. On the Create an Account or Login page, enter your username and password, and click Login or, if you don't have an account already, create a new account.
7. At this point, you should be in the test bank site with your new test bank listed at the top of the page. If you do not see it there, please refresh the page or log out and log back in.